T.L.S.

ESSAYS AND REVIEWS FROM

The Times Literary Supplement · 1972

II

T.L.S.

ESSAYS AND REVIEWS FROM

The Times Literary Supplement · 1972

II

London
OXFORD UNIVERSITY PRESS
New York   Toronto
1973

Oxford University Press, Ely House, London W.1.

GLASGOW NEW YORK TORONTO MELBOURNE WELLINGTON
CAPE TOWN IBADAN NAIROBI DAR ES SALAAM LUSAKA ADDIS ABABA
DELHI BOMBAY CALCUTTA MADRAS KARACHI LAHORE DACCA
KUALA LUMPUR SINGAPORE HONG KONG TOKYO

ISBN 0 19 211552 9

Printed in Great Britain by
Alden & Mowbray Ltd
at the Alden Press, Oxford

CONTENTS

NOTE

TLS 11 is a selection of review articles which first appeared in the *Times Literary Supplement* during 1972. They vary as much in style as they do in subject-matter, but together they represent both the diversity and the intellectual rigour at which the *TLS* always aims. The subjects covered are political, social, philosophical, historical, and scientific, as well as specifically literary; and there is also a selection of reviews of the year's more durable novels and volumes of poetry. The Index refers not only to the contents of *TLS 11* but also to other important reviews printed in the *TLS* in 1972.

I

SPIES AND COUNTERSPIES
(a) TREASON IN BOHEMIA

GUY BURGESS will remain as a minuscule, but distinct, figure in the comedy of our times. For a few weeks he lurched on to the stage of history, established himself in his role, and slouched off again. But what was his role? Was he a cunning intriguer who used his own instability as a mask for his activities? Or was he a schlemiel pretending to be a spy? Was he Wallenstein, Mephistopheles or Felix Krull?

To a few he may appear as a dedicated idealist, paradoxically enough devoted to a notion of the greatness of his country—and correspondingly despondent at what he regarded as its decline—erratic no doubt in his private life, but never deluded or tempted to stray from the course on which he had set himself in his youth, that course being service to communism, which, he believed, was the only antidote to the loathsome exploitation and inefficiency of Western capitalism. Many others will see him as a virus infecting the liberal intelligentsia and the evil genius of numbers of men in public life; the squalor of his private life being reflected in the squalor of his resolution to accept sums of money to betray both his country and his friends in order to promote the interests of one of the two vilest tyrannies of our time.

Some, however, will judge that neither of these assessments begins to depict a character who was indeed insubstantial, trivial and, in any serious sense, unimportant, but whose very eccentricity illuminates the oddity of our age with its fierce ideological conflicts which force individuals into calamitous situations the like of which have not been seen in Europe since the seventeenth century.

(a) GORONWY REES: *A Chapter of Accidents*. 270 pp. Chatto and Windus. £2.75.

(b) J. C. MASTERMAN: *The Double-Cross System in the War of 1939 to 1945*. 203 pp. Yale University Press. £2.95.

1

In the years between the wars there were two particularly fashionable ways of demonstrating your rejection of the customs and ethos of British society, both of which could be guaranteed to shock the Establishment. Either you became a homosexual or you became a communist. Burgess was remarkable in becoming both. He was not, of course, unique in so doing; but the number of Christian de Claverings who successfully became Chris Clays were few. When one recollects that to tolerate homosexuals in the 1920s, and communists in the 1930s, was considered to be the mark of being civilized if one did not share these tastes or beliefs—and all the more so if one detested them—it is not surprising that someone of Burgess's gifts was taken up and got around at a time when the older generation took particular pleasure and pains to open doors to the young, and the young were eager to be escorted through them.

He had very special gifts. He radiated charm and vitality. He had the good looks of a boy, resembling the drawings of Harry Wharton of Greyfriars in the Billy Bunter stories; he was merry, with a mind like quicksilver, ready to be amused and to amuse. He was quite unlike the undergraduate Marxists of those days. Whereas they had learnt their Marxism and selfconsciously applied the concepts to their society, like John Cornford or Christopher Caudwell, Burgess seemed to have been born a Marxist: his Marxism was not an intellectual exercise, a lesson learnt and regurgitated, it emerged as a genuine vision of life. The secret of his success later, as a talks producer in the BBC, where he would sometimes re-write the scripts of MPs who came to give talks on his programmes, rested in his ability to express ideas in an unaffected way. He understood the springs of political action and related the personalities of the day, their motives and policies to a set of rational principles which he could always embody in historical generalizations without falling into Marxist jargon. This ability made his conversation attractive, gave weight to his political pronouncements and, indeed, seemed to his listeners to give a dignity to contemporary politics which they had never glimpsed before.

Already as an undergraduate he had formed judgments about literature, music and painting, which impressed those who had just met him by their originality. In 1930 he was declaring George Eliot to be the greatest of English novelists because she saw so clearly how her middleclass characters were held in the powerful grasp of the morality of their class which in turn was dictated by economic causes beyond their control. His favourite opera was the *Marriage of Figaro*—and indeed in his contempt for the politicians and governing-class acquaintances whom later he helped or pimped for, he resembled Figaro himself. At the height of Lytton Strachey's fame, Burgess denounced him as infinitely inferior to the Eminent Victorians whom he pilloried. Indeed Britain's imperial past, the Royal Navy, the Victorian age were for him all evidence of the decline of his own country into an enfeebled capitalism, in which managerial incompetence was not improved by doses of spurious humanitarianism. His contempt for Halifax and his policies was unbridled: not so much at Munich, as earlier in India; and after the war he was to denounce the British withdrawal from India as a characteristic betrayal of her historic role. In his curious way he was a patriot, proud of the days when Britain was the leading power in the world and contemptuous of the ruling class of the present, which in his view was behaving with all the folly born of those inner contradictions which Marx had predicted. He was a true Stalinist in hating liberalism more than imperialism, in admiring ruthlessness and denouncing scruples as sentimentalism.

He appeared to be completely self-assured and devoid of shame. Numbered among each generation of undergraduates are its liberators, students who appear to their contemporaries more mature, more vital, and more confident that they can explain the nature of things. They liberate their friends from the conventions of their families, school and class by the strength of their personality, by their power of ridicule and charm, and by their freedom from anxiety and guilt. Some continue to grow and become the leaders of their peer group. Others, early-flowerers, fade as the days of their undergraduate triumphs recede.

In one sense Guy Burgess remained a clever undergraduate all his days, reading the same books, listening to the same music, expounding year in year out the importance of George Eliot, his gargantuan sexual appetite unassuaged. He would go to bed with anyone he could, of any class, though for preference the working class; and he regarded it as his duty to liberate as many of his own class as possible from the thrall of bourgeois sexual inhibitions. As he grew older, he went in for rougher and tougher trade, but seemed immune to blackmail or black eyes, the twin hazards of the predatory homosexual. It was a point of pride with him to be more reckless and full of effrontery than any competitor. But it was also his pride to be a notable friend with a keen sense of what friendship meant—a confidant, a willing adviser, who would be above any petty censoriousness or conceit.

This was the Cambridge undergraduate whom Goronwy Rees, as a newly elected Fellow of All Souls, describes meeting in 1931. Mr Rees was the son of a well-known Calvinist Methodist minister and had come from Cardiff High School by a scholarship to New College. Staunchly heterosexual, he had a number of affairs as a young man, but none more edgy than his affair with Oxford. Oxford welcomed and wooed him, offered him friendship, prizes and the most prestigious of fellowships; but he was never entirely won over. Elizabeth Bowen, describing, in *The Death of the Heart*, the impact of Oxford upon a character from somewhat the same background, wrote: "Eddie was taken up, played up, played about with, taken down, let down, finally sent down for one idiotic act." Mr Rees escaped some of these processes and in the end sent himself down by resigning his All Souls fellowship, preferring to live the more mondain, exacting and precarious life of London journalism. He was not to be seduced by the academic embrace: he found Oxford too frivolous, too dominated by the upper-middle classes and too insulated from what, with an admirable prescience, not shared by his mentors, he judged to be the issue of the times—the convulsion of the capitalist world in the epidemic of the Depression and the disease in the shape of fascism which it caught during its weakness.

In being a communist sympathizer Mr Rees was characteristic of much that was most ardent and high-minded in his generation, and it is easy to see why he was attracted to Guy Burgess. But almost at once his new friend became shrouded in mystery. Burgess ostentatiously broke with his communist past, became secretary to an extreme right-wing politician, who shared his sexual tastes and, sprightly as ever, began to peddle some sophisticated quasi-fascist notions of power politics. By 1935, however, he seemed to be back on a left-wing tack from which he was never again to be deflected. He remained a man of mysteries: the curious and extremely varied company he kept; the wildness of his drinking; the secret assignations which filled all his holidays abroad. Oddest of all was the time in 1937 when Burgess told Mr Rees that he was in fact a Comintern agent and tried to recruit him. Why else, Burgess asked him, should he have suddenly disengaged from the Party before going underground? Why else should he have borne the contempt of those whom he most admired—the open supporters of the left—at the time of his cover-story? But Mr Rees declined to swallow the bait; principally, as he says, because he could not take Burgess as an entirely serious character.

Nobody could. Mr Rees's portrait of Guy Burgess in *A Chapter of Accidents* is a triumph. The incalculable nature of his behaviour is always several leagues ahead of the analysis needed to explain it, and the description of the mounting bewilderment, amusement, anxiety and exasperation which it provoked in Mr Rees is masterly. Burgess was a King in Bohemia. He used to cook in a heavy iron saucepan a thick grey gruel compounded of "porridge, kippers, bacon, garlic, onions and anything else that may have been lying about in the kitchen", a dish which sustained him over each weekend. Chewing raw garlic was only one of his minor social disabilities: in his Foreign Office days a minute was circulated requiring him to desist.

Perhaps it would have taken too long to describe in full the shambles of his Bond Street flat. There he used to keep a flitch of bacon hanging on a string outside the window which was hauled up when he needed to hack off a slice, and was then consigned again to outer space. Grime covered everything. Every table, lampshade, sheet and blanket was scarred with burns, the stigmata of so many drunken evenings. The bath had no plug: in its place was a sock, once white but by now dark grey with dirt, into which a squash ball had been thrust. Screams rent the air at night in the building because his flat was sandwiched between two others inhabited by prostitutes: but it was a moot point whether the traffic in and out of their rooms was any heavier than that in and out of his.

His habits were filthy, going far beyond those of negligent bachelors: in his Foreign Office days he was often sodden and sweaty. Maurice Bowra in a characteristically vigorous phrase used to complain that he had "shit in his finger-nails and cock-cheese behind the ears". Even Evelyn Waugh's imagination did not dare to create such a monster of improbability. How was it possible to believe that such a person had the self-control to be a spy? Was it not more natural to assume that his mysterious comings and goings, his odd but impressive contacts in politics, and his self-confident assurance that he was in the know were clouds in a dream world in which he lived?

And yet he was a spy; and the suspense which Mr Rees creates as he tells the story of his relationship with Guy Burgess is gripping: how it developed so that Burgess became godfather to his twin children, how he kept on going back to that evening when Burgess declared he was an agent, how every time he began to ask himself—for since the Nazi–Soviet pact Mr Rees had turned strongly against the communist cause—whether he ought to convey his suspicions to someone; and then some new grotesque escapade (which seemed in no way to disturb the confidence of his superiors) persuaded Mr Rees that his fears were follies. Eventually there came the final telephone call to his wife from Burgess, the disappearance, and then the discovery that the suspicion which had gnawed at his mind for so long was true.

The suspense is all the more telling because his relationship with Burgess still continued. Like a ghost the invisible Burgess in Moscow haunted him and became an obsession—an obsession which was to end in personal catastrophe for Mr Rees. By this time Mr Rees, a victim of his own romantic temperament, had decided unwisely to return to his own people. He had accepted an invitation to become Principal of University College, Aberystwyth, the town of his birth where he had spent his early childhood. It was a community still dominated in the mid-1950s by the spirit of the primitive Methodism of his father and by the narrowest manifestations of Welsh nationalism. The Students' Union was not allowed to have a bar; and the atmosphere instead of being intellectually stimulating was too often of an insufferable gentility, so that the Principal and his wife felt closer to the students who for all their naivety and clumsiness cared about learning and knowledge. Suddenly one February day in 1956 Mr Rees heard the news that Burgess and Maclean had given a press conference in Moscow, the first firm indication that they were there, nearly five years since their flight.

At this point Mr Rees lost his head, and his obsession destroyed him. He sat down and wrote an indictment not only of Burgess but of his friends, and in particular all those friends who were in high places or had been in the security service during the war. His literary agent did what agents are supposed to do: he got the best price for the articles from *The People*, part of the contract being the horrifying stipulation that the newspaper should be entitled to re-write the material. Mr Rees insanely agreed to this condition. The articles contained the material used in this book but they were also a call for action. They declared that Burgess had blackmailed people to obtain secrets; that he was protected by his homosexual friends in MI5, and that his behaviour had been scandalous for so long that he should have been expelled from the service on several occasions. Some were mentioned by name as associates of Burgess, others were easily identifiable; and the last article closed with a plea to root out the traitors in our midst since it was certain that Burgess and Maclean were not the only people in positions of trust who had been recruited into the Soviet spy ring.

The explosion detonated by these articles was atomic; but the blast-walls of the Establishment are so cunningly constructed that the person who was most hideously wounded was Mr Rees himself. With some notable exceptions, such as John Sparrow, his Oxford friends rounded on him. Maurice Bowra wrote to suggest that he should plant Judas trees round the playing fields; and when a London literary lady cancelled an invitation to dinner, he realized that he was no longer, as he puts it, *salonfähig*. His friends took the line that to start a witch-hunt five years after the birds had flown was inexcusable, and they put it about that Mr Rees, fearful that Burgess would make some malicious and false statement about him, had made the error of trying to get in first and denounce his former friend.

Meanwhile his puritanical opponents at Aberystwyth realized that their chance had come. Checked at first, they finally succeeded in getting a court of inquiry into their Principal's behaviour set up. The committee's report was so hostile but so palpably unable to find misdemeanours in Mr Rees's conduct at Aberystwyth that the council refused to endorse it.

But the damage was done. Mr Rees, who until then had refused to resign, believed that he could no longer work there profitably. He was now forty-five, homeless, jobless and with the hiss of the world in his ears; and a month later he was knocked over and dragged by a passing car, nearly died from his injuries and spent months in hospital. That was the end of the chapter of accidents.

Mr Rees is not as personal in his book as he was in his newspaper articles: most of the references to people are discreet, and he mentions few names. But he is unrepentant. For him it is still scandalous that MI5 were unable to identify Burgess, Maclean and Philby; scandalous that, the first two having fled, a far-reaching inquiry was not set on foot at once; scandalous that the Establishment closed its ranks although the existence of a Burgess within its most sacred precincts affronted all it stands for.

Yet Mr Rees's self-justification is the weakest part of the book.

Even if we think of *A Chapter of Accidents* purely as a tale, he has made the same mistake in craftsmanship which Joe Ackerley made when he wrote about his father. The mistake was to write primarily about himself instead of about the situation.

Ackerley did not see that he had a situation shaped like an hour-glass: himself the pursuer of guardsmen, he discovers in the end that his father owed his rise in the world to a chance encounter when as a guardsman he was picked up by a well-to-do homosexual who bought him out of the Life Guards and made him his companion. Ackerley ruined what could have been a miniature work of art by self-commiseration. Mr Rees is stoical, not lachrymose. But the centre of this book should not have been himself. It should have been the calamity of his relationship with Burgess. Something needed to be said about his father and his childhood, but his book should not have taken the form of an autobiography.

Mr Rees does indeed explain his conduct in 1956 in terms of his relationship to Guy Burgess. He believes that they were drawn to-gether by Burgess's indictment of the etiolated English ruling class and intelligentsia, which struck a chord in Mr Rees's Welsh heart. The new elite after the war were not much better. They were perhaps more humane, progressive and enlightened, but where were the rough-hewn qualities they needed? When wrestling with the problem of whether to denounce Burgess to MI5, having been told he had dis-appeared, Mr Rees consulted a close friend, who reminded him of E. M. Forster's dictum that if a choice had to be made between betraying one's country or one's friend, he hoped he would have the guts to betray the country.

Mr Rees protested that this was a false dichotomy: one's country was a dense nexus of social relationships of which loyalty to one person formed only a single strand. The polite but unenthusiastic reception by MI5, when finally he decided that he must voice his suspicions about Burgess, heightened his conviction that the authori-ties were anxious only to hush the matter up, horrified that two upper-class officials were traitors, but unable to grasp that there might be dozens of other traitors within the old-boy network. Mr Rees had been offered in his disquiet, as it were, a cup of tea. But, like Saki's bishop, he was out for blood not tea.

Yet there are two reasons why this explanation is unsatisfactory. Perhaps Oxford had a more penetrating influence on Mr Rees than he will allow. Certainly by his own account he appears to have behaved in his various positions exactly in the way which he accuses a member of that intelligentsia which he disdains to have behaved. After the war he became a director in an engineering business, the great attraction being that it gave him ample time for writing. Not a very dynamic approach to industry.

In 1952 he became Estates Bursar of All Souls, which owned thirty thousand acres of agricultural land. Did he take steps to move the investments out of land and into equities to take advantage of the great equities boom during the decade? He did not. Instead he was impressed by the "ancient wisdom" of Lord Brand of Lazards, at that time one of the least aggressive and most stuffy of merchant banks, who declared that if equities had existed in the Middle Ages, no Oxford college would have survived. Not the reaction one might expect from someone who believed that Britain's economy had been paralysed by such ancient wisdom.

Nor for that matter did he apparently question what All Souls should do with its wealth—a question which became acutely embarrassing at the time of the Franks Commission. No one can doubt that at Aberystwyth he was a liberal, humane Principal with the interests of his students at heart, who brought to them some of the blessings of the Oxford tutorial system. But he does not appear to have had any other ideas about higher education: all the more strange since, on the grouch again, he has in recent years flayed the new universities for being liberal arts colleges (instead of business schools), quite out of touch with the needs of a technological society. He was, in fact, as fine a flower of the Oxford culture of his day as, each in his way, are Warden Sparrow and Warden Hampshire.

The second reason is concerned with democracy and the rule of law. Mr Rees is correct in saying that British security was slow to react to the implications of the Fuchs and Hiss cases and to introduce positive vetting. Western intelligence was always more susceptible to penetration when it switched during the war from thwarting communism to subverting fascism, in the course of which communist sympathizers almost inevitably had to be employed, some of whom proved to be lethal. He is surely right to criticize the Foreign Service for retaining Burgess and Maclean after their scandalous drunken bouts. But is he right to be incredulous? Civil servants are protected from dismissal by processes minutely laid down in Estacode in order to protect them against the venom of their superiors or a mere dislike of unorthodoxy. This again is a British democratic freedom.

(How often in fact are heavy and aggressive drinkers sacked from any profession?)

In that boastful and malevolent book, written so as to sow the maximum number of seeds of distrust in British intelligence by conveying the impression of verisimilitude, Philby mocks the ineffectiveness of the attempts of MI5 to pin anything on him.

He conceals the fact that nothing would have suited the Soviet Union better than to have seen the British public service—for the investigation would not have stopped at the intelligence and diplomatic services—hobbled and paralysed by a McCarthyite purge. It would not have stopped at the public service. The Beaverbrook press, and certain left-wing journalists who shrieked for the head of Mr Big who was said to have shielded the missing diplomats, would have been delighted to halloo the hounds along and tear at the universities, the entertainment industry, the media and all those circles where people who had known Burgess could be found. Titus Oates and Pemberton Billing can be found in every age. But on this Mr Rees is silent.

Mr Rees also neglects to state that although MI5 were certain that Philby was the Third Man, as Philby admits, he could not be detained. In England proof of guilt is required in the courts, and that kind of proof was lacking. Public opinion is strongly against giving parliamentary or quasi-judicial inquiries the latitude that committees of Congress possess, in which the reputation and livelihood of individuals can be destroyed without hope of redress. Nor will public opinion readily tolerate strong-arm tactics during interrogation: it is even critical of the pressure put upon those detained in Ulster during armed subversion.

It is odd that Mr Rees, who is a columnist and member of the advisory board of *Encounter*, fails to recognize that what distinguishes British democracy from a communist society is precisely this unwillingness to pillory individuals and sacrifice them to the dubious value of making the state that bit more "secure". He still seems unable to grasp why, at a time when Senator McCarthy's exploits had scarcely passed into history, his friends disapproved of his articles in *The People* for making reckless innuendos and calling for a witch-hunt. It is all the odder since he himself was the victim of a witch-hunt.

Had he consulted the most powerful and elegant analysis yet made of the Philby affair, by Hugh Trevor-Roper, he would have found solutions to many of the problems which still obsess him. He would also have found an assessment of why it took so long to reorganize the Secret Service after the war: not because it was riddled with homosexual lefties anxious to protect their friends, but because it had reverted to its amateur, inefficient state of hidebound conservatism. But where Burgess is concerned, perhaps Mr Rees would have been better comforted by the judgment of A. J. P. Taylor or Graham Greene and others who, sceptical of the value of espionage, regard it as a grotesque and useless comedy. Certainly Guy Burgess operated in his adopted profession on a level of farce unattained by any of Malcolm Muggeridge's reminiscences. Whatever moral judgment may be passed on this scamp who became a scoundrel, there is something memorable in the effrontery of one who, as a junior Foreign Service official, having in his possession the first volume of the Kinsey Report on the sexual behaviour of the human male, at that time unobtainable in England, kept it in the most secure place he could find: namely stuffed at the back of the private safe in Ernest Bevin's room in the Foreign Office. But he was not a man worthy of serious consideration, as Philby made clear enough.

There were highly professional and efficient spies, Lonsdale and Philby certainly being among them. Lower down the scale there were the seedy, unstable, riff-raff among whom Guy Burgess, with his Old Etonian ties and the appearance of someone who had just stepped off the Golden Arrow after a night in the rue de Lappe, was one.

Yet in the end Burgess emerges as a more sympathetic figure than Maclean brutalized by drink; or than Philby, whom Graham Greene has compared to a Jesuit living in Elizabethan England. He nursed illusions. In the long romance which he had with communism, he used to declare that Stalin was genuinely tolerant of homosexuals. Unlikely as this hypothesis was, he was in fact permitted, as he slid downhill in Moscow, to live his last year with a working-class friend whom, he maintained, he had picked up while living illegally in the capital. (Whether or not the friend has now been given another assignment by the secret police is unknown.) He treasured illusions.

His friends were for ever receiving messages and hearing with mixed feelings that Guy had been speaking affectionately about them to the journalists and travellers who visited him. He protested that he was still a dedicated communist; but, having announced to his guest that he knew well that his flat was bugged, he would burst out in his last years into bitter denunciations of everything Russian and express his hatred of the Slav mentality. He was always asking to be re-assured that his friends still cared for him.

But on one matter he was under no delusion. He used to say that if he returned to England he would be able to take up with all his friends where he broke off, with one exception. He was most uncertain what E. M. Forster would say to him. Perhaps Forster might have said that Guy Burgess had at least the distinction of showing that it was possible to betray both one's friends and one's country simultaneously.

This book covers the old ground worn flat by Anthony Purdy and Douglas Sutherland, and by Tom Driberg, but due to Mr Rees's skill it is compulsive reading for the over-fifties. There is a frontispiece of Mr Rees looking immeasurably Welsh.

(b) THE DOUBLE AGENCY GAME

"BY MEANS of the double-agent system *we actively ran and controlled the German espionage system in this country.*" The claim is a startling one, and Sir John Masterman is justified in departing from his usual decorous and cool narrative style to indulge himself for once in italics. It is all the more stimulating because the official origin of this book stamps it with a patent authenticity, and truth wins another of its victories over fiction.

Before the Second World War, Sir John was a don at Christ Church; he has since been Provost of Worcester and Vice-Chancellor of Oxford. In 1940 he was recruited into a branch of MI5, the counter-espionage service, and was occupied from then until 1945 in the large section which ran double-agents in Britain. Just before he left the service, during the months of July-September of 1945, he was asked to write an official narrative of the activities of his section, to be printed for an extremely restricted circulation among experts as a manual for future use. More than a quarter of a century later he has obtained official permission to publish it; his motive, he says, is to restore confidence in a service whose failures receive publicity and criticism but whose successes are never known except to a small circle. As a good historian he has published the original document and not attempted to expand or to modify it in the light of later experience. As a result the general reader is provided, for the first time, with the real thing, elegantly presented with all due amplitude.

To control the whole of the enemy's espionage system at the most vital point meant that the British Government and services had in their hands a most powerful instrument. The details of how it was acquired are entertaining and instructive, but more important are the uses to which it was put. Various as they were—Sir John lists seven— they group themselves in essence under three principal heads which may be briefly categorized as counter-espionage, positive intelligence, and deception. The system's achievements under any one of these heads would have been enough to justify the trouble and expense. The latter item, as he sardonically remarks, was largely cared for by the Germans themselves, who went to great pains to pay our controlled agents handsomely.

The counter-espionage expert would no doubt assert as his ideal the denial of all information to the enemy; but this is something probably beyond reasonable expectations even in a country such as wartime Britain. It follows as the next best thing that, if the Germans were to have information at all through agents, it was preferable that those agents should be controlled rather than uncontrolled. Admittedly, in order to preserve their credibility you must allow them to pass on information to their masters, and the bulk of it must be true. Even so, you have the benefit of knowing what the enemy knows and what he does not know; and from time to time you can slip in false information to help your deception plans along. Secondly, if you allow the enemy to have, as he believes, an active network of agents in your country, he is likely to be content, and not make the great effort required to augment that network; if he does, you will get early news of any fresh arrivals. Thirdly, by your knowledge of the traffic which your controlled agents send, you obtain information about the personalities and working methods, including the ciphers, of the enemy service, and this is not only of value for your other two purposes but also puts you in a position to trip up and expose other enemy agents when they appear.

The vital point about this control of enemy agents in Britain was, from the first, whether we could be sure that it was total. As Sir John explains, we were at the beginning uncertain of this, and no doubt missed many opportunities because of the fear that the Germans might have uncontrolled agents here whose reports would confute those of the controlled agents. It soon, however, became clear that these apprehensions were unfounded. As H. R. Trevor-Roper has revealed, from quite early on we were able to read the ciphers of the

Abwehr, the German intelligence service, and to prove by this means that the double-agents we were running were not only their only source, but that they had the highest regard for them. Still, the habits of caution ingrained from the period of doubts remained valuable because other more straightforward sources of information were always available to the Germans, such as prisoner-of-war interrogation, aerial reconnaissance, wireless intercepts, and reports from neutral diplomats in London.

The second achievement of the system arose from the fact that we controlled both ends and knew not only what the agents were sending but also what questions were asked. The latter were first-class evidence for German intentions. It was clear, for instance, when they stopped inquiring about fighter airfields and asked about bomber airfields instead, when they went over to questions about food stocks and food supplies, and also when they told their agents to lie low and take no risks, that they had given up ideas of invasion and were relying on the blockade.

A sensational example of how positive information could have been but unfortunately was not derived from the questions put to agents has an American angle. In August, 1941, the double-agent TRICYCLE, a patriotic and pro-British Yugoslav who had been working in England since the previous December, was ordered by the Germans to go to the United States via Lisbon to start a large-scale espionage network there. He took with him a long questionnaire, a third of which was devoted to Hawaii, and to Pearl Harbor in particular; moreover, while the questions about the rest of the country were vague and general, those about Pearl Harbor were specific and detailed. Admittedly it was for the Americans to draw the deduction which is now so obvious, but Sir John feels that, if relations had been as intimate as they later became, his own service should have taken the initiative in pointing it out, even at the risk of a snub from their friends.

The third, the best known and historically the most classic use of double agents is for the purposes of deception. It is a justifiable British boast that in the Second World War we elevated deception, on a strategic scale, to a fine art, highly systematized. It all began, as Sir John acknowledges, in the Middle East but its greatest triumph was undoubtedly FORTITUDE, the cover plan for the invasion of France. The general outline is already familiar: how German attention was diverted to the Pas de Calais, and kept there even after the

Normandy landings. Of course many other techniques were employed besides Sir John's speciality, though there is no doubt that the Germans relied more on agent information than on anything else. It was one of their weaknesses.

What Sir John reveals, which is new, is how close we came to losing our advantage. The agents had been well built up during 1943, but things began moving against them in 1944. With the removal of Canaris, the German intelligence service began to move jerkily in the direction of greater efficiency. The unavoidable spread of knowledge about the double-agent system increased the possibility of leaks. Above all there was the tendency of Abwehr officials to desert the sinking ship. This was the greatest danger, for if one of their men came over to the other side the Germans must expect that he would compromise all their agents; if nevertheless they went on transmitting as though nothing had happened they would at once be assumed to be under control. "In short the German turncoat, trying to assist us, would in fact destroy our entire system." As it was, one German agent in Portugal who had already made tentative contacts was tricked into returning to Germany, and we were only saved by the fact that there was not enough time before D-Day for OVERLORD for the Germans to unravel the tangled skein. One network had to close, but the others performed successfully.

The "Grand Deception Plan", as Sir John calls it, was designedly the apotheosis of the double-cross system. It was with hopes of this that MI5 kept the show alive during the years of waiting, coaxing the various services and home departments to feed them with the true information necessary to give credibility to their controlled agents. It was also confidently expected to be its Götterdämmerung; for surely, after being so grossly deceived, the Germans would realize exactly how it had been done. But not at all; with quiet satisfaction Sir John records that "those agents who took a leading part in the Grand Deception were more highly regarded after it than before". Partly this was because of German inefficiency, of which MI5 should by then have had experience enough. Unlike Lady Bracknell, they had tried once to undeceive the Abwehr by "blowing" an agent. One with the code-name SCRUFFY had been chosen to demonstrate how they would like the Germans to think they would work a double-agent; he was made to send messages full of the stupidest gaffes, but his German controls continued to be credulous and the case had to be closed down before the embarrassment became too painful. And in the second place, by then, and occasionally even earlier, many German intelligence officers had taken to shutting their eyes wilfully to suspicions about their agents. They thought it better for selfish reasons to have corrupt or disloyal agents than to have no agents at all. So it came about that TATE, the doyen of the double-agents, was able to go on transmitting to his control in Hamburg from the autumn of 1940 until a few hours before the city was captured by British troops. The last message back from control was in the most appreciative terms, with a thoughtful postscript on a personal matter.

The mention of TATE's personal problems is a reminder that, for all Sir John's sense of the dignity of historical writing, and for all his skill in Whitehall prose—which is, in fact, subtler in style and drier on the palate than many outsiders realize—animation enters when he comes to deal with personalities. Normally he preserves a judicious austerity. TREASURE, who had been of enormous help over FORTITUDE, "proved exceptionally temperamental and troublesome", a verdict which strikes home to those who have read the book she published in 1966 under her real name of Lily Sergueiev (*Seule face à l'Abwehr*, translated in 1968 as *Secret Service Rendered*). TATE, who landed by parachute with an unserviceable wireless set right into the hands of a reception committee tipped off by his predecessor SUMMER (a moody and unsatisfactory character), is Sir John's ideal of the Industrious Apprentice. SNOW, who started it all, even before the war, he calls his W. G. Grace, but his heart goes out to his Bradman, GARBO. He was a Spaniard, equally anti-Fascist and anti-communist, who took the kingdom of heaven by storm by setting himself up in Spain as a one-man intelligence agency and forcing us to take him on, to be the pride of the artificers of deception. He was a man who took grave pains over his work and developed a florid, imaginative prose style which acted like catnip to a cat on the highest levels in German intelligence. All these characters, despite their code-name masquerade, come strongly to life as proofs of the doctrine Sir John lays down: that the good case officer must live the life and think the thoughts of the agents he controls.

A summary can do only scant justice to a book so full of wisdom on a subject about which so much nonsense has been written. There are, for example, hilarious stories about how it was necessary to keep up German faith in the men they had sent as sabotage agents by actually letting them blow up part of a food store and a generating station; how hard it was for instance to rouse the sleeping night-watchmen and inveigle them to a safe place out of sight of the controlled saboteurs. There is a thoughtful disquisition on the advantages of notional as opposed to real agents for purposes of deception. There is a pregnant allusion to the labour and thought that went into building up dummy formations, with divisional and corps shoulder-patches carefully supplied to the Germans through the Spanish diplomatic bag, and mustering them into a false order of battle under that queen of all bogus formations, the First United States Army Group or FUSAG, which the Germans believed was waiting in Kent all ready to spring across the Straits of Dover when OVERLORD had done its diversionary work.

Sir John Masterman scores because he is a skilled writer. But he has the advantage over his rivals that he is writing about things that really happened with all the vivid actuality of contemporary experience. There is no better book than *The Double-Cross System* on wartime intelligence.

2

THE PICARESQUE PHALLUS

THE NAME Casanova has been a generic term for the promiscuous male for so long that, in most people's minds, it has probably become completely fused with the Don Juan myth. Critics of the recent new English divorce law dubbed it "the Casanova charter", because it was thought to facilitate the activities of the conquering fornicator or stud who moves on from one woman to another, with little or no regard for the hearts he may be breaking or the messes he is leaving behind. In other words, Casanova is taken to be the outstanding real-life exemplar of "male chauvinism", as Don Juan is its legendary representative. But, as usual, when one looks into the matter, the apparent stereotypes turn out to be more complex than one had at first supposed, and in this instance neither the myth nor the reality is adequately covered by any simple concept of masculine selfishness.

Don Juan is a vast and nebulous character who has been variously interpreted. Is he a crypto-homosexual, frantically hiding his femininity from himself? Or an oedipal obsessive vainly returning to many wombs in the hope of finding the true, original one? Or a modern Prometheus who thinks that, by flouting the moral law and flashing his little creative stump at God, he is somehow getting his own back on the great Creator for the absurdity of the universe? In these and other manifestations, he seems to be less concerned with establishing his dominion over individual women than with mounting an attack on the feminine principle in order to satisfy some other, and more obscure, urge—psychological, sociological, or metaphysical.

Giacomo Casanova, an actual historical figure, who was born in Venice in 1725 and died in Bohemia in 1798, was quite unlike this. He

GIACOMO CASANOVA: *History of My Life*. Translated by Willard R. Trask. Volume 1: 349 pp. Volume 2: 330 pp. £3.50 the set; Volume 3: 346 pp. Volume 4: 358 pp. £3.50 the set; Volume 5: 313 pp. Volume 6: 322 pp. £3.50 the set; Volume 7: 338 pp. Volume 8: 317 pp. £3.50 the set; Volume 9: 415 pp. Volume 10: 392 pp. £3.75 the set; Volume 11: 370 pp. Volume 12: 459 pp. £4.20 the set. Longman.

was not at the demonic end of the seducers' scale, with the God-defying Don Juan, or with Lovelace, the Marquis de Sade, and Laclos. He seems to have had no metaphysical dimension and little or no psychological perversity. He was first and foremost an eighteenth-century picaresque adventurer, with a great fund of un-directed energy, a huge appetite for sex, and an all-consuming love of women. The word "love" needs to be emphasized; there can be no doubt that he was passionately fond of women as women.

He would go to no end of trouble for them, would lavish time, money and conversation on them, and always measured the quality of his current affair or affairs by the degree of sentimental harmony accompanying the sexual demonstrations. He keeps repeating, with apparent sincerity, that he always preferred love to lust, although he constantly surrendered to the latter when the former was not available. He insists that love depends on the face and the voice of the beloved, and that an anonymous tussle in the dark is not love:

I saw, as so many times before, that *sublata lucerna nullum discrimen inter feminas*. A true proverb as far as physical enjoyment goes, but false and very false in regard to love. The soul's loadstone lies in the face; this may be strong proof that man has a soul entirely different from that of the animals . . . when a face . . . has made a man fall in love . . . if he succeeds in enjoying the possessor of it, no deformity or ugliness in her body repels him; he even manages to find beauty in what, if he examines it, is ugly; but he does not care.

In confirmation of this, it may be noted that his most touching ex-perience was with a girl called Charlotte Lamotte, who was never his mistress in the technical sense; she was six months' pregnant when a fellow-adventurer abandoned her to his care; Casanova looked after her tenderly until she died in childbirth three months later, and he keeps referring back to her in his narrative as a sad loss.

Another sign of his kindly nature was that he had the gift of friendship in love; his ex-mistresses were usually delighted to see him again, and often took up with him where they had left off—at least that is what he says, and he cites chapter and verse so convincingly that it seems churlish not to believe him. Realizing that his own character was unreliable—"I knew myself too well not to foresee that in a settled way of life I should become unhappy"—he had frequently wangled marriages for them with more dependable, less mobile individuals and, in a typically eighteenth-century way, he presents these arrangements as triumphs of virtue. On several occasions, he describes scenes that Greuze could have turned into *tableaux de genre*, with the inscription, "Casanova, shedding benevolent tears, as he marries off an ex-mistress".

It is true that in the matter of pregnancies he was unscrupulous, and only occasionally practised contraception (usually, in fact, as an additional item in the erotic ritual), but in the eighteenth century the general attitude towards births was somewhat different from what it is today. Such a high proportion of children died in infancy while in the care of wet-nurses or in foundlings' homes that Nature herself gave the impression of obligingly wiping out the results of the urges she had inspired.

However, it would be excessive to try to rehabilitate Casanova as an exponent of relative sexual morality. He may have come to represent the latent promiscuity in all men, but even if only a sizable minority were as promiscuous as he organized society would become impossible, just as the picaresque hero in general supposes the existence of a large mass of the non-picaresque. He himself knew that his temperament was exceptional and was driving him relentlessly on, regardless of any social prudence: "All my life long I have been absorbed in vice and a worshipper of virtue."

Until his powers began to wane at the age of thirty-eight or so, he appears to have operated like a priapic machine-gun. But at least it can be said that his insistent phallus was not altogether divorced from the rest of his personality, and that this personality, as it rises from the printed page, is warm and likable in its amorousness and roguery. He would certainly never have echoed the sex-degrading, male-chauvinist remark of a philanderer in a twentieth-century French novel: "On ne crache pas qu'avec la bouche." His metaphors for semen are "nectar" and "soul", and although they are conventional ones in eighteenth-century erotica, they are not quite as out of place as might be supposed in the context of his writing.

The importance of the new edition of his *History of My Life* is that it allows the English-speaking reader to appreciate for the very first time, what exactly Casanova said about himself. All previous English versions were based on the early nineteenth-century text edited by Jean Laforgue, a teacher of French in Dresden, from the original manuscript in the possession of the Brockhaus firm. Laforgue was a bowdlerizer and an adaptor who, according to the evidence supplied by Willard Trask, made devastating alterations to both style and content.

Curiously enough, no one appears to have thought of checking with the manuscript again, until it was found to have survived the bombing of Leipzig during the Second World War. It was eventually published in France by Plon, in 1960, in a scrupulously exact edition which respects Casanova's mistakes, mis-spellings, and marginalia. His writing is sprightly and direct—". . . the public is not a lady and I like to be instinctive"—but as a Venetian who had picked up French haphazardly in the course of his career, he had a very uncertain command of idiom and gender, as he freely admits. The same solecisms and Italianisms occur with irritating frequency. Since Mr Trask has turned this slightly broken text into plain American prose, with only a few Gallicisms here and there, this is one of the rare cases of a book being perhaps more palatable in translation than in the original. The American version has the advantage of providing the contents without the distracting linguistic irregularities.

Casanova says at the beginning that he is using French because that language is more widely known than his native Italian, and it is true that French was the general cultural vehicle of the Europe of his day. He adds, in a chatty passage in one of the later volumes, that he began writing only to prevent himself dying of boredom and frustration during his unhappy retirement as Count Waldstein's librarian at the castle of Dux in Bohemia. But a great French book may have been his unacknowledged source of inspiration. Rousseau's *Confessions* was published in two parts in 1781 and 1788; Casanova began writing in 1789, at the age of sixty-four, and he must have read Rousseau, because he makes a disparaging reference to a statement contained in the *Confessions*, and some of the early episodes in his own narrative have a suspiciously Rousseauistic air. He does not present himself as an admirer of Rousseau, but it is possible, and indeed probable, that the *History of My Life* is an offshoot of the *Confessions*, just as much as Restif de la Bretonne's *Monsieur Nicolas* (1796). Moreover, there is some resemblance between Restif and Casanova: each is a slightly manic, sex-obsessed character with a vague, neo-Rousseauistic philosophy of Nature and a very fluent pen.

It may be that the *Confessions* helped both of them to realize their identities as eccentric individuals and to have the courage to reveal themselves in writing. But whereas Rousseau is a literary genius with a marvellous sense of poetic and psychological detail, Restif and Casanova are no more than minor writers. Although they can make us feel the reality of their own characters in a rough and ready way, they haven't the gift of bringing other people fully to life, or of composing great, archetypal scenes, as Rousseau does. Casanova's pages teem with names; in the course of his career, he had dealings with hundreds of people, from emperors and kings, aristocrats and rich merchants, to peasant girls, common prostitutes, rogues and card-sharpers; yet few of them are strikingly portrayed. Even the three mistresses to whom he devotes most space—Henriette, M.M., and Mme Dubois—remain fairly blank, so that when their names crop up in later contexts the reader is usually hard put to remember who exactly they are. He gives a wealth of non-significant detail about times of day, travelling arrangements and prices of meals, but when it comes to people he hardly breaks away at all from neo-classical generalization—"alabaster globes", "perfect beauty", "charming wit", etc. If one nevertheless goes on reading, it is because the sheer accumulation of incident adds up to a fascinating account of a particular picaresque adventurer in the context of eighteenth-century European society.

Rousseau's *Confessions* is undeniably the supreme work in the genre, because Jean-Jacques's picaresque existence was accompanied by an intellectual and emotional itinerary of enormous importance in the formation of the modern mind. Casanova has to be classified as one of the lesser talents but larger temperaments. Among real-life figures, he is reminiscent not only of Restif, but also of Beaumarchais, the Chevalier d'Eon, Abbé Prévost and John Law; and, in fiction, of Gil Blas, Jacob in Marivaux's *Le Paysan Perdu* and Moll Flanders.

Since no authoritative social historian appears to have dealt with the subject, one can only surmise why the eighteenth century was so rich in picaresque figures, particularly in engaging rascals who could make the kind of statement that occurs in Casanova's first volume:

So here I was in Rome, with a good wardrobe, a fair amount of money, some jewelry, and a fair amount of experience, with good letters of recommendation, completely free, and at an age when a man can count on the help of fortune if he has a spark of courage and a face which disposes those whom he approaches to look on him with favour. It is not beauty, but something more valuable, which I possessed but which I cannot define. I felt that I was capable of anything.

All during the Middle Ages and the Renaissance there had been travelling scholars, craftsmen and musicians, pilgrims and strolling players, itinerant mercenaries and rogues. But the picaresque figure, as opposed to these various characters or to the external type, the navigator or colonist, became dominant only in the eighteenth century, and his existence is more specifically reflected in French literature, although the term and the basic literary form were of earlier Spanish origin.

Casanova's story, like Rousseau's and numerous others, helps us to see how the emergent individualism of the post-Renaissance era coincided with a tradition-ridden, hierarchical yet exploitable society. There was a peculiar balance between the mobility of the individual and the fragmentation of political authority ("Heureux temps des lettres de cachet!" as Casanova was to write in 1789, without apparent irony, as he looked back on the pre-Revolutionary period). In spite of absolutism, the big nation state did not yet exist in its modern form. Europe was still for the most part a mosaic of principalities and duchies.

Even within the larger units, such as France and Russia, local *seigneurs*, whether great or small, enjoyed an autonomy that is unimaginable today. It follows that the adventurer, although he might fall foul of arbitrary authority (as Casanova did, when he was imprisoned in the Leads by the Venetian State Inquisitors, or in a jail in Barcelona by a regional governor), was not dealing with the all-pervading, faceless bureaucracies of the modern world. He could bring pressure to bear through his protectors and play off one source of power against another.

The universal inequality in rank, wealth and influence was an insurance for the clever man. Each little local lord had a kind of court; he kept open house for amusing guests; he might even serve pensions to people in whom he took an interest (for years, Casanova, in tight corners, depended on two elderly patricians, Bragadin and Dandolo, who had taken a fancy to him in his youth and who would send him money across Europe). The *seigneur*'s salon was often a private gaming-room, where the adventurer, through the discreet manipulation of chance, could reline his purse. He could win credit by posing as a physician, an astrologer, or an alchemist.

If his temporary protector had the ear of the King, the Prince, or the Duke, he might even be proposed for the carrying out of diplomatic missions, the management of financial deals or the setting up of new institutions, since there was usually no organized civil service or trade union spirit to stand in his way. If he came to grief in one locality he could always move on to another, where his reputation might take some time to catch up with him. Being equipped with letters of recommendation and a ready flow of conversation, he could expect, on arriving in a new place, to dine out every day for some weeks at least. The ladies and gentlemen of the town might be waiting for some fresh mental or sexual stimulus, and there was no mechanized entertainment for him to compete with. It was the habit, in all European countries, for the members of the leisured classes to visit each other constantly, morning, afternoon and evening, in drawing rooms, bedrooms and theatre boxes, so that a newcomer found himself immediately in the swim.

As one reads about the endless round of meals, card-parties, receptions, orgies, excursions and masked balls that Casanova attended in Italy, France, Holland, Germany, Russia, England and Spain, one realizes how closed and departmentalized twentieth-century society has become. Nowadays, only at two opposite ends of the social scale—in the international jet-set or the hippy underworld —could an individual enjoy the freedom of movement and participation that Casanova took for granted over the whole social scene. Very revelatory, for instance, of the international network of influence is the way, as a young man, he obtained his first employment. He was still in his native Venice; his mother, an actress who had been working for some time in Dresden, persuaded her protectress, the Queen of Saxony, to bring pressure to bear on the Queen of Naples, her daughter, to persuade the Pope to appoint a certain priest to a bishopric in Calabria so that Casanova could be his secretary.

He did not keep this post, or any other, for very long, because— unlike Beaumarchais, for instance—he was not the sort of picaresque hero who makes good, marries into the upper-class and establishes himself on a firm, financial basis as a new aristocrat. He had many opportunities to cleanse himself of the stigma of having been born among the classless parasites of the acting profession (he did, in fact, become a Papal Knight, for what that was worth), but he threw them all away, either because of the natural instability of his temperament which made it impossible for him to think about the future until it was too late, or because the central interest in his life was not material success or power but the lyrical and physical satisfaction of his genitals. Occasionally, in the intervals between beds, he mentions literary ambitions, but he had no definite talent and did not start writing for publication until very late. So long as, by fair means or not too foul, he had enough money to play the aristocrat and court the ladies, his days were full enough:

Since in this life nothing is real except the present, I enjoyed it, dismissing the images of the past and loathing the darkness of the always dreadful future, for it offers nothing except death, *ultima linea rerum* . . .

Despite myself, I knew, and I was forced to admit, that I had wasted all my time, which meant that I had wasted my life.

Sometimes, he expresses the same truth by means of an Italian proverb, "la cazza non vuol pensieri" (the penis does not wish to think). Before he died, at the age of seventy-two, he had taken the narrative of his life up to his forty-ninth year; plainly, even at that fairly advanced age, his indomitable organ was still coming between him and his wits, as well as stimulating them.

Here again, it has to be noted that the circumstances of the time favoured his temperament. Although the eighteenth century usually respected the outward forms of social decorum, morality among the upper classes was even more permissive than is the case today. Since most unions were *mariages de convenance*, any wife was fair game for the seducer, and indeed expected to be courted. The social prestige of the nobility was such that a man with the bearing of an aristocrat could approach a middle-class or lower-class girl and count on turning her head with a mixture of blandishments and gifts. She, for her part, might look upon this initiation as a useful prelude to marriage, rather in the manner of those girls of certain native tribes who prostitute themselves to earn their dowries. Masks, disguises, and the curious eighteenth-century passion for transvestism facilitated intrigues.

Also, before the invention of modern hygiene and mechanized transport, everyday living was much more physical and intimate than it is now. Travellers were jostled together for long periods in closed carriages; total strangers would share rooms or even beds in country inns; the universal practice of the *table d'hôte* was very different from the impersonality of the modern dining-room. A lady or gentleman could hardly travel without a servant to empty the chamber-pot and arrange toilet facilities, and such a servant might be less of a guardian of virtue than an active go-between. Girls, more often than not, slept two in a bed and, as Casanova explains for the benefit of naive parents, two curious sisters, cousins or friends were often easier to seduce than one, since they would egg each other on and think that what both of them did together was more excusable than what one of them might have done alone.

In any case, the whole century was bathed in a glow of eroticism; poised as it was between the old pastoral world of Europe and the new dawn of rationalism, individualism and technology, it had a peculiar intensity which may, as a kind of side-effect, have produced a diffused genital excitement. And Casanova, in his jovial way, tries to cover the whole non-pathological erotic range, from "L'Embarquement pour Cythère", by way of "L'Escarpolette" to Aretino's positions and the cures for venereal disease.

It is in this connexion, even more so than with regard to some other incidents in the narrative, that the question of Casanova's truthfulness arises. He presents himself frankly, and in so many circumstances, as a fluent and ready liar, that he must have got into a habit of mythomania that was very hard to break in old age, even when he was writing his confessions for posthumous publication (besides, there is evidence that he had some slight hope of issuing them in his lifetime). The notes to Mr Trask's translation show that many of his stories are probably true, while others seem to be manifest inventions. It is difficult to say whether, in sexual matters, he is describing his own experiences scrupulously or amplifying them with the help of the more or less clandestine literature of the day. In writing up his exploits he may have amused himself by making them approximate to erotic stereotypes. It is clear that a great deal of his narrative cannot be literally accurate, since he gives what purport to be verbatim transcriptions of conversations which occurred twenty, thirty, or forty years earlier; that is, he often casts his stories into the pseudo-novel form, as a novel-writer might, conversely, use the pseudo-memoir form.

Again, some episodes sound much more convincing than others. In the quite outstanding chapters describing his imprisonment in, and escape from, the Leads, every detail has the ring of truth, and one would expect this to be the case, since the tiniest events of such a dramatic experience must have been indelibly imprinted on his memory, and there would in any case be little point in falsifying them. But when he expatiates on a sodomitic and masturbatory scene with a Turk in a Constantinople summer-house, while the naked ladies of the Turk's harem bathe in a pool outside, one has doubts; similarly, when a novice, in blushing wonderment, treats him to fellatio through the grid of a convent parlour, or he falls in love with a castrato, mistaking the eunuch for a girl, or with a pretty person in male attire who is passing herself off as a castrato with the help of a false penis. These things may be true, but they could also be imaginary incidents in a pornographic novel that Casanova is combining with the story of his life to cheer himself up in the dreary, flaccid solitude of Dux. Since a lot of the amorous *badinage* is reminiscent of *La Nuit et le Moment* by Crébillon fils, some of the physical exploits may have been titivated with the help of such books as *Felicia ou mes fredaines* or *Le Portier des Chartreux*.

On the other hand, he may genuinely have attracted a wide spectrum of experience, because his philosophy of nature, as he hints at it from time to time, embraces everything except sadistic cruelty and masochistic submission; he does not, like the Marquis de Sade, make these things the important features of nature. He sometimes refers to sodomy as being anti-natural, but this seems to be an automatic use of the adjective, since he apparently engaged in the activity without any scruples. Nor was he opposed to incest, voyeurism, multiple sex, or any of the non-aggressive variations, almost all of which he describes with gusto. In short, in his case as in some others, it is impossible to tell whether pornography followed the amorality of real life or whether real life followed the imaginings of pornography. This, after all, is what one would suppose to be the case with his kind of picaresque hero. Courageous and dashing, but without any definite social or moral principles, he was very far from being a precursor of the modern Existentialist *révolté*, like Rousseau or Figaro; he was just a sort of freelance, self-appointed aristocrat with a *membrum supervirile*.

3
CULTURAL REVISIONS
(a) THE DREAM IN RUINS

EDMUND WILSON writes in the 1957 chapter of *Upstate*:

Looking out from my window on the third floor, I saw the change made here by autumn in the landscape and the atmosphere: they become distinctly more serious, Nature begins to warn us, reassuming her august authority; the luxury of summer is being withdrawn.

In context, this passage carried many times the weight of any ordinary nature-note: the book is already half over, a splitting head of steam has been built up and the reader is by now in no doubt that the luxury of summer is being withdrawn from the writer himself, from the historical district in which he writes, from all the artists he has ever personally known and from the America which he has for so long chronicled and which he is now ceasing even to distrust— *Upstate* shivers with the portent of an advancing ice-cap. Wilson's monumental curiosity and zest of mind have not grown less, but by now they are like Montaigne's, exiled within their own country and awaiting, without real hope, a better age which will know how to value them. Self-confidence remains, but confidence in one's function ebbs; one's books do not seem to have been much use; the public weal has proved itself an illusion and private life is running out of time. "C'est icy un livre de bonne foy, lecteur", wrote Montaigne, dampening the reader's ardour,

Il t'advertit dez l'entree, que ie ne m'y suis proposé aulcune fin, que domestique et privee: ie n'y ay eu nulle consideration de ton service, ny de ma gloire; mes forces ne sont pas capables d'un tel dessein.

Just so long as we understand each other.

(*a*) EDMUND WILSON: *Upstate*. Records and Recollections of Northern New York. 386 pp. plus 14 plates. Macmillan. £4.50.

(*b*) LIONEL TRILLING: *Sincerity and Authenticity*. 188 pp. Oxford University Press. £3.

Wilson's tone is similarly self-sufficient. "The knowledge that death is not so far away", he writes in 1963,

that my mind and emotions and vitality will soon disappear like a puff of smoke, has the effect of making earthly affairs seem unimportant and human beings more and more ignoble. It is harder to take human life seriously, including one's own efforts and achievements and passions.

That was the year in which he was writing *The Cold War and the Income Tax*—a profound growl of dissatisfaction about owing the United States Government a swathe of back-taxes which it would only have wasted on building and dropping bombs if he had handed it over. Dealings with the revenue men were prolonged and wearying, making a general disappointment with life understandable. In 1966 things were going better, but his view of existence didn't much lighten. To go with his Kennedy Freedom Medal he was given a $1,000 award by the American Academy of Arts and Sciences and a $5,000 National Book Award, but he found himself feeling let down rather than puffed up. "They make me feel that I am now perhaps finished, stamped with some sort of approval and filed away. . . ." He is hard on himself, and no softer on humanity as a whole. "Reading the newspapers, and even the world's literature, I find that I more and more feel a boredom with and even scorn for the human race." In such ways his darkening mood is overtly stated, but what gives it power—and makes *Upstate* such an elegiac and at times unmanning book—is the way in which the selectivity of his impressions presents picture after picture of decay, confusion and loss. Talcottville, NY, is presented as a last vestige of the old, hopeful America, and Wilson—not hiding or even sheltering, just waiting—takes up residence there each summer to find that the new and vengeful America has always moved a bit closer. Not that it matters much any more.

By the end of the book we're a long way from the mood in which Wilson first evoked Talcottville, in his "The Old Stone House" essay of 1933, later collected in *The American Earthquake*. In the first place, that essay recalled the hopes of the New Englanders who had grown sick of narrowness and were all for pushing on into the realm of unlimited opportunity:

I can feel the relief myself of coming away from Boston to these first uplands of the Adirondacks, where, discarding the New England religion but still speaking the language of New England, the settlers found limitless space. They were a part of the new America, now forever for a century on the move.

The thrill of the great American experiment is still there in the
writing, and even though this old essay was just as disenchanted as
the new book is, the disenchantment worked in reverse: Talcottville
was the opposite of a refuge, representing a past that needed to be
escaped from, not returned to.

Thirty years or so later, in *Upstate*, he is cricking his neck to get
back to it, but it is too late. Material progress has already made its
giant strides. Juvenile delinquents and uproarious bikers maraud
and destroy. The John Birch Society slaps up flagrant stickers.
Treasured windows on which poet friends have inscribed verses with
a diamond pen are shattered in his absence. The Sunday *New York
Times* is too heavy for him to carry. There is a spider in the bathtub
of a motel. An old acquaintance, Albert Grubel, keeps him abreast of
the ever-escalating car-crash statistics. His daughter Helena grows up
and starts having car-crashes of her own. In 1963 he finds out that he
has for all this time been living virtually on top of a SAC air-base,
and is therefore slap in the middle of a prime target area. By the end
of the book there is a distinct possibility that a four-lane highway
will be constructed a few inches from his front door.

The detail is piled on relentlessly, and if there were nothing else
working against it, then *Upstate* would be a dark book indeed. But
several things stop it being disabling. First, there are revelations of
the Wilsonian character, as when he faces the bikers and asks them
why they can't ride on the highway instead of around his house, or
when he argues about iambic pentameters with Nabokov (who insists
that Lear's "Never, never, never, never, never" is iambic), or when he
tells Mike Nichols that Thurber is not alone in lacking self-assurance
and that he, Wilson, often gets up at four o'clock in the morning to
read old reviews of his books. In bits and pieces like these there is
enough singularity and sheer quirkiness to keep things humming.

Second, there is evidence of the Wilsonian curiosity, as when he
deepens his knowledge of the county's history, or when he becomes
interested in the founding and the subsequent fate of the old Oneida
community. Wilson can't stop learning things, and it's worth remembering at this point that the curious information which crops up
in the book is only the topmost molecule of the outermost tip of the
iceberg. In the period covered by *Upstate* (1950–70), Wilson was
producing exhaustively prepared books like *The Shock of Recognition*
and *Patriotic Gore*, breaking into new cultures with books like *The
Scrolls from the Dead Sea*, *Apologies to the Iroquois* and *O Canada*,

turning out important investigatory pamphlets like *The Cold War and the Income Tax* and *The Fruits of the MLA* (a crucially important attack on boon-doggling academicism which has yet to be published in Britain) and editing *A Prelude* and the second and third in his series of literary chronicles, *The Shores of Light* and *The Bit Between My Teeth*—the first, *Classics and Commercials*, having appeared in 1950.

Only the European panoptic scholars come near matching Wilson for learning, and for sheer range of critical occupation there is no modern man to match him, not even Croce. If *Upstate* tends to give the impression that his wonted energy now only faintly flickers, the reader needs to remind himself sharply that the mental power in question is still of an order sufficient to illuminate the average city. Seemingly without effort, Wilson dropped *A Piece of my Mind* (1957) somewhere into the middle of all this hustle and bustle, and in the chapter entitled "The Author at Sixty" announced:

I have lately been coming to feel that, as an American, I am more or less in the eighteenth century—or, at any rate, not much later than the early nineteenth. . . . I do not want any more to be bothered with the kind of contemporary conflicts that I used to go out to explore. I make no attempt to keep up with the younger American writers; and I only hope to have the time to get through some of the classics I have never read. Old fogeyism is comfortably closing in.

Taking him at his word on this last point, most critics and reviewers were relieved, which was very foolish of them.

But on the first point, about feeling himself to be an eighteenth-century or nineteenth-century figure, Wilson was making a just estimate, even if he meant only that he didn't drive a car and couldn't bear to pronounce the word "movies". As Alfred Kazin argued in his review of *The American Earthquake* (collected in his fine book *Contemporaries*), the men to compare Wilson with are the literary artists driven by historical imaginations—men like Carlyle.

The third thing which lightens the darkness of *Upstate* is the author's gradually revealed—and revealed only gradually even to himself—interest in a local young woman striving to better herself. Perhaps without really willing it, Wilson is telling a subtle story here: flashes and fragments are all we get. But by the time the book is over, we are convinced that her story is the story of the book, and that the story has gone against the mood. Kazin suggested that Wilson's secret was to gaze at America with a cold eye without being cold on

America. *The American Earthquake* inexorably recorded the shattering effects of industrialism and the spiritual confusion of the New Deal, but it was not a hopeless book—it responded to the period's vitalities, even (while castigating it) the vitality of Henry Ford. *Upstate* very nearly *is* a hopeless book, and for a long while we suspect that Wilson *has* gone cold on America. But finally we see that he hasn't, quite: as the girl Mary works to establish herself in a way that her European origins would probably not have allowed, the American adventure haltingly begins all over again, at the eleventh hour and in the fifty-ninth minute.

Against the Stygian background of the book's accumulated imagery it is not much hope to offer, but it is not nothing, and Wilson was never in the consolation business anyway. Which leaves us—as we shelve *Upstate* beside *A Prelude* and prudently leave room for the books dealing with the thirty uncovered years between them—with the question of what business Wilson *has* been in.

What does Wilson's effort amount to? Is there an atom of truth in his dispirited suggestion that his books have dated? Supposing—as seems likely—that Wilson belongs with the great, copious critical minds like Saintsbury, Sainte-Beuve, Croce, Taine: is he doomed to survive like them only as an emblem of the qualities a mind can have, Saintsbury for gusto, Sainte-Beuve for diligence, Croce for rigour, Taine for drama? Wilson makes Van Wyck Brooks's output look normal, Eliot's look slim, Empson's, Trilling's and Leavis's look famished. Just how is all this avoirdupois to be moved forward? We need to decide whether critical work which has plainly done so much to influence its time vanishes with its time or continues. To continue, it must have done something beyond maintaining standards or correcting taste, important as those functions are: it must have embodied, not just recommended, a permanent literary value. And we do not have to re-read much of Wilson's criticism—although it would be a year of perfect pleasure to re-read all of it—to see that it does embody a value, and embodies it in a way and to a degree that no other corpus of twentieth-century work has approached. But this value, so easily sensed, is very difficult to define, since it must perforce reside in whatever is left after opposing high estimations of Wilson have cancelled each other out. Lionel Trilling (in "Edmund Wilson: A Background Glance", collected in *A Gathering of Fugitives*) says that an interest in ideas is the very essence of Wilson's criticism. Alfred Kazin, on the other hand, says that ideas are things Wilson is not at home with. If both these men admire the same thing in Wilson, what is it?

The answer is that Wilson has a mental style—a mental style which reveals itself in the way he writes. He is proof by nature against metaphysics of any kind (sometimes to the damaging extent that he cannot grasp why men should bother to hold to them), and this characteristic gives his work great clarity. He never has to strive towards perspicuity, since he is never tempted even momentarily to abandon it. And in more than fifty years of activity he has put up such a consistent show of knowing what he means—and of writing it down so that it may be readily understood—that he has invited underestimation. The most difficult escape Houdini ever made was from a wet sheet, but since he was in the business of doing difficult-looking things he had to abandon this trick, because to the public it seemed easy. What Wilson was doing was never easy, but he had the good manners to make it look that way. If he could only have managed to dream up an objective correlative, or a few types of ambiguity, or if he had found it opportune to start lamenting the loss of an organic society, he would be much more fashionable now than he is. But we can search his work from end to end without finding any such conversation-piece. What we do find is a closely argued dramatic narrative in which good judgment and misjudgment both stand out plainly. The dangerous excitement of a tentatively formulated concept is absent from his work, and for most of us this is an excitement that is hard to forgo: the twentieth century has given us a palate for such pepper.

But there is another, more durable excitement which Wilson's entire body of work serves to define. There is a clue to it in *Upstate*, in the passage where Wilson discusses the different courses taken by Eliot and Van Wyck Brooks:

They were at Harvard at the same time, Brooks of the class of 1908, Eliot of 1910, and both, as was natural then, went, after college, to England. Eliot took root there, but Brooks said that, during the months he spent in England, he found himself preoccupied with American subjects. This difference marks the watershed in the early nineteen hundreds in American literary life. Eliot stays in England, which is for him still the motherland of literature in English, and becomes a European; Brooks returns to the United States and devotes himself to American writing, at the expense of what has been written in Europe. Eliot represents the growth of an American internationalism: Brooks, as a spokesman of the twenties, the beginnings of the sometimes all too conscious American literary self-glorification which is part of our American imperialism.

As it happened, Wilson was to go on to cover American subjects with all Brooks's thoroughness and more; and to parallel Eliot's internationalism while yet holding to the tacit belief that the American achievement could well be crucial in the continuity of that internationalism; and to combine these two elements with a total authority of preparation and statement. For that preparation, he had the brilliant education available in prewar Princeton to a young man ready to grasp it. For that statement, he was obliged to evolve a style which would make his comprehensive seriousness unmistakable in every line. Out of these two things came the solid achievement of judgments based on unarguable knowledge ably supplied to meet an historical demand. From the beginning, Wilson was a *necessary* writer, a chosen man. And it is this feeling of watching a man proving himself equal to an incontestably important task—explaining the world to America and explaining America to itself—which provides the constant excitement of Wilson's work.

Commanding this kind of excitement his prose needed no other. Wilson grew out of the great show-off period of American style. He could not have proceeded without the trail-blasting, first performed by Mencken and Nathan, but he was fundamentally different from them in not feeling bound to over-write.

Wilson's style adopted the Mencken–Nathan toughness but eschewed the belligerence—throwing no punches, it simply put its points and waited for intelligent men to agree. It assumed that intelligence could be a uniting factor rather than a divisive one. In the following passage (from "The Critic Who Does Not Exist", written in 1928 and later collected in *The Shores of Light*) this point is made explicitly:

What we lack, then, in the United States, is not writers or even literary parties, but simply serious literary criticism (the school of critics I have mentioned last, ie, Brooks, Mumford and Joseph Wood Krutch, though they set forth their own ideas, do not occupy themselves much with the art or ideas of the writers with whom they deal). Each of these groups does produce, to be sure, a certain amount of criticism to justify or explain what it is doing, but it may, I believe, be said in general that they do not communicate with one another; their opinions do not really circulate. It is astonishing to observe, in America, in spite of our floods of literary journalism, to what extent the literary atmosphere is a non-conductor of criticism. What actually happens, in our literary world, is that each leader or group of leaders is allowed to intimidate his disciples, either ignoring all the other leaders or taking cognizance of their existence only by distant

and contemptuous sneers. H. L. Mencken and T. S. Eliot present themselves, as I have said, from the critical point of view, as the most formidable
figures on the scene; yet Mencken's discussion of his principal rival has, so
far as my memory goes, been confined to an inclusion of the latter's works
among the items of one of those lists of idiotic current crazes in which the
Mercury usually includes also the recall of judges and paper-bag cookery.
And Eliot, established in London, does not, of course, consider himself
under the necessity of dealing with Mencken at all . . . Van Wyck Brooks,
in spite of considerable baiting, has never been induced to defend his
position (though Krutch has recently taken up some challenges). And the
romantics have been belaboured by the spokesmen of several different
camps without making any attempt to strike back. It, furthermore, seems
unfortunate that some of our most important writers—Sherwood Anderson and Eugene O'Neill, for example—should work, as they apparently do,
in almost complete intellectual isolation, receiving from the outside but
little intelligent criticism and developing, in their solitary labours, little
capacity for supplying it themselves.

Wilson's innovation was to treat the American intelligentsia as if it
were a European one, speaking a common language. "For there is
one language", he wrote in the same essay, "which all French writers,
no matter how divergent their aims, always possess in common: the
language of criticism." That was the ideal, and by behaving as if it
had already come about, he did a great deal to bring it into existence.
The neutral, dignified tone of his prose was crucial here: it implied
that there was no need for an overdose of personality, since writer
and reader were on a level and understood one another. As Lionel
Trilling has convincingly argued, Wilson's years in an editorial chair
for *The New Republic* were a big help in getting this tone right—he
was in action continuously (more than two-thirds of the pieces in *The
Shores of Light* first appeared in *The New Republic*) before a self-
defining audience of intelligent men, all of whom were capable of
appreciating that opinions should circulate.

The literary chronicles, especially *The Shores of Light*, are commonly valued above Wilson's more integrated books, and although
it seems likely that the people doing the valuing have not correctly
judged the importance of the latter, the evaluation nevertheless
seems just at first glance. As has often been pointed out, there is
nothing in criticism to beat the thrill of hearing Wilson produce the
first descriptions and definitions of the strong new American literature that was coming up in the 1920s—the first essays on Fitzgerald
and Hemingway will always stand as the perfect objects for any
literary journalist's envy and respect. But here again we must remem-

ber to avoid trying to nourish ourselves with condiments alone. What needs to be appreciated, throughout the literary chronicles, is the steady work of reporting, judging, sorting out, encouraging, reproving, and re-estimating. The three literary chronicles are, among other things, shattering reminders that many of the men we distinguish with the name of critic have never judged a piece of writing in their lives—just elaborated on judgments already formed by other men.

A certain demonstration of Wilson's integrity in this regard is his ability to assess minor and ancillary literature about which no general opinion has previously been built up: *The Shock of Recognition* and *Patriotic Gore* are natural culminations of Wilson's early drive towards mining and assaying in territory nobody else had even staked out. Wilson is a memory: he never at any stage believed that the historic process by which writings are forgotten should go unexamined or be declared irreversible. Remembering is one of the many duties the literary chronicles perform: not so spectacular a duty as discovering, but equally important. For Wilson's self-imposed task of circulating opinions within an intelligent community (a community whose existence depends on such a process for its whole existence), all these duties needed to be scrupulously carried out, and it is the triumph of the literary chronicles that they were carried out in so adventurous a way.

Unless all these things are held in mind, the true stature of the literary chronicles cannot be seen, even by those who value them above the rest of Wilson's work. In *The Shores of Light* it is necessary to appreciate not just "F. Scott Fitzgerald" and "Emergence of Ernest Hemingway", but also pieces like "The Literary Consequences of the Crash", "Talking United States", and "Prize-Winning Blank Verse". In *Classics and Commercials* we need to cherish not only the standout hatchet-jobs like "Who Cares Who Killed Roger Ackroyd?" and "Tales of the Marvellous and the Ridiculous" but also the assiduous labour of weighing up—never impatient, even when repelled—which went into essays like "Glenway Wescott's War Work" and "Van Wyck Brooks on the Civil War Period". And unless we can get rid of the notion that picking winners was Wilson's only true calling in life, we will have no hope at all of reaching a true estimation of *The Bit Between My Teeth*—a book disparaged as tired and thin by reviewers who in the full vigour of youth could not have matched the solidity of the least piece in it. "The Pre-Presidential T.R." and "The

Holmes-Laski Correspondence" are masterly examples of what Wilson can accomplish by bringing a literary viewpoint to historical documents; and "The Vogue of the Marquis de Sade" got the whole Sade revival into focus and incisively set the limits for its expansion.

The literary chronicles would have been more than enough by themselves to establish Wilson's pre-eminence: to a high degree they have that sense of the drama of creativity which Taine had been able to capture and exploit. If people are going to read only some of Wilson instead of all of him, then the chronicles are what they should read. But it is one thing to say this, and another to accept the assumption—distressingly widespread in recent years—that *Axel's Castle* and *The Wound and the Bow* and *The Triple Thinkers* have in some way done the work they had to do and may be discarded, like used-up boosters. There is not much doubt about how such an idea gained currency, books of long essays being so much harder to read than books of short ones. But there is no reason for anyone who has actually read and understood a book like *Axel's Castle* to go along with such a slovenly notion. When, in the Yeats chapter of that book, Wilson compared the Yeats of 1931 to the Dante who was able "to sustain a grand manner through sheer intensity without rhetorical heightening", he was writing permanent criticism, criticism which can't be superseded, certainly not by pundits who are boning up their Dante from a parallel text instead of learning it the hard way from a teacher like Christian Gauss. It is barbarism of a peculiarly academic kind to suppose that truths of this order—not insights, explications, or glosses, but truths—can be appropriated to a data-bank or dismissed as obsolete. A Dantesque "epigrammatic bitterness" is *precisely* the quality to see in the mature Yeats, and in 1931, before the last poems were written, it was virtually prescient to be able to see it, since that quality had not yet reached its full concentration.

Wilson paid heavy penalties for being plain—or rather we paid heavy penalties for not seeing the force of his plainness. In the Eliot chapter of *Axel's Castle* he said something about Eliot that forty years of theses and learned articles have done their best to bury, something which we are only now capable of seeing as criticism rather than conversation, the intervening hubbub of academic industry having revealed itself as conversation rather than criticism:

We are always being dismayed, in our general reading, to discover that lines among those which we had believed to represent Eliot's residuum of original invention had been taken over or adapted from other writers. . . .

One would be inclined *a priori* to assume that all this load of erudition and literature would be enough to sink any writer, and that such a production as "The Waste Land" must be a work of second-hand inspiration. And it is true that, in reading Eliot and Pound, we are sometimes visited by uneasy recollections of Ausonius, in the fourth century, composing Greek-and-Latin macaronics and piecing together poetic mosaics out of verses from Virgil. Yet Eliot manages to be most effective precisely—in "The Waste Land"—where he might be expected to be least original—he succeeds in conveying his meaning, in communicating his emotion, in spite of all his learned or mysterious allusions, and whether we understand them or not.

In this respect, there is a curious contrast between Eliot and Ezra Pound.

With Pound, Wilson was like Tallulah Bankhead faced with a tricksy production of Shakespeare: he wasn't afraid to announce, "There's less in this than meets the eye". With Eliot, he was bold enough to say that things were simpler than they appeared at first blush. Both these judgments were backed up by a deep learning which had nothing to fear from either man, by a sense of quality which knew how to rely on itself, and by a seriousness which was not concerned with putting up a front.

There is no need to go on with this part of the argument. It's more merciful simply to state that Wilson's entire critical corpus will go on being read so long as men are prepared to read widely and well. His strategy of using magazines—first *The New Republic*, later the *New Yorker*—as shipyards in which to assemble books was triumphantly successful. He is the ideal of the metropolitan critic, who understood from the beginning that the intelligence of the metropolis is in a certain relation to the intelligence of the academy, and went on understanding this even when the intelligence of the academy ceased to understand its relation to the intelligence of the metropolis. When Wilson called the Modern Language Association to order, he performed the most important academic act of the postwar years—he reminded the scholars that their duty was to literature.

For Wilson literature has always been an international community, with a comprehensible politics of its own. He learnt languages not just out of passionate curiosity but out of quasi-political purpose, becoming acquainted with whole literatures in the same way that a man who carries an international passport proves himself a part of the main. As late as the mid-1950s Wilson was apologizing for not having done enough in this line: he has always been a trifle guilty about failing to get interested in Portuguese and Spanish. But to a chastening extent he had already made himself the universal literatus, and in the later decades of his life we find him becoming increasingly conscious that this is his major role—if he has any significance in the realm of action, then this is it. Modesty has never been among Wilson's characteristics, but a certain diffidence does creep in, of which the quietism and resignation of *Upstate* are the logical culmination. The central paradox of Wilson remains unresolved: he has put himself above the battle, inhabiting an Empyrean of knowledge by now fundamentally divorced from an unworkable world. The paradox was vicious from the beginning, becoming more and more so as modern history unfolded in front of him. Wilson was a born internationalist in literature and a born isolationist in politics, and there is a constant tension between the achieved serenity of his literary judgment and the threatening complexity of his self-consciousness as an American.

A patrician individualist by nature, Wilson was automatically debarred from running with the pack. His radicalism in the 1920s and 1930s had a decisive qualitative difference from any Marxist analyses currently available: it was elitist, harking back to the informed democracy of the American past, and therefore on a richer historical base than the hastily imported European doctrines which bemused his contemporaries. Wilson's reports on Detroit are as devastating as Marx on the working day, but the intensity is the only connexion. Wilson was revolted by industrialism's depredations—if the ecological lobby ever wants to put a bible together, there are sections of *The American Earthquake* which could go straight into Revelations—but the revulsion was just as much on behalf of what America had previously been as on behalf of what it might become. Marxism is future-directed metaphysics: Wilson's thought was bent towards the literary recovery of the estimable past.

Making no commitment to communism, Wilson was never compelled to scramble away from it, and he maintained his dignity throughout the 1930s. By 1940 he had completed his analysis of the revolutionary tradition in Europe and published it as *To the Finland Station*. In the final paragraph of that book he declared it unlikely that the Marxist creeds would be able to bring about

a society in which the superior development of some is not paid for by the exploitation, that is, by the deliberate degradation of others—a society which will be homogeneous and cooperative as our commercial society is not, and directed, to the best of their ability, by the conscious creative minds of its members.

America went to war again, and again Wilson was isolationist: as
with the First World War, so with the Second, he saw no point in
America becoming involved. He was still explaining such phenomena
by market pressures and the devious conniving of Big Business—it
was a Fabian position, never much altered since he first picked it up
from Leonard Woolf.

Wilson has difficulty in understanding how irrational forces can be
so potent. In *Europe without Baedeker* and *A Piece of my Mind* he
came close to holding the Europeans collectively responsible for
pulling their own houses down in ruins about their heads. It was the
high point of his isolationism, further reinforced by a commitment
to the American past amounting to visionary fervour. In his admiration for Lincoln we find Wilson getting very near the mysticism he
spent a lifetime scrupulously avoiding. Finally he found an historical
base solid-seeming enough to justify the relieved rediscovery of a
Platonic Guardian class. "To simplify", he wrote in *A Piece of my
Mind* (1957),

one can say that, on the one hand, you find in the United States the people
who are constantly aware . . . that, beyond their opportunities for money-
making, they have a stake in the success of our system, that they share the
responsibility to carry on its institutions, to find expression for its new
point of view, to give it dignity, to make it work; and, on the other hand,
the people who are merely concerned with making a living or a fortune,
with practising some profession or mastering some technical skill, as they
would in any other country, and who lack, or do not possess to quite the
same degree, the sense of America's role.

That was as far as he got: the Republic he loved began to be overwhelmed by the Democracy he had never been sure about, and in the
new reality of the 1960s he found himself taxed but unrepresented.

In *Upstate* Wilson is faced with the ruins of the American Dream,
and appears to be forgetting what we are bound to remember: that
the fragments can be built with and that this fact is in some measure
due to him. The intellectual community which is now fighting for the
Republic against its own debilitating tumours was to a considerable
extent his personal creation. That Americans of good will, in the
midst of wearying political confusion, can yet be so confident of their
nation's creativity is again in a large part due to him. As Christian
Gauss was to Wilson—master to pupil—Wilson is to nobody:
nobody he can see. He now doubts the continuity he helped to
define. But, beyond the range of vision now limiting itself to Cape

Cod and Talcottville, there will always be young men coming up who will find his achievement a clear light. He is one of the great men of letters in our century.

(b) REAL AND SOCIAL SELVES

Now and then it is possible to observe the moral life in process of revising itself, perhaps by reducing the emphasis it formerly placed on one or another of its elements, perhaps by inventing and adding to itself a new element, some mode of conduct or of feeling which hitherto it had not regarded as essential to virtue.

THIS IS the opening sentence of Lionel Trilling's Harvard lectures, *Sincerity and Authenticity*, and it is easy to recognize in it a constant preoccupation of his writing. It has been his special mission to observe those moments when culture turns over in its sleep and adopts a new posture, and to study the works in which such revisions of attitude become evident. It is a concern that attaches itself naturally to the Arnoldian ideal of criticism, something more than the reassessment of established classics, or the scrutiny of new additions to the canon; a critical ideal which aspires to survey the tendency and direction of a whole culture, sometimes at a turning-point in the past, but always with an eye to the urgencies and actualities of the present.

At a time when so much criticism has lost itself in fiddle-faddle or pedagogy the gravity and dignity of this purpose stand out with welcome clarity. If anything is to vindicate the ambitious claims that literary criticism was accustomed to make for itself some years ago it must be some such aim as this. Professor Trilling, like Matthew Arnold before him, has always been immune to the more evident dangers of such a programme. He has never been tempted to instant diagnoses or patent-medicine remedies. Yet there are other dangers, and to these it is precisely the most discerning practitioners who are most exposed. For a writer unprotected by obtuseness or indifference it is possible to react too sensitively to the signs of the times, to respond too readily to immediate pressures. This sometimes happened with Arnold; his vivacities at the expense of the Rev William Cattle or the British College of Health in the New Road, though still delightful to amateurs of the nineteenth century, were directed at rather transitory targets; and in our present world of global convulsions the pertinacity and seriousness of his criticism seem after all to have been focused on a very English cultural crisis—crisis as felt by the son of Dr Arnold of Rugby. Its configuration would hardly have been acknowledged by his contemporaries Marx or Baudelaire. And it is so in some of Professor Trilling's earlier work; the cultural crisis of the twentieth century is projected from the viewpoint of a professor of modern literature at Columbia University—not always recognizable in the same proportions from Western Europe, even by those somewhat ambiguous Europeans, the English.

But attacks of cultural malaise succeed each other with such rapidity in our century that they breed in the end a dumb resistance. Professor Trilling's mind seems by nature to move more slowly than the kaleidoscope of circumstance, and he is obliged to search out the unobserved constants among its changing images. It is notable that the themes of *Sincerity and Authenticity* are still in large part the same as those of his earlier book *Beyond Culture* (1965). The same texts and the same authors occupy the same prominent positions— *Le Neveu de Rameau*, Jane Austen, Nietzsche, especially *The Birth of Tragedy*, Conrad's *Heart of Darkness*, the later writings of Freud. But much has happened since 1965, both outwardly and inwardly, to set them in a new light. The position of America in world esteem has radically altered, and old half-conscious assumptions are no longer possible. The earlier, rather surprising, concurrence in Clark Kerr's vision of the super-university as the natural home of creative effort has now disappeared—for obvious reasons, one supposes. The more patent and immediate symptoms of *das Unbehagen in der Kultur* are still indeed observed, but they are placed in a much longer historical perspective and treated with more firmness. English writing on matters of this kind tends to high-table mumble or the chatter of NW1, American to the New York or Californian apocalyptic style.

Professor Trilling has always written with too much delicacy and scrupulousness to fall into any of these modes; and he has now found a manner of presentation that quite transcends local deformations. It is always a problem for the writer of cultural criticism to address his special audience and at the same time to make his observations properly available *urbi et orbi*. *Sincerity and Authenticity* is a beautifully written book, its tone admirably judged and perfectly sustained.

The discussion moves within wide historical limits. It is not easy to say with any precision when sincerity first makes its appearance as a new element in the moral life. We cannot, Professor Trilling remarks, reasonably ask whether the patriarch Abraham, or Achilles, or Beowulf, was sincere; but we can ask this question about the young Werther or Marianne Dashwood. It is when society begins to be conceived as an entity set over against the individual that the question of sincerity becomes a matter of concern. It begins, that is to say, with a period of increased social mobility, when the individual is no longer simply fixed in a predetermined and unarguable state, but becomes aware of himself as a mobile unit in a system that can to some degree be viewed objectively. In England this means the end of the sixteenth century, and Professor Trilling cites in evidence the number of villains in Elizabethan and Jacobean tragedy who are dissemblers—unwilling to be what they are, pretending to be something else, in order to become something else again. Even when a measure of social fluidity is seen as natural or desirable the actual process of moving from one status to another is always fraught with danger and attended by moral suspicion. The ideal is what seventeenth-century France called the *honnête homme*, and what Hegel later (though probably not quoting this phrase) was to call "the honest soul"—the man who can be what he is, show himself to others as he is, and regard the authorities and institutions of his society with equanimity and respect.

A key place in Professor Trilling's argument is occupied by Diderot's *Le Neveu de Rameau*, with its contrast between Diderot-*Moi*, as the honest soul, and Rameau the nephew, the failed man of talent, the outcast from the system, a fawner, a flatterer, a conscious hypocrite; the man with no assured centre of personality. Such a man is precluded from sincerity since he has to be all things to all men; and the brilliant picture of his hopelessly fragmented character reaches its climax in the scene where, in a frenzy of motility, the nephew enacts a whole opera in his own person, playing all the parts, imitating all the instruments, becomes a hurricane, a cataract, the night itself. This is the character, fundamentally untrue to himself because there is no self to be true to, that is referred to by Hegel in the *Phenomenology*, and becomes his prime example of what he calls Spirit alienated from itself, or the disintegrated consciousness. It is Hegel's commentary as much as the original *nouvelle* that takes the central place in Professor Trilling's discussion. The honest soul for Hegel is "noble", the disintegrated consciousness is "base". The honest soul can conceive and aspire to possess a moral and social resting-place. Its vision of the good life is honour, peace, order and beauty; a vision seen equally as the goal in Shakespeare's last plays and the novels of Jane Austen.

It is a defect in the culture of Anglo-Saxons that very few of them carry the whole argument of *The Phenomenology of Spirit* in their heads; and Professor Trilling does well to remind us (if we knew it we are apt to forget) that Hegel comes down decisively against the "noble" consciousness and in favour of the "base". He rules wholly in favour of the nephew, wholly against Diderot-*Moi*. The honest soul is rejected by Hegel because it is defined and limited by its "noble" relation to the external power of society; the "base" is saluted because it represents the effort of Spirit to resist the conditions imposed upon it by the "noble" ethos. Once this realization has acquired a foothold, sincerity as an ideal is on the defensive. It is defended by Rousseau in his argument against role-playing in the *Lettre à M d'Alembert sur les Spectacles*. It lives on in England in the novel; and Professor Trilling at this point sensitively extends his earlier discussions of Jane Austen—that uncompromising defender of the "noble" consciousness who is yet aware of the dialectic between its acknowledged superiority and the forces that are continually threatening to disrupt it.

From this time on England has always been apt to linger in an earlier historical phase than the rest of Europe, and we might remark (though Professor Trilling does not) the contrast between the English and the French novel throughout the nineteenth century—between *David Copperfield*, say, and *L'Education sentimentale*: the one leading to an "honest" reconciliation between the self and the world, the other showing that any such reconciliation is impossible. By now we are approaching the age of Nietzsche, and already foreseeing the age of Freud.

As the ideal of sincerity, the honest soul and the noble consciousness becomes progressively more difficult to entertain, the second of Professor Trilling's new moral elements makes its appearance. This is the rival ideal of authenticity—a notion that depends radically on the recognition of a divided consciousness. Beneath the surface of functioning social life and the accepted relations of man to man lurks a rival system of forces, destructive and uncontrolled. The exemplary text here is Conrad's *Heart of Darkness*, with its hero Kurtz, the possessor of every civilized accomplishment, the fine flower of European cultural idealism, betrayed by the depths of his own nature to bestial savagery and cruelty and an end of pure horror. The succeeding discussion does not take us into the computerized wasteland where even Mr Kurtz is dead. The presiding geniuses of the latter part of the book are Nietzsche and Freud, and the subject under examination is the state of our own cultural imagination. It is indeed this process of self-examination that the whole discussion has been leading up to; and that is its strength.

The Apollonian and the Dionysian principles in Nietzsche are historically conditioned foreshadowings of the Ego and the Id in Freud, and the daunting requirement of authenticity is that these obscure forces shall be brought back from banishment and recognized as part of our lives. Needless to say, Professor Trilling does not fall into the vulgar error of regarding Nietzsche and Freud as mere champions of Dionysus and the Id. He knows very well that the argument of *The Birth of Tragedy* is weighted as much in favour of Apollo as of Dionysus, that the argument of Freud is for the assumption of the Id into the manageable daylight of the Ego. But he knows equally well that this is not the way they have been read. The contemporary reader sees Dionysus as the almost undisputed protagonist of *The Birth of Tragedy*, and Apollo as a rather tiresome ancillary. Freud is commonly thought to authorize the unbinding of exactly those forces that it was his purpose to control.

Here, as in *Beyond Culture*, we find Professor Trilling asking himself in some bewilderment what strange imperative it is that drives the modern imagination to this blatant misinterpretation of two of its patron saints. He gives a partial answer in the present book. Sincerity in the old sense is not possible to the characteristic aesthetic attitudes of the modern imagination,

whose masters took the position that, in relation to their work and their audience, they were not persons or selves, they were artists, by which they meant that they were exactly not, in the phrase with which Wordsworth began his definition of the poet, men speaking to men.

Not men speaking to men, through the nexus of custom and institution by which men commonly speak to one another. The modern artist is the possessor of an impersonal shamanistic power, the transmitter of a message that comes from beyond the bounds of rational consciousness.

Here it is appropriate to desert Professor Trilling's argument and speak of the quality of his own writing. It is wide, fastidious and deeply thoughtful in its range of reference. Temperate, controlled and delicately scrupulous, it is a tribute if ever there was one to the

"honest" consciousness. Yet these qualities exist in a state of acute
tension because they can find no anchorage in the present cultural
scene. The art that has spoken most powerfully to Professor Trilling
is the classic literature of our century, from which the "honest soul"
has been banished as a pitiable and inauthentic survivor. Its songs
have had one theme—"Things fall apart, the centre cannot hold";
"Uber diese Lieder lacht der Bürger beleidigt, der Heilige und Seher
hört sie mit Tränen." Well, Professor Trilling does not assume the
role of saint or seer, and he does not show us his tears; but his
writing in this latest phase gains an unwonted poignancy from the
sharp divergence between the natural tendencies of his mind and the
tendencies of the living culture to which he has responded most
deeply. At earlier dates he seemed to entertain the possibility of some
actual resting-place for the spirit—the university perhaps or some
corner of the civilization of his own country. These refuges never
looked very plausible, and now, it appears, he looks to them no
more: he has become a lonelier writer and a stronger one.

If this is so, it is not surprising that he should pay much attention
to Freud's *Civilization and its Discontents*. He notes the movement
away from the Freudian position in recent years. There is Sartre's
argument that we are conscious of our unconscious all the time, and
that it is mere "bad faith" to place the unconscious beyond the
bounds of responsibility, as though it were not part of ourselves.
Professor Trilling points out that this objection has been partly
anticipated by Freud himself; and for the rest it is largely a matter of
terminology. We have only to posit the antithesis in other terms—
two consciousnesses, both ours, but the one inaccessible to the other
by introspection. The bad faith disappears and the problem remains
the same. As he has done before, Professor Trilling examines the
Freudian arguments with some minuteness, and in Freud's last communications he finds a kind of sombre nobility. The self-division of
consciousness is not a twentieth-century disease curable by alterations
in the social system: it is inherent in man's development that he
turn part of his energies against himself in punitive guilt. More for-
bearing and gentle in its manner than most of Freud's earlier pronouncements, that is his last message. And Professor Trilling asks
why Freud brought his intellectual life to its climax with this dark
doctrine. He proposes an answer—that Freud, for whom religion was
an illusion, needs a surrogate for the hardness, the acceptance of
suffering, that runs through the Jewish and Christian traditions.

The last pages of *Sincerity and Authenticity* deal with some post-Freudian nostrums. Marcuse sets out expressly to deny the contentions of *Civilization and its Discontents* in the name of social hope, but with a startling internal contradiction—for he remains signally dissatisfied with the relaxation of character engendered by his own libertarian principles. Last there are the writers—R. D. Laing, David Cooper and Norman O. Brown are cited—who find in total alienation, the literal alienation of insanity, a guide through the modern labyrinth. This is a turbid area, and anything like a *prise de position* on such matters would fall short of both sincerity and authenticity.

But there is a line to be drawn, and finally Professor Trilling draws it. The exaltation of insanity as a means to the profoundest authenticity derives perhaps from an unjustified inflation of the doctrine of this anti-psychiatric school of psychiatrists; but it has been encouraged by their ill-controlled vaticinations and the frantic incoherence of their elected style. Professor Brown is not worth much powder and shot, but perhaps he serves the same purpose as the Rev William Cattle. Professor Trilling displays a damaging passage from David Cooper—one of those well-chosen citations that does not require destructive criticism; it destroys itself. He offers a guarded salute to Laing, and finds some seeds of cogency in the view that proposes an antinomian reversal of all accepted values.

But he follows it with a moving and impressive rebuke:

Who that has spoken, tried to speak, with a psychotic friend will consent to betray the masked pain of his bewilderment and solitude by making it the paradigm of liberation from the imprisoning falsehoods of an alienated social reality.

Who will consent to

the appalling belief that human existence is made authentic by the possession of a power, or by the persuasion of its possession, which is not to be qualified or restricted by the coordinate existence of any fellow man?

In short, he finds the position of these counsellors, whatever suasions to it our present state may offer, deeply tainted with cant. And, with a severity that is both rare in his writing and greatly to be welcomed, he says so.

4

THE OUTLOOK FOR ULSTER
(*a*) A MEASURE OF LOYALTY

DECENT PEOPLE in England who have given earnest, but not very prolonged, thought to the Northern Ireland question sometimes come up with the idea that the solution would be the appointment of a Catholic Tory Lord as Executive Governor. The Catholics would love him for his religion, the Protestants for his politics. The process would be helped on by a combined visit of the Pope and the Archbishop of Canterbury, to recommend religious peace.

Direct contact with the area, and conversation with members of the two communities, brings the depressing discovery that a Catholic Tory would be the most unpopular of all possible governors. The Catholics, it is true, would not necessarily dislike him much more for being Catholic as well as Governor. If he were an English Catholic, the weight of additional dislike would hardly be perceptible, since the Catholicism of the English is not felt to be the same as the religion of the same name practised in Ireland. There would just be the embarrassment which is generally felt when a gesture intended to be agreeable falls flat. But if the new Governor were an Irish Catholic he would be regarded by many Catholics as a traitor—an Irishman representing an English monarch in Ireland—and would be high on the assassination lists. As for the Ulster Protestants, the appointment of a Catholic—of whatever provenance—as Executive Governor would appear to many of them as the worst insult and threat to the province since the reign of James II, and since the arch-traitor Lundy was governor of Londonderry.

(*a*) RICHARD ROSE: *Governing Without Consensus.* 567 pp. Faber and Faber. £6.

R. S. P. ELLIOT and JOHN HICKIE: *Ulster.* A Case Study in Conflict Theory. 180 pp. Longman. £2.80.

CONSTANTINE FITZGIBBON: *Red Hand: The Ulster Colony.* 367 pp. Michael Joseph. £3.

(*b*) CONOR CRUISE O'BRIEN: *States of Ireland.* 336 pp. Hutchinson. £3.25.

So far as the Pope and the Archbishop of Canterbury are concerned, the undoubted pleasure of Belfast Catholics at seeing their Holy Father would be marred by the spectacle of tens of thousands of their fellow citizens trying to get at that venerated figure in order to drown him in the Lagan (together with the Archbishop for coming with the Pope, and thereby becoming, in Protestant eyes, what an Irish Catholic Governor would be in Irish Catholic eyes—a traitor). The whole ecumenical exercise, if carried out, would produce riots and mayhem on a scale far exceeding anything that even Belfast has yet known. Fortunately, the Pope, whether infallible or not, has sense enough to keep out of Belfast.

Components and variants of the Catholic/Governor/Pope/Archbishop cure have been heard from more than one member of Parliament, and from a newspaper magnate. Their disaster-fraught suggestions were the result, not of stupidity or ill-will, but of superficial information. It is probable that if they had read the first of the three books reviewed here they would not have offered these suggestions, and indeed that they would have refrained altogether from utterance on this grim, complex and impracticable subject.

Richard Rose's *Governing Without Consensus* is probably the most illuminating book ever written about Northern Ireland. Its core is made up of the responses to what Professor Rose called a "loyalty" survey carried out by him over "a multi-stage stratified random sample of 1,500 households". The stratification of areas was "by religion, partisanship, and urban, semi-urban or rural character". A total of 757 Protestants and 534 Roman Catholics were interviewed: 58.6 per cent Protestant and 41.4 per cent Catholic— approximating the actual balance of the two communities, with a slight inflation of the Catholic component.

The inflation is not significant for the survey, since results are presented separately for Protestant and Catholic respondents. It was carried out during the period March to August, 1968. The results therefore relate to the last months of what we may now call "The old Northern Ireland". The period of the survey was not only before the coming of serious violence, but also before the Civil Rights Movement entered its active phase of non-violent militancy, in October, 1968. It must not, therefore, be assumed that the attitudes recorded by Professor Rose are those now held by the same proportion of the two communities. In many cases they almost certainly are not: a hardening of attitudes, in both communities, throughout the period between 1968 and 1972 is something which almost all observers agree in discerning. The true extent, character and distribution of what is vaguely described as "hardening" could, however, only be found out by means of a new survey, conducted as closely as possible on the lines of Professor Rose's 1968 survey.

Fortunately Professor Rose was very happy in his choice of dates; a survey finished in the summer of 1968 forms the perfect baseline against which to measure the effects of the years of challenge and of violence. Unfortunately, it would probably not be safe to attempt such a survey either in present conditions, or in any conditions likely soon to exist in the province; and if a new survey were attempted its results might not be reliable. A climate of fear, suspicion, intimidation and violence is unfavourable to the carrying-through of any kind of public opinion survey, but especially of one on so "hot" a subject as loyalty.

The material in this long book—more than 550 pages including the notes—is rich in detail. No attempt will be made here to summarize a book which everyone seriously interested in Northern Ireland will want to read for themselves, but attention should be drawn to certain aspects of Professor Rose's findings which seem particularly significant.

The first concerns the degree of alienation of the Catholic minority from the Northern Ireland regime, in the forty-ninth year of that regime's existence. This survey shows that that alienation—while greater than certain Unionist spokesmen, in their more euphorically "Rhodesian" moments, suggested—was less, indeed considerably less, than nationalist spokesmen were accustomed to claim. Professor Rose's single most startling finding is that 33 per cent of the Catholic part of his sample said they approved the constitutional position of Northern Ireland; 34 per cent said they disapproved; 32 per cent said they didn't know. (We aren't told what happened to the other 1 per cent.) Among Protestants the proportions were: approve 68 per cent; disapprove 10 per cent; don't know 22 per cent (apparently Protestants are more amenable to being added up than Catholics are).

Even in 1968, 34 per cent was almost certainly inadequate as an index of Catholic alienation. Many of the 33 per cent "don't knows" could probably be added to it. Professor Rose indicates that they were "persons of limited education", and it seems they just failed to understand a rather fancily-worded question. But even if we make the extreme assumption that all the "don't knows" can be lumped with the "disapproves", we are still left with the fact, as it was then, of approval of the Northern Ireland Constitution by one third of the Catholics. In present circumstances it may safely be assumed that that figure would be greatly reduced.

It might be thought that the 33 per cent who approved were the upper crust of the Catholic community. Other parts of the survey, however, show little reason to believe that there is much class difference between them and the 34 per cent "disapproves" (although most of the "don't knows" presumably fall in a lower class than either of the deciding groups). Professor Rose finds a strong correlation between political views and religion; and a weak correlation between political views and social class. These facts are of course obvious to anyone who has spent any time in Northern Ireland, but like many other obvious facts they have been partly concealed from view by a froth of rhetoric. Professor Rose blows away much of the froth.

In so far as class differences are more important than religious differences, then Ulster people of the same class should have more similar regime outlooks than people of different classes but the same religion. The data from the loyalty surveys clearly rejects this hypothesis. The difference between middle-class and working-class Protestants in support for the constitution is 4 per cent and 3 per cent in endorsement of an Ultra position. Similarly, among Catholics, there is only a 2 per cent difference across classes in support for the constitution, and a 5 per cent difference in readiness to demonstration against the regime. The differences between religions are much larger. Within the middle class, Protestants and Catholics differ by 36 percentage points in their readiness to support the constitution. And manual workers differ by 30 percentage points. In refusal to comply with basic political laws, about half of each class group is ready to endorse extra-constitutional actions against others who share class but not regime outlooks. It is particularly noteworthy that there is no consistent tendency for middle-class Ulster people to be readiest to endorse the constitution and refrain from extra-constitutional politics, notwithstanding their relative advantage in terms of status.

Governing Without Consensus is a rather depressing book—as any objective book on Northern Ireland has to be. One can pick from it, for consolation, two straws of potential hope. One is the fact that, whereas the Catholic hierarchy have rejected integrated education— Catholics and Protestants together—no less than 69 per cent of the Catholic part of Professor Rose's sample are in favour of integrated education. (This is, even so, a frail little straw for the author also finds that "while attendance at mixed schools tends to reduce Ultra and rebel views, it does so only to a very limited extent". The figures he cites, however, are a little more encouraging than his "very limited" would suggest.)

The second relatively hopeful finding—and a much-needed ray of hope at the present time—is that people who recalled "actively bad" community relations showed the least propensity to endorse violence. "This suggests", says Professor Rose, "that while sectarian bitterness will make people fighting mad, some who see its consequences in bloodshed and disorder will react against it." Let us hope the "some" will become "many".

The factual content of *Governing Without Consensus* is presented with admirable lucidity and fairness. Professor Rose's theoretical formulations based on the material seem to be less satisfactory, being both over-elaborate and excessively noncommital: a combination favoured by too many social scientists. There is one other small carp. The photographs included relate mainly to a period later than the loyalty survey, and may mislead the unwary reader by their topicality. Professor Rose does comment on events later than 1968, but it is from the survey he then directed that all the attitudes analysed by him are taken. Yet the merits of this book overwhelmingly outweigh its deficiencies, and all concerned with Northern Ireland owe a deep debt of gratitude to Professor Rose.

Ulster: A Case Study in Conflict Theory is the kind of book that brings conflict-theory studies into disrepute. The authors set out by raising hopes that they are about to bring to bear on the Northern Ireland conflict more precise and sensitive terminology and more rigorous methods than have yet been applied to it. We could do with this. But in reality nothing is brought to bear on anything. The book consists in the main of slices of theoretical verbiage alternating with slices of popular and highly inaccurate history and social description. There is little or no interpenetration between the theoretical bit and the narrative-and-descriptive bits, and the conclusions, so far as they concern Ulster, are not based either on the theory or on the narrative. Some of them are merely the sort of thing the weariest leader-writer could have thought up without "scientific" assistance:

This indicates that until constructive steps are taken it seems unlikely that there will be any progress in relations between the two communities and therefore in bringing an end to the trouble.

Others are mere wish-fulfilments, flying in the face of the observed facts: "This is because there is now a chance of a radical re-structuring of the political division—away from religion, towards a class framework."

The book also contains the insignificant results of an embarrassingly amateurish survey conducted in March, 1969, by means of interviews with some politicians in Belfast and a few in Dublin. The politicians talked their heads off, it seems, and the interviewers, having neither shorthand nor tape-recorders, wrote down bits here and there. "All the answers", as the authors disarmingly observe, "are an edited version distorted in terms of what the interviewer thought most important."

The interviewers could scarcely have been competent to edit this material nor would the authors have been competent, because they do not seem to know their chosen field of study well enough, as appears at many points. That they mugged up their subject hastily and approximately is shown, for example, by a reference to "the 1789 Irish Socialist uprising"; the statement that "during the war Southern Ireland gave support to the German cause and it was then [*sic*] that the slogan 'England's danger is Eire's [*sic*] opportunity' was coined": by the appearance of distorted proper names like "Warroughk" and "Whittacker"; by the definition of the Dáil as "the Dublin Houses of Parliament" as well as by more subtle evidences of unfamiliarity. Moreover, the standard of proof-reading is so bad that it is often hard to know whether the authors mean what they actually appear to be saying, or the opposite, or something in between: for instance, "cases of violent conflict between communities of roughly the same size are rarer than those where there is equality". On the whole, "inequality" seems the more likely reading.

Red Hand: The Ulster Colony is a rather easy-going, informal discussion of the historical roots of Northern Ireland. Many people are likely to find it readable and informative. Others will find it rather difficult reading because of Constantine FitzGibbon's tendency to slip from period to period, with very little notice; and his frequent and rather strange comparisons with outside phenomena. Very little of this book deals with contemporary Northern Ireland, and Mr FitzGibbon is not at his best in this section: "It would seem that the Red IRA being now under the control of International Communism as directed from Moscow, has been ordered to hold its hand for the time being. . . ." In fact it does not appear that either the "Green" or the "Red" IRA is under the control of anything—certainly not of anything so remote and exotic as "International Communism . . .

directed from Moscow". This is the equivalent of the theory that the men of 1916 were in the pay of Berlin. In reality, Irish rebels have responded to Irish situations in their own way, sometimes borrowing rhetoric or ideology from abroad, and often looking there for weapons and other aid, but seldom amenable to outside advice. In any case, Moscow, like Rome (or even Dublin), would find it difficult to assess each crisis arising in Ardoyne or Andersonstown in time for its advice to have much relevance. Things move quickly, under pressure of local competition.

(*b*) SHARING AN ISLAND

When Conor Cruise O'Brien gave up his prestigious professorship in New York to join the political menagerie in Dublin there was much speculation about what he would make of it, and it of him. That his presence in Leinster House would cause the Dáil debates to blossom occasionally from Billingsgate into literature was a prediction which has more than once been fulfilled. It was also reasonable to suppose that the impact of his strong personality and cosmopolitan experience upon that stalwart body of conservatives known as the Irish Labour Party would be considerable, though now that the initial euphoria has worn off it is difficult to be sure how these excellent geese are reacting to the swan so suddenly decanted upon them in 1969.

What could not have been expected in 1969—at least until the bloody August of that year—was that Northern Ireland would rush so fast along its murderous course of self-destruction that this continuing crisis would become the obsessive preoccupation of all Irish politicians North and South. Dr Cruise O'Brien, as his party's spokesman on the Ulster question, has been more deeply involved than most and *States of Ireland* is the result.

It is a rather strange book, which is both typical and untypical of its author. It is typical in its irony and wit and pugnacity, untypical in its apparent shapelessness. One needs to say "apparent" because the different sections cohere more closely than a casual reader might discern, but the overall effect remains somewhat confusing. The book consists of some general history, fragments of literary criticism, spasms of autobiography, an extract from Dr Cruise O'Brien's political diary for the ominous summer of 1970, an extended account of the developing situation in Northern Ireland and, by way of appendix, a splendid diatribe against Sinn Fein which was intended to flatten the President of that organization (Official wing) in public debate and by all accounts did just that.

Described thus baldly, the book seems a bit of a mess. This, however, is by no means fortuitous. The mess, so to speak, is the message. Dr Cruise O'Brien is writing out of the depths of a world where ignorant armies clash by night (sometimes, also, in broad daylight) and he wishes us to understand that confusion is an essential part of that nightmare. He has sometimes been confused himself and, with his usual honesty, does not hesitate to tell us when what he had earlier said or written now strikes him as false or inadequate. Yet, although this exposes *States of Ireland* to the criticism that it too may be a transitional document and that Dr Cruise O'Brien may be adopting a different stance some time in the future, such a criticism would be unjust. It would be unjust because the important things he is saying here he has been saying for several years—at this moment he carries his political life in his hands for saying them—and because the book is at bottom a deeply reflective one, being founded on his own highly intelligent and perceptive view of Irish history.

It is not necessary to agree with everything he writes in order to appreciate the significance of his interpretation. He probably overestimates the effect of the fall of Parnell in 1890–91 on the generation which grew up in the shadow of that event. It is customary among historians—and broadly correct—to derive from that traumatic experience both the Irish disenchantment with constitutional politics and the revival of romantic nationalism. But there is a danger here of under-stressing the hold which the parliamentarians continued to have on Irish opinion and also of minimizing the fact (which Dr Cruise O'Brien mentions, albeit briefly) that up to 1941 the real threat to Home Rule came not from romantic revolutionaries but from Ulster Unionists and British Conservatives. However, it is plain that Dr Cruise O'Brien is more than a little obsessed with Parnell, so much so that he even indulges in a little "transference", apparently believing that it was only his family connexions which saved him from getting the "1891 treatment" at the general election of 1969. It must be admitted though that his Parnellite sensitivity is not unjustified. He has indeed had the "1891 treatment" once already. It was from the British Right over Katanga, and it may be that he will get it again, but, irony of ironies, this time from the Irish Left.

If this happens it will be because his reading of the past and present, together with his own mixed origins, makes him more aware than most Southern politicians of the differences which separate Protestants and Catholics in Ireland. (Like other civilized commentators he abhors that "religious" nomenclature but cannot do without it.) Because he is so conscious of these differences he insists that the present demand for Irish unity is irresponsible. Indeed, he goes further and suggests that none of the main sections of the population of Ireland actually wants unity. "In short", he writes, "what has been coming across to ordinary people is that our problem is *not* 'how to get unity' but how to share an island in conditions of peace and reasonable fairness, and that such conditions *preclude* unity as long as the Ulster Protestants reject that."

It may well be that he is right, at least for the foreseeable future, though whether, writing, as he says, from the "Catholic" side of the fence, he is wise to exclude even a remote prospect of the promised land is another question; where there is no vision, the people perish. Certainly, an immense weariness and sadness are manifest these days among these same "ordinary people" of whom Dr Cruise O'Brien writes and to whom on public platforms he is now so constantly appealing. But he knows very well—it is a major theme of his book— that even ordinary people are imprisoned in their myths and that in North and South there are strong vested interests in the continuance of those myths. Whether the figure in the shadows is Cathleen ní Houlihan or King Billy is immaterial; on both sides of the border the existing states of mind constitute a standing danger to peace.

It is not surprising, therefore, that Dr Cruise O'Brien, who has dared to question the sanctity of "1916 and all that", should be assailed with every kind of vilification, though it is surprising to find him apparently regarded in some quarters as a crypto-Unionist. He is certainly not that. Indeed, despite the breadth of his experience, one suspects he does not know the Protestant mind in either part of Ireland as well as he thinks he does. But this does not stop him from affronting the traditional nationalist pieties, hagridden as he is by his convictions that to seek unity by force, or even to superimpose the unity issue on the separate issue of civil rights for Northern Catholics, is to risk imminent civil war for the whole island. Nor is he one to shelter behind the printed word. Not content with castigating the woolly thinking of his fellow-politicians, he has confronted Sinn Fein face to face and his showing up of Tomás Mac Giolla is a piece of polemic of which Burke might not have been ashamed. These actions and this book are the testimony of a very brave man. He deserves our respect and our sympathy.

5

AN ART OF POSSIBILITIES

THE HERO of John Berger's new novel, *G*, is an Anglo-Italian Don Juan whose short but dedicated life between the sheets spans the turn of the century. The bastard son of an Anglo-American heiress and an ugly Italian merchant of Livorno, he becomes as an adult a self-absorbed and self-possessed sexual "devil" with a recurrent leer. G neither demands nor repels our sympathy; although presented as a radically alienated product of bourgeois hypocrisy, he also emerges as a type of existential hero completely devoid of bad faith.

When the heiress Laura announces her pregnancy, the obese purveyor of candied fruits, Umberto, pleads with her to settle in a neighbouring Italian city so that he may love his only son as a father should and, more important, so that his only son may love him as a son should. But Umberto is married to a barren woman: refusing to play second fiddle or kept mistress, Laura haughtily returns to England resolved to devote her life to her child. Yet the society to which she belongs—mother, nurse, and maid—intervenes. In a nicely ironical twist, Mr Berger causes the mother simultaneously to embrace Fabianism and to discard her son. The boy, who is given no name for 127 pages, then called G, is reared on a farm by a brother and sister, Jocelyn and Beatrice, whose relationship he only later discovers to be incestuous. Thus he becomes a privileged orphan whose expensive upbringing can never atone for the stigma, the offence, of the primal parental abandonment.

His character develops accordingly. At the age of five he falls sexually in love with his governess, Miss Helen, without expecting any return. Otherwise he accommodates to superior force, to the tutor who beats him by rota, to the ragged strangers who one day lead him into the woods and enact an obscure passion play over the bodies of two dray horses, to the public schoolboys who in later years bait the Italian side of him with the jibe that his mother must have

JOHN BERGER: *G*. 316 pp. Weidenfeld and Nicolson. £2.50. *Selected Essays and Articles*. Edited by Nikos Stangos. 249 pp. Penguin. Paperback, 40p.

been Garibaldi's mistress. G learns to isolate and immunize himself, to achieve self-sufficiency; conscious of no resentments as a child, he will devote his adult life to an unremitting saga of vengeance.

So much for the first half of Mr Berger's novel, which is fluent, touching, convincing and often brilliantly expressed. But already there are signs that the author intends to baffle and frustrate the clients of a conventional narrative. Declining to be God, he disclaims omniscience at crucial moments. After the dray horse episode, obviously formative because later recalled, we read: "His fear is overcome, both his fear for himself and (for it is different) his fear of the unknown . . . overcome by another, stronger revulsion. It is beyond me to create a name for this revulsion: the ones I can think up all simplify." A comparable termination occurs when, at the age of eleven, G is abruptly taken to Milan to meet his father. It is 1898, and the boy not only witnesses but becomes swept up in the ferocious revolutionary fighting and the savage repression which stabilized the bourgeois-parliamentary system of Giolitti. At the height of the battle, when G is being cradled by an unknown and ugly Roman girl, who pretends that he is her fiancé, Mr Berger brings down the curtain: "I cannot continue this account. . . . From this point on everything I write will either converge on a full stop or else disperse so widely that it will become incoherent."

Three years later a new twist occurs. Beatrice, having married an officer and been promptly widowed in the course of the Boer War, returns to the farm and seduces the fourteen-year-old boy. A trauma? Hardly. Assured yet gentle, G takes her almost as an inheritance, a right. When we next meet him he is already an adult, a wealthy young man for whom aviation is a peripheral hobby, now staying in Domodossola to witness the first airborne crossing of the Alps. But the purpose proves to be as contingent as the hobby is peripheral. While the intrepid Peruvian flyer, Geo Chavaz, heroically braves the meteorological hazards of the Alpine peaks and valleys, G sets his mind to seducing a hotel maid. The existential paradox of the man becomes clear: a cynical and ephemeral frivolity masks the most serious and human of drives:

His desire, his only aim, was to be alone with a woman. No more than that. But they had to be deliberately not fortuitously alone. . . . In the company of others women always appeared to him as more or less out of focus . . . because they were continuously changing in their own regard as they adapted themselves to the coercions and expectations of the others around them.

Thus the orphan abandoned by his mother chooses in order to be chosen, and the seducer who apparently treats females as objects in reality invests them with self-determination. In one of his many discursive passages, Mr Berger further explains: "The stranger who desires you and convinces you that it is truly you in all your particularity whom he desires, brings a message from all that you might be, to you as you actually are."

After the maid, and in rapid succession, G seduces the wife of a wealthy Parisian motor-manufacturer who puts three bullets in his shoulder and despatches him to hospital just at the time when the hero, Chavaz, who has crashed inexplicably on landing, is dying amidst universal admiration and mourning. But Chavaz's death moves G no more than the thought of his own; so thoroughly has he been lagged by life that he is insulated against his own mortality. He is without a sense of history, either past or future. The final act takes place in Trieste in 1915, on the eve of Italy's declaration of war, in an imperial city populated by haughty Austrian officials, opportunistic Italian merchants, irredentist Italian nationalists and, providing the immediate context of G's own tortuous dénouement, by violent Bosnian separatists. By this time G's permanent rebellion has transcended the flesh which is still its vehicle, its occasion. Aspiring to seduce the wife of an Austrian banker, and completely assured of success, he prefers in the event to penetrate the society rather than the woman by bringing to a posh ball a simple Bosnian working girl, Nusa. In this city of smouldering animosities and proud causes, G's isolation and indifference achieves its final, fatal political translation; because he is distrusted as a spy, as a clandestine foreigner, by every faction, the ultimate agents of his death emerge at random from the last roulette.

When *G* was still a work in progress, Mr Berger remarked of it: "I do not know whether it will be eventually categorized as an essay, a novel, a treatise, or the description of a dream." Which reminds us that Mr Berger himself is not so much a star as a galaxy of talents in search of a centre of gravity and a literary form which can synthesize his gifts as art critic, essayist and novelist. At a time when the traditional boundaries of fact and fiction, of imagination and intellect, are in a state of flux, no one is better equipped than he to lay minefields across the borders, to cancel the poet's proverbial licence and to pluck the authorial eye (and "I") from a privileged anonymity. *G* is a work which raises questions of great critical interest. It does not, however, always succeed in fashioning convincing connexions, whether causal or structural.

In *Permanent Red* (1960), Mr Berger remarked that every painter must discover his own personal point of departure, whether it be geometry, the density of pigment or whatever, and then push his creativity beyond it. But Mr Berger himself, arriving at the stadium burdened by an abundance of talents, found himself entering simultaneously for the sprint, the mile, the shot, and the pole-vault. Performing extremely well at all but winning none, he finally reached a solution: *G* is the pentathlon. Put in a more realistic idiom, Mr Berger's dilemma, rather rarer in this country than in France, is that of the *intellectual* who is *also* an artist. One thinks of a Jean Cassou, an André Chamson, a Simone de Beauvoir. And although the painter's eye might seem to be Mr Berger's most distinctive characteristic as a writer, it would probably be more useful to regard the intellectual's fierce analytical intelligence and seriousness of moral purpose as his true point of departure. Certainly *G*, which is almost totally devoid of humour, is fundamentally an exploration of morality.

In *Permanent Red*, Mr Berger defined the critic's task, but it must also apply to the artist: "First, you must answer the question: What can art serve here and now? Then you criticize according to whether the works in question serve that purpose or not." As a humanistic Marxist who believes that the artist's proper duty is to overcome the fragmentation, alienation, and despair endemic to a decadent bourgeois culture, he has argued that the nature of all art is an attempt to define and render unnatural the distinction between the actual and the possible, to express the inadequacy of the given state of things, sometimes with horror, sometimes by presenting the desirable ideal. (It is possible to quarrel with his denial of art as ever being a mimetic celebration of nature.) One recalls Mr Berger's biting descriptions, in *A Painter of Our Time* (1958), of the commercial acolytes of art, and his portrayal of a talented Hungarian émigré painter who lives in poverty for years because his work lacks the bright trendiness necessary for success. In a later book *The Success and Failure of Picasso* (1965), Mr Berger does not spare the great artist during his two phases of relative flippancy: the period after the First World War, when he entered the *beau monde* and imitated Ingres, and the years after 1944 when he relapsed into an easy, sentimental invitation to Arcadia.

In *G*, the serious moral purpose underlying the hero's promiscuity is frequently made explicit. For example: while plotting to seduce Monsieur Hennequin's wife, G directs the following thoughts at the husband:

You chose this woman as you made her your own. At any moment the degree of conviction in your choice depended on your estimate of how exclusively she belonged to you. . . . You chose Camille's innocence, delicacy, maternal feeling, spirituality. She emphasized these for you. She suppressed the aspects of herself which contradicted them. She became your myth. The only myth which was entirely your own.

In other words, she became your property. Mr Berger's hostility towards private property, particularly as it affects works of art, quite legitimately extends to woman-as-property. The role of woman in G's society merely exemplifies the general social structure, so that G himself can be regarded as an anarchist revolutionary (propaganda by deed), or, to use a phrase that Mr Berger, borrowing from Ortega y Gasset, applies to Picasso, as a "vertical invader" (even if his occupation is mainly horizontal).

Determined to situate G in his social and historical context, Mr Berger frequently resorts to an alternative narrative, describing in considerable detail the significance of Garibaldi, life in the trenches during the early months of the First World War, or the political intrigues of Trieste. Part montage, part "living-newspaper", these excursions too often represent a failure of tact and discrimination. So obvious are the social juxtapositions that the reader may feel himself taken for a fool incapable of making connexions; at the same time Mr Berger robs his own narrative of homogeneity. In the event it is never quite clear whether G-as-Don Juan is being presented as an alienated product of a specific society, or whether his fundamental existential rebellion merely acquires its specific form, its particular life-style, from the age in which he lives.

Such an ambiguity is the more surprising in that Mr Berger here gives himself full rein as a didactic essayist, shifting without a blush from the implicit to the explicit. His high talents as an essayist are confirmed in his new collection, *Selected Essays and Articles*, which contains, apart from "The Moment of Cubism", pieces on Guevara, Jack Yeats, Le Corbusier, Victor Serge, and Walter Benjamin. The volume closes with three connected reports on the Czechoslovak crisis in the wake of the Soviet invasion, which are models of acute political observation and compassionate understanding. As an essayist, however, Mr Berger does not always resolve connexions to the extent he achieved in his brilliant analysis of a dedicated country doctor, *A Fortunate Man* (1967). One notices in his *Picasso* a hiatus between the painter and the backcloth, between a genius the nature and source of whose inspiration is wonderfully captured on the one hand, and the existence of Lenin, monopoly capitalism and exploitation of the Third World on the other. Aimé Césaire is introduced— because he is quite different from Picasso. Of course Marxist historians and essayists, more than most, are tormented by the difficulty of explaining the precise links between the artist and his environment, between the "base" and the "superstructure". In "The Moment of Cubism" Mr Berger again wrestles with the problem, promotes heuristic enthusiasm above discretion, and then, retreating, admits that the Cubists were not interested in politics, "were not aware of all that we are now reading into their art", and were joined to their time by a route which "remains unknown".

The main connexion which Mr Berger as an essayist has to make in *G* is between sex and history. One must say here that his skill and subtlety in matters of sex is by no means anticipated in his earlier work, although both *A Painter of Our Time* and *The Foot of Clive* (1962) display, as subsidiary themes, an ironic understanding of the brash and banal ad man's image of female allure. Yet *G* treats sex quite differently. Indeed not only is G himself physically unprepossessing, but not one of his conquests is described in a way likely to arouse the reader's erotic interest. But the main dilemma is this: that having offered himself full didactic scope to discuss as well as describe sex-within-history, to approach the matter both analytically and imaginatively, Mr Berger seems to recoil from these possibilities: "All generalizations", he writes, "are opposed to sexuality." He then adds: "That is the only poem to be written about sex—here, here, here, here—now." And why? Because, he argues, "extreme single-mindedness . . . accompanies sexual desire . . . the conviction that what is desired is the most desirable possible. An erection is the process of total idealization." (Presumably Sartre never said this, but one often senses his shadow hovering over Mr Berger's search for essences; nevertheless, fortunate is the writer whose occasional ghost is Sartre.) The odd thing about this generalization (apart from the preceding statement that all generalizations are hostile to sexuality) is that it seems to turn truth inside out.

Imagine the sailor's angry penis hurrying from the ship for a one-night stand, and the whole edifice collapses. Mr Berger's assertion that the true equation of sex is "the experience $= I + $ life", and is therefore "inexpressible in the third person and in the narrative form", flies in the face of all experience except those privileged encounters which are so rare. And if sex is really as he says it is, then surely he is wasting his energy writing about it. In fact he is not wasting his energy or ours, because he writes so well, but one must admit that this book's commentary on itself is often marred by a distrust of the written word so radical as to be, in a stubbornly professional writer, downright perverse.

Yet this perversity is the child of a genuine creative tension and of a spirit of experimentation which rejects easy solutions. The painter's eye confronts the dialectician, the naturalist recognizes that the illusion of mimesis is a sham, and the disciple of Cubism searches for a literary equivalent of Fernand Léger's geometrical optimism. These remarks can be developed less elliptically by once again returning to the early Berger. Take, first of all, the writer-as-painter.

Mr Berger was once a student at the Central and Chelsea Art Schools. The early chapters of *A Fortunate Man* are essentially inspired by visual factors, by the shifting appearances and surprising angles of small men trapped within a larger nature. In the first short sketches of *Selected Essays*, he once again indulges his delight in watching and seeing: no obvious dramatic content is required. But these are doodles: in *G* he must paint, he must integrate the shape of things with human causality, with feeling and knowing (as Alain Robbe-Grillet did in *La Jalousie*). How? Clearly aspiring to the stark, unsentimental precision of Cubism, he must suppress the naturalistic-documentary impulses so apparent in *The Foot of Clive*, *Corker's Freedom* (1964) and *A Fortunate Man*. In the first two of these books, both novels, Mr Berger married naturalism to its second cousin impressionism by juxtaposing and overlaying sharply recorded images of humdrum behaviour, associating inner landscapes with physical objects and allowing consciousness a free flow. More than a literary style was involved here; the obligation to life carried a moral weight —as with Zola. Consider only the years of steady observation which supported the portrait of the country doctor, or the exacting compilation of data about card indexes, filing systems, and styles of deference which brought the thwarted Corker's little employment agency to life.

Why does Mr Berger feel constrained to suppress this heritage?

Naturalism encourages empathy by suggesting a direct congruity between life and art. In *Art and Revolution* (1969), a study of the Soviet artist Ernst Neizvestny, he voiced a critical estrangement from naturalism which was bound to exact its price in his creative writing. Art, he said, must be transformation. While disapproving of the spineless decadence which infects modern art, he has nevertheless accepted the tacit modernist premise that the old Renaissance-Enlightenment certainties about reality and perspective are dead. The work of art ceases to be nature and becomes artifact; the spectator becomes nature. Searching within the modernist school for an affirmation of optimism and human solidarity compatible with his own ideology, his admiration settled on the post-revolutionary Russian avantgarde and on the prewar Cubists. In these circles a faith in the social relevance of art was reconciled with an honest approach to the medium itself, to the *process* of art. Here is the launching-pad for *G* as a literary structure.

About Cubism Mr Berger has written extensively. The real subject of Cubism, he argues, is sight itself. The two-dimensional surface of the picture serves as the constant by which we approach the variables, the hidden surfaces and dimensions. Claiming that the Cubists were the first to paint totalities rather than agglomerations, and tracing the movement back to the confident materialism of Courbet and the reluctant scepticism of Cézanne, he made bold to describe Cubism as the only example of dialectical materialism in painting. Mr Berger is too sensible a writer to reduce *G* to a single stylistic label, but the emphasis clearly emerges:

I isolate parts in order to follow my eyes, instant by instant, faithfully. . . . The fresh evidence of each part, of each new sight of her, contributes to my perception of her as a whole, and makes this whole continually move and pulsate like a heart, like my own heart.

Or consider this:

Whom were we walking?/I was a knee which wanted the thigh on the other leg./The sounds of my most tender words were in your arse./Your heels were my thumbs./I was hiding in one corner of your mouth.

The resemblance to Braque or Picasso in the years 1907–14 is certainly very striking. Elsewhere the author offers a fuller explanation of his literary philosophy:

But I have little sense of unfolding time. The relations which I perceive between things . . . tend to form in my mind a complex synchronic pattern.

I see fields where others see chapters . . . I write in the spirit of a geometri-
cian. . . . One of the ways in which I establish coordinates extensively is by
likening aspect with aspect, by way of metaphor.

The confession about "unfolding time" is a revealing one: probably
it accounts for the lack in all of Mr Berger's novels of a certain
dramatic urgency. But in so far as we are concerned with the overall
style or structure of *G*, one notices that Mr Berger attempts to translate Cubism into literary terms by employing and rather over-taxing
many of the devices used in recent years by Sarraute, Sollers, Butor
and the other novelists who have said farewell to naturalistic certainty
and divinely certified mimesis. Mr Berger's entire narrative is broken
up into hundreds of double-spaced sections, some of them constitut-
ing only a single line or phrase, thus deliberately exposing the hiatus
between conception and achievement. The gear shift in which he
moves from "he" to "I" to "you" is so well greased as to be virtually
automatic. This is alienation with a vengeance.

With increasing frequency Mr Berger imposes himself on his own
story. Turning the page, one may suddenly come across a personal
dream having no direct bearing on the action, or an account of a
recent visit to a Paris laundry. The message is twofold: work in
progress; torment. As the confessions of difficulty multiply, the
reader may begin to wish books were sold with a guarantee: "The
way my imagination forces me to write this story is determined by its
intimations about those aspects of time which I have touched but
never identified. I am writing this book in the same dark." There are
also passages which stretch the reader's credibility:

Armed with the entire language of literature we are still denied access to
her experience. There is only one possible way, of, briefly, entering that
experience: to make love to her. Then why do I want to describe her
exhaustively, definitely, when I fully recognize the impossibility of doing
so? Because I love her. I love you Leonie. . . . It was he who said this.

Was it? The paradox here is that in *G* Mr Berger once again displays
a high talent for set-scenes and dialogue of a conventional kind. One
remembers the impact, in *A Painter of Our Time*, of the episode in
which Janos Lavin and his friend the narrator John visit the private
art collection of Sir Gerald Banks. Perhaps Mr Berger now regards
such victories as Pyrrhic ones.

He may be right. But the modern writer must either yield some
territory to the *dramatic* heritage of fiction or risk alienating his

readers in the wrong way. To emphasize that the failings of *G* are the result of a rich endowment of talents and of a bold, experimental intelligence which distrusts the safe, mediocre and provincial, is not to explain these failings away. One comes away from *G* as from many modern paintings: provoked and stimulated, yet baffled and faintly resentful.

6

FICTION OF 1972

(a) E. M. FORSTER

The Life to Come

LONG BEFORE E. M. Forster's death in 1970, rumours were common in academic and literary circles of the manuscripts that he would leave for posthumous publication. There was a novel, too daring in its homosexual theme, one heard, to appear during Forster's lifetime; and there were stories—though these were less often mentioned, and less confidently described. The rumours were repeated, were contradicted, reappeared; and their persistence was a kind of comfort to Forster's admirers, for if these stories were true, then his talent had not in fact dried up, but had simply moved into territories where the general public was not yet prepared to follow. To literary minds, the death of a talent may seem worse than the death of a writer, and it was nice to know that Forster's gift was still alive at King's.

After such a long pre-existence as gossip, *Maurice* when it appeared was a profound disappointment (see the *TLS*, October 8, 1971). The same inhibitions that had prevented Forster from publishing it during his life had prevented him from writing it at the full stretch of his imagination; it emerged as a flat and un-Forsterian narrative of an Edwardian homosexual's search for sexual freedom—therapeutic, perhaps, for Forster, and historically interesting, but imaginatively lifeless.

The Life to Come virtually completes the record: it contains all Forster's completed short stories not included in *The Celestial Omnibus* or *The Eternal Moment*. These include one, "Albergo

---

(a) E. M. FORSTER: *The Life to Come*. 240 pp. Edward Arnold. £2.50.

(b) MARGARET DRABBLE: *The Needle's Eye*. 368 pp. Weidenfeld and Nicolson. £2.25.

(c) BERNARD MALAMUD: *The Tenants*. 230 pp. Eyre Methuen. £1.95.

(d) JOHN UPDIKE: *Rabbit Redux*. 406 pp. André Deutsch. £1.95.

(e) DORIS LESSING: *The Story of a Non-Marrying Man*. 318 pp. Cape. £1.95.

Empedocle", which appeared in *Temple Bar* in 1903 (it was his first story to be published) but was judged not good enough for the first collection, and one contribution to a serial story that ran in *Wine and Food* in 1948. The rest are published here for the first time.

The stories are of two kinds, and come from two distinct periods in Forster's life. The first five are from his early years, the years of the novels and published stories, and in subjects and treatment they resemble the other work. Most of the Forsterian situations and themes are here: his resentment of maleheartiness, his cold dislike of Anglo-Indians, his taste for affection between white and dark men. There is one of his castrating mothers, and one of his wet Cambridge young men, a warm-hearted rustic, and an English lady who writes about Renaissance art. The scenes are Italian *pensiones* and English country houses. We have been here before, but in more interesting company. For none of these stories is as good as the best of the *Collected Short Stories* and the worst deserve the judgment that Forster himself made of one of them: "It was a complete flop. . . . My inspiration had been genuine but worthless."

The case for publishing these minor pieces must depend on one's judgment of Forster's importance as a writer: if he is indeed a major English novelist, then it is worth having even his discarded work; but if he is something less, then this is an act of supererogation. Certainly these five stories add nothing to his stature, though they don't detract much, either. They are simply more of the same.

The eight stories that follow are a rather different matter. They concern sexual relations between males, and they were written much later—the earliest in 1922, the latest in 1957–58. Apparently there had been others, dating back to 1907, but Forster had burnt them in 1922—"not a moral repentance", he noted in his diary, "but the belief that they clogged me artistically. They were written not to express myself but to excite myself. . . ." But the "indecent" writing continued, and so did the clogging. In the thirty-five years that followed Forster could still write to excite himself, and did, as these surviving stories testify; but he could not express himself, at least not through fiction.

To write in order to excite is, of course, to write pornography, and that is what, in a strict sense, these eight stories are. They have the essential qualities of pornography: that is they substitute sexuality for character, and they treat sexual action apart from the common, shared life of human beings. The sexual act is treated as an act of violence—a desired sodomic rape—or it is a fit of madness, or a fatal disease, or it is a bit of sudden and unconsidered fun. But it is always a sharp deviation from ordinary life, a break in the order of things. There is no reciprocity of feeling here, no relationship for which *love* seems the right word. There is *mystery* (a word Forster was partial to), but there is no affection. But when one thinks of it, there is little enough affection in the novels, either. "Only connect" was an injunction that Forster found insuperably difficult, or so his fiction suggests, and he was not able to imagine convincing instances of connexion. He worried about Englishmen's undeveloped hearts, but that is the kind of character he could create. And the literature of the undeveloped heart, in its most explicit form, is the literature of pornography.

This is not to say that any of these stories is likely to corrupt or even stimulate any reader, for Forster is here, as always, reticent and decent. There is none of the hard-core pornographer's sexual gigantism, none of the hard-breathing purple prose of the Soho bookshops; the nearest he comes to describing a sexual member at all is in the phrase "a muscle thickened up out of gold" (did he really think it was a *muscle*?). It is all very pale and circumspect. And that is the saddest thing about these saddening stories—that such shy, uncertain imaginings should have been necessary to a gifted man's sexual life.

And how are we to relate these poor stories to the drying-up of Forster's talent? For there is nothing here to contradict the statement that his ability to write fiction died with *A Passage to India*. It had always seemed reasonable to accept Forster's own explanation, that he had stopped writing because his Edwardian subject evaporated in the war. But now another account seems possible: Forster stopped writing for the public because he felt he wanted only, or was able only, to write about homosexual love, and society would not allow him to. And of course he was right, society would not have allowed him to, as the *Well of Loneliness* and *Boy* cases demonstrated. "I should have been a more famous writer", he noted sadly in his diary in 1964, "but sex has prevented the latter." His *crise de quarante* was, then, simply his acceptance of his own nature as his only subject. It was an honest and honourable commitment, the sort of decision one might expect of Forster. But it meant the end of his talent, for though he could live with his homosexuality, he could not write well about it, even in private.

Only one of these stories approaches the quality of Forster's other short fiction. "Doctor Woolacott" is a parable of a very Forsterian sort, which treats homosexuality as a disease that separates the sufferer from life; the beautiful young man in the story is death, and health is the enemy of love. T. E. Lawrence, one of the friends who read this story, admired it extravagantly, and told Forster that it had helped to reconcile him to his own sexual nature. It is perhaps not quite *that* good, but it is the best of the lot, and the most like Forster's earlier parables of constraint and freedom, stories such as "The Story of a Panic" and "The Other Side of the Hedge" (and among the early stories in this volume, "Albergo Empedocle"). And it suggests, by its similarities, that those other stories might best be read on the same terms.

Obviously, for Forster—shy, inhibited, and desirous of social approval—the most personal and painful example of constraint was society's disapproval of his sexual impulses. When Eustace bolts into the trees (freed, characteristically, by a working-class Italian youth), when the unnamed narrator slips through the hedge, when Kuno leaves the Machine, they are escaping the confining and distorting effects of conventional society upon a deviant personality. Indeed, it does not seem extravagant to say that "Doctor Woolacott" expresses in slightly more explicit terms the principal theme of all Forster's fiction—the yearning for free expression through male love, and the repressive power of society. In his public writings Forster concealed that theme, as Oscar Wilde did in his plays; in Wilde there is always the hidden secret, the shameful revelation, in Forster there is always the impulse towards free action, and the fear of it. The love that dared not speak its name was always there in disguise.

Forster called his published stories "fantasies", and so they are, and in that sense they belong to a different order of imagination from the novels. They make free use of the improbable and the visionary, and they pay little attention to the texture of ordinary English social life; they are, as Leonard Woolf said, "Pan-ridden". These private, homosexual stories are also fantasies, but in a different and less interesting way. They are the sexual fantasies of a man who wanted, he said, "to love a strong young man of the lower classes and be loved by him and even hurt by him. That is my ticket. . . ." The strong young man appears again and again, and so does the hurting. But the private fantasies remain private; they will help Forster's admirers to understand his nature and his limitations, but they will not add anything to Forster's stature as an artist.

"Our lower nature has its dreams", Forster says in "The Rock". And characteristically, he preferred that nature: "As long as I have flesh and blood I pray that my grossness preserve me." Perhaps it did. Who is to say that these stories gave him less pleasure, or less sustenance, than his finest novel? But they will not sustain us.

One should add a kind word for the new Abinger edition of Forster's works, of which *The Life to Come* is Volume Eight. The little green volumes of Arnold's earlier edition had a seemly plainness, and no doubt Forster approved of their pocket-sized modesty, but it is good to have his books in a uniform library format, well bound, readable, and handsome. Oliver Stallybrass has edited this volume with admirable care, and one can be sure that the rest of the edition—which will include another twenty volumes—will, under his editorship, be as well and generously treated.

(b) MARGARET DRABBLE

The Needle's Eye

MARGARET DRABBLE writes with a rare passion; rare not so much in its intensity (though there is more pretence of strong feeling than the thing itself around in English writing today) as in its object: a passion for justice. She has what Sartre recommended for a novelist: moral obsession. In some of her earlier books, the quality was repressed in the more genial pursuit of a social sketch (*Jerusalem the Golden*) or a romantic portrait (*The Waterfall*). In *The Needle's Eye*, it is finally given its head.

A stock Victorian character was the aristocrat who acquired a stern morality from an Evangelical nanny. (Every schoolboy learns this of Wilberforce.) Miss Drabble's contemporary equivalent is Rose Vassiliou, a rich girl who got her name from her London Cypriot husband, and her money from one of those English families where county origins and business success are profitably mixed. But she was brought up by Noreen, a maid soaked in life-denying non-conformity, and quick with its more embarrassing texts. Hence the needle's eye; hence Rose's decision to give away a trust fund of £20,000 to build a school (soon destroyed by civil war) in an obscure African country; hence her determination to stay with her three children in a shabby house in a "bad area" of London after divorcing her ambitious, unfaithful, quarrelsome, violent husband.

She isn't, of course, exactly plumbing the lower depths. "Quite often, as she was buying a tin of beans or a box of eggs, she would see an old lady buying herself a single egg." But at least she sees it: unlike her smart friends, living not in poor but in fashionably mixed districts,

as though they licensed seedy old ladies and black men to walk their streets, teaching their children of poverty and despair, as their pet hamsters and guinea-pigs taught them of sex and death.

Rose can enter such company (and the opening pages of the novel) with a debby line: "I couldn't get a taxi because I live in such a ridiculous place." She has her privileged qualities still, does Rose. (She likes constructing her sentences like this, does Miss Drabble. It lends a certain kitchen-sink tartness to moral subtleties.) The freedom of riches combined with the rigid values of poverty make for considerable wilfulness, and Rose can chatter, or even prattle, about her own behaviour in a tone more self-indulgent than self-critical.

Nevertheless, she stands out from the self-advancing ruck of smart communicators and successful professionals whom Miss Drabble delights to dishonour. (Bitchiness can sweeten priggishness, and there are plenty of put-downs for the contemporary elite.) Specifically, she stands out enough to attract the attention and sympathy of Simon Camish, a barrister who has "arrived" from provincial poverty, and is even more ill-at-ease than Rose in this String-along world of chocolate mousse and goose-shit walls.

Simon admires both Rose's moral strictness (so different from his rich wife's mindless sociality) and her warm scattiness (so different from his own unnourishing sense of duty). She consults him on her legal difficulties: her husband wants the children, and threatens to exploit her decision to keep them in this working-class dump. A mutual interest gathers force, whose development takes up the bulk of the book. Simon sees in Rose, as the novel's epigraph from Yeats has it, "the fascination of what's difficult". The sparse pleasures of integrity revisit him. Their relationship is resolutely non-sexual, although Simon finally plucks up enough devilry to advertise yet another act of renunciation:

"If I had been free", he said, "I would have asked you to marry me."
"Ah", she said, gently, tenderly, "ah yes. What a nice time we would have had. I too have thought of it, you know."

The writing—as in this extract—trembles on the edge of sloppiness, and sometimes tumbles right over. "O lovely Miss Lindley", concludes one paragraph of rhetoric about an admirable school mistress. "O almost confident apostrophe." In the long run, such excesses are all to the good. Miss Drabble can write drily, or wittily, or intelligently, with no trouble at all. It would be smug to rest on this established talent; and it is the flights of lyricism in pursuit of moral feelings which give *The Needle's Eye* its most distinctive, if not its most obvious, successes.

The ending is another matter. Not for the first time, Miss Drabble appears to be shaping course for a catastrophe (the abduction of Rose's children by the husband) which she then shies away from. Does she believe that, finally, "people don't do such things"; or is she afraid of the difficulties of describing them? The husband's character—an obstinate dottiness quite as strong as Rose's own—is interesting enough, and central enough to the story, to deserve some of the space lavished on Rose's tears or Simon's resolutions. As it is, he is a *deus ex machina* designed to frustrate, rather than promote, a happy ending. He moves back with Rose, their shabby district suddenly goes up in the world (a brilliant half-page cameo), she and Simon remain just sad friends. It is as if the effort of joyless virtue had exhausted author and characters alike.

Although this is a very ambitious, marvellously written, morally admirable book, its final impact is less than the sum of its parts. Its conclusion is not only a further concession but a defeat. Rose, reflecting on her weakly patched-up marriage, tells herself that she did it "in the dry light of arid generosity. . . . Her duty, that was what she had done. For others. For him, for the children." Like a true Puritan, Miss Drabble is sounder on pain than pleasure, on self-denial than on achievement. "To those that suffer", Rose tells herself, "is given the strength to endure suffering." Or not, as the case may be. Yeats also wrote: "Too much sacrifice can make a stone of the heart." And a stone is not even an acceptable sacrifice.

(c) BERNARD MALAMUD

The Tenants

THE MERIT of seriousness is not much to claim for a writer these days. At a time when sundry public figures, from politicians to television playwrights and religious pundits, can achieve bloated eminence merely by throwing around a few perennially profound questions and finding ready answers among their own prejudices, there may, indeed, seem little point in maintaining intellectual gravity before the world audience. The urge to abandon pin-striped dignity and caper hilariously across the international literary arena has been particularly strong upon Jewish writers in recent times, but there is a limit to what can be done with the-laugh-that-hides-the-tears; so it is almost cheering to return every so often to the work of a man so dedicatedly, but healthily, gloomy as Bernard Malamud.

The Tenants is not the best of Malamud, for a fable-cum-metaphor as schematized as this one does not stretch happily to 230 pages, but it is a highly respectable attempt to define the spiritual conflict between black and white cultures without making over-specific reference to issues of social policy. Harry Lesser, a Jewish novelist, lives in an otherwise uninhabited tenement, using his legal rights to resist the attempts of his landlord, Levenspiel, to dislodge him and redevelop the site. The familiar Jewish comedy here—Levenspiel writes pathetic letters, in which mounting threats coexist with ever more desperate pleading and a steadily increasing cash offer to Lesser—establishes the book's foothold in a recognizable social world. Lesser acknowledges its realities by keeping them at bay. Having written two books, one good, one bad, he must now prove himself, triumphing over the mediocre implications of his name. The novel he is struggling to finish has taken almost ten years to write, the ten years that have seen his fellow-tenants' departure and the arrival of the rats and roaches. All this is cleverly done; nothing too apocalyptic, nothing complacently gentle.

The sound of a second typewriter in one of the disused, befouled apartments signals the onset of Malamud's dialectic. Willie Spearmint, the black ex-convict, ex-drugpusher and aspiring writer who has moved in brings Lesser not only the technical problems of a black American's vigorous but unformed writing but also his belligerent presence, his friends and in particular his white Jewish girlfriend Irene. The first of Lesser's fatal errors comes when he slips away from a party where he and Irene are the only whites, and goes to bed with the sad black girl Mary. He is discovered, and in the novel's most tautly-written scene, he faces the sullen black assembly. Challenged by Willie to "Play the dozens", the insult-game for which Lesser has no taste ("What good is a contest of imprecation?" he pleads in fear), he is humiliated; but Willie later explains that only "the dozens" saved the white interloper from physical attack. Lesser hardly cares, having fallen in love with Irene, Willie's girl.

As the necessity of insisting here upon plot-lines and narrative details implies, Malamud by this time has settled down single-mindedly to the task of engineering the final clash between Lesser and Willie. From this point, in fact, the two writers are locked in an undisguisedly symbolic single combat. Willie asks Lesser's opinion of a chapter; Lesser dismantles it, and at the worst possible moment confesses, in an attempt to explain his unease, his deep involvement with Irene. Willie breaks up Lesser's flat, destroys his ten years' work; Irene leaves town, but Willie eventually moves back into Lesser's tenement. He and Lesser, armed with razor and axe, prowl the building, bound to collide. In terms of Malamud's fable, it is clear that they will destroy each other.

It is interesting that Lesser chooses at one point to quote at Willie from Coleridge: "Nothing can permanently please which does not contain in itself the reason why it is so and not otherwise"— interesting because this is precisely the standard by which *The Tenants* fails. It is the unlikely tactlessness of Lesser that invites catastrophe, not the hostile incompatibility of his consciousness and Willie's. Their clash might have been inevitable for other reasons, but Malamud's novel deliberately avoids the wide-ranging view which would call for a statement of these.

But although the reader is likely to resent feeling trapped by suspiciously faulty machinery at the climax of the novel, it is written with a sharpness that continually reasserts Malamud's humane intelligence. Perhaps the most vivid incidental pleasure here lies in his use of Harlem slang. Even in his first novel, *The Natural*, Malamud threatened to rival Ring Lardner in his manipulation of comical baseball jargon. He is no less precise in evoking the sounds that issue from under an Afro haircut. When ambitious Willie Spearmint declares: "They gon gimme a million bucks of cash", one feels at once Malamud's sensitivity to language. The little word "of" makes all the difference.

(*d*) JOHN UPDIKE
Rabbit Redux

JOHN UPDIKE's characteristic hero-figure spends most of his life switchbacking from guilt to bliss, from sexual guilt to spiritual bliss, from spiritual guilt to sexual bliss—except that neither brand of bliss is the real thing. The only bliss that properly deserves the name is that which is (in both spiritual and sexual ways) most guilty. We remember the ringing of church bells that accompanied Rabbit Angstrom's inauguration into the mysteries of oral sex and, at a subtler level, we remember the prettily clouded lyricism which has always contrived to suck the blood from even Updike's most determinedly detailed reports of physical excess. Updike's has always seemed a rather comfortable confusion—with wit (a genuinely sharp and worldly wit) to hand as a counterbalance to religiose effusing, and with a cutely soaring linguistic colourfulness forever ready to evaporate brutality.

Nowhere has his "confusion" (or can we now describe it as a fully formulated paradox?) been more comfortable than in this new book, in which the unfortunate Rabbit—as if he had not been punished enough in *Rabbit Run*—is resurrected for another cosmic beating. At the beginning of *Rabbit Redux* we find our hero, still bemused and accident-prone, back with his wife Janice; indeed, he has been back for some years and now spends most of his time in gloomy contemplation of his marriage's gradual attrition. Rabbit works as a typesetter in the same printing works that his father has been toiling in for years and now and then his melancholy reflections on his domestic situation are broken into by the old man's bulletins on his mother's incurable ill-health. In the evenings—Janice tends to be out a lot these days—he sits with his unengaging son Nelson watching television and chewing television suppers. The newscasts aptly buttress Rabbit's general sense of hollowness and defeat. It's a grim picture: the erstwhile athlete, slightly paunchy now, slumped in suburban pointlessness, and long past fighting it.

Or so it seems. In fact, Rabbit still has some buried vigour and when news unsurprisingly arrives of Janice's involvement with a Greek car salesman, he begins to manifest a few flickers of rebellion. Charlie Stavros is not only a terrific lover, he is also a terrific Lefty. Rabbit's response to both qualities is one of mild reawakening. Sexually, he begins taking another look at his dull wife (and indeed at the whole subject); politically, he discovers that his prejudices, when forcibly and wittily articulated, can be passed off as opinions—opinions which are, needless to say, thoroughly right-wing. (There is a fine scene in a restaurant in which Rabbit comes face to face with

Stavros and engages him in violent argument about Vietnam—
Updike keeps it excitingly agile and naturalistic as an argument but
doesn't neglect a single nuance of the basic sexual rivalry that is
animating the dispute). We are meant to see that Rabbit's sexual
humiliation is at the back of his aloofly ugly politics.

When Janice leaves him for Stavros, Rabbit drifts—frustrated,
sardonic but still essentially inert. And guess what he drifts into?
By a single stroke of engineered good fortune, he encounters both
the Youth thing and the Black thing. Taken out for an evening by a
Black colleague who thinks he's going to seed, Rabbit is introduced
to Jill, a juvenile druggy who has fallen in with a set of fierce Black
Powerites. She is handed to him on a plate; he accepts and she, in the
morally slovenly way of her generation, doesn't object—doesn't,
that is, care. Rabbit takes her into his house and she is later joined
there by one of her (now fugitive) Black chums. And from this
point on, the novel turns into the *Reeducation of Rabbit*; the whole
spectrum is covered—race, Vietnam, drugs, capitalism, sex—and at
each point Rabbit is forced to relax his guard, is persuaded by his
guests' naked extremism to reformulate his stock objections. It's a
long job, and rather longer for the reader than it seems to be for the
characters taking part—lengthy, hip-talking seminars on the history
of slavery tend to make their point long before they know they've
made it and Rabbit's conversion is both instantly predictable and
interminably wordy. When the talking stops we get treated to bouts
of sexual or narcotic eccentricity but, again, these are only stirring
(and then not all that stirring) first time round.

Converted though, in some measure, he becomes, Rabbit is still a
long distance from the world of either Jill or Skeeter. About the same
distance as he's now become from the solid neighbours who petition
him to get rid of his unsavoury companions. As a kind of compromise between the two worlds, he makes slickly offhand overtures to a
nearby, known-to-be-frustrated wife, and is languishing in her bed
when (in old-style Rabbit style) news of disaster reaches him. A
long time ago, Rabbit's baby was drowned when he was in the arms
of "another woman". This time, the news is that his house has been
burned down (presumably by the solid neighbours). Jill, asleep and
drugged, is killed, and Skeeter callously runs, leaving her to meet
her whitey fate. Another seminar for Rabbit, and one more step
towards the sad, illuminated settlements he's finally obliged to settle
for.

It's an obvious progression and Updike only rarely manages to disguise its obviousness; he does so, when he does, by exercising those gifts of laconic social observation which he too infrequently gives rein to—Rabbit in the world is so much more powerfully alive than Rabbit ruminating in his bed (soliloquy is always a cue for Updike to plunge into his verbal rose-bath). As with *Couples*, the small-scale successes could have been made large-scale had not Updike been bent on some other, infinitely larger, scale right from the start. *Rabbit Redux* could have been both tight and expansive; as it stands, it's grandiose and claustrophobic. And plump, plump and comfortable, with wordy self-display.

(e) DORIS LESSING

The Story of a Non-Marrying Man

ONE OF the great rewards of reading Doris Lessing's novels has always been a sense of sharing with the writer herself the experience of growing older, of discovering new ideas and questioning old values. This is not merely to say that, in her best-known and most substantial books (the Martha Quest series and *The Golden Notebook*) Mrs Lessing has given us an unforgettable account of her generation's involvement in world violence and a good deal of insight into her own writing experience; it is her peculiar gift to write with the kind of honesty and generosity that suggest to the reader he is privileged to be a friend, to feel he knows something of the true ideals, the private agonies and delights, that have inspired her writing. And, like any real friendship, this appreciation is more acute where those ideals are shared and the brave spirit of inquiry and challenge that Mrs Lessing's work always shows seems to the reader in itself a wholly admirable thing.

Although a collection of short stories is not normally the form in which one finds integrated self-revelation, Mrs Lessing's new volume is quintessentially part of her sharing of experience, a marvellous scrapbook of old and new memories and discoveries. Whether she is simply describing, in three short vignettes of solitary walks round Regent's Park, how a moorhen's nesting or the falling leaves seemed heavy with meaning and the images infinitely precious; or chronicling the bizarre chance that led a Rhodesian post-office clerk of thirty years ago into political prominence; or accompanying old Hetty Pennefather and her cat with their pramful of rags to a derelict's death in Hampstead; or imagining the reactions of interplanetary reconnaissance officers to a pop group in Cornwall—without obtruding, she leaves us in no doubt what, for her, gave a particular experience its paradoxical, often bitter, significance.

For instance, the accepted attitude—that welfare suits all the needy, that domesticity is better than roving bigamy, that love can be measured by sexual fulfilment, that there is a "norm" of sane and proper social conduct—often stirs Mrs Lessing to irreverent challenge. Or, sometimes, to almost Waugh-like cracks at conformity: the secretly scandalous ménage of two young doctors and their pretty wives ("Not a Very Nice Story") is summed up like this:

They soon established (like showing each other their passports, or references of decency and reliability) that they shared views on life—tough, but rewarding; God—dead; children—to be brought up with the right blend of permissiveness and discipline; society—to be cured by common sense and mild firmness but without extremes of any sort.

She is also increasingly fond of the casual aside—"which reminds me of the actress who, playing a nun in a stormily religious play, used to take the habit home with her. . . . She wore the habit for ironing, washing up, rinsing out her underclothes"; "it *is* odd how often authors cause characters to insult dollar bills, roubles, pound notes"; "well, but even the best of marriages can hardly be described as honey"; and so forth. The style is plain, often harshly abbreviated, until Mrs Lessing lets go on the chestnut trees or the moorhen's nest or the precious stones that little Ephraim in Johannesburg collects for a rich Alexandrian merchant's daughter thousands of miles away.

Almost a short novel, and certainly the most telling story in this collection, is "The Temptation of Jack Orkney", a saddening, affectionate account of the dark night of an old socialist's soul. Practical, prolific in successful committed journalism, benevolent to all good progressive causes and rediscovering a happy middle-aged love for his wife, Orkney is summoned to his dying father (thus missing a Trafalgar Square Twenty-Four-Hour Fast on behalf of Bangladesh). And, precipitated by the enforced reconsideration of what eternity might mean, what religious belief offers the old and—in his pretty daughter and niece—the fervent young, what *use* should be made of his remaining energy, Orkney suffers a nightmarish

Damascus *coup de foudre*. Mrs Lessing's own agnostic doubts, and the self-questioning that only the brave dare attempt in middle age, combine to give Orkney a poignancy that many readers will surely recognize; not only is he a symbol of his generation, the "Old Guard" for whom "six million Jews" had summed up the worst of which humanity was capable (only now, here were *nine million* starving in Bangladesh), who had taken the same stands on Korea and Kenya, Cyprus, Suez, Hungary, the Congo, Nigeria, Ireland, Vietnam. . . . He is also the man who has seen a pit of negation, a change in the younger generation he cannot dismiss or be useful to, and the story ends, "facing into the dark", with the knowledge that he no longer has at his fingertips the answers to any of the world's problems.

7

DEGREES OF JUSTICE
(a) THE SOCIAL CONTRACT

IT IS A COMMON criticism of Kantian theories of ethics, including Kant's own, that they founder on a dilemma: either the injunctions derived from them are purely formal, in which case they offer no guidance as between rival substantive moralities, or they depend on the invocation of material axioms about the nature and workings of the good society which have to be justified on other grounds. But Kant himself gives a vigorous rejoinder in his argument against Hobbes. The notion of the social contract, says Kant, necessarily presupposes an "external right" whereby "each individual's freedom is so restricted as to harmonize with that of everyone else". This a priori requirement, so far from being purely formal, enjoins equality before the law and universal suffrage and prohibits not only paternalism, however benevolent, but any restriction of opportunity to the talented and the industrious. From the hypothesis of the social contract, conceived not as a fact but as "an idea of reason", it follows that the legislator should so frame his laws "that they could have been produced by the united will of a whole nation"; and those laws will, it turns out, be the laws of a society recognizable as an open liberal democracy.

It is an argument very similar to this which is revived and defended by John Rawls as the basis for his theory of justice. He is quite explicit about its Kantianism, and in his preface even goes so far as to disclaim any originality for his views. But in this he is more virtuous than truthful. Although he too emerges as the advocate of a qualified liberalism, he has not merely resuscitated the idea of the social contract in the face of the long dominance of Utilitarianism but has elucidated a conception of justice which goes beyond anything to be

---

(a) JOHN RAWLS: *A Theory of Justice.* 607 pp. Clarendon Press: Oxford University Press. £5.

(b) HUGH LLOYD-JONES: *The Justice of Zeus.* 230 pp. University of California Press (IBEG). £4.05.

found in Kant or Rousseau. It is a convincing refutation, if one is needed, of any lingering suspicions that the tradition of English-speaking political philosophy might be dead. Indeed, his book might plausibly be claimed to be the most notable contribution to that tradition to have been published since Sidgwick and Mill.

The principal ideas developed in it have already been advanced in a series of articles which Professor Rawls has brought out over a number of years, and the book is thus the fruit not merely of long reflection but of careful attention to criticism. Since 1958, when the first of these articles appeared, his interpretation of "Justice as Fairness" has been no less widely debated in Britain than in the United States. Its strengths and weaknesses have been argued in the leading journals both of philosophy and of political science, and several books on moral and social issues have been explicitly influenced by it. Some of its critics may continue to question whether it has been adequately buttressed to withstand their objections. But it is unlikely that there is any criticism of a more than incidental kind of which Professor Rawls is not already aware and which he has not either conceded or rebutted to the degree which, in his own view, is required.

The essence of his theory is as follows. Justice is the primary virtue of social institutions, and the requirement of a theory of justice is that it should yield a general and intuitively acceptable standard for the assessment of the distributive aspect of social organization as either fair or unfair. This cannot be done by means of either classical Intuitionist or Utilitarian conceptions of justice. But it can by means of the idea of the social contract, for we can discriminate between alternative standards in the light of the principles which would have been chosen by rational persons as yet ignorant of the contingencies of natural endowment and social circumstances. Such persons would, Professor Rawls claims, be bound to assign priority to two principles. The first, which takes precedence over the second, is that "each person is to have an equal right to the most extensive total system of equal basic liberties compatible with a similar system of liberty for all". The second is that "social and economic inequalities are to be arranged so that they are both: (a) to the greatest benefit of the least advantaged, consistent with the just savings principle, and (b) attached to offices and positions open to all under conditions of fair equality of opportunity".

Much, of course, depends on how these deceptively straightforward formulae are to be interpreted. But the interpretation which Professor

Rawls wishes to place upon them is at the same time fundamentally liberal (since liberty is to be restricted only for the sake of liberty) and fundamentally egalitarian (since inequalities are justified only if they are to the advantage of the least favoured).

The sense in which this conception of justice constitutes a "theory" is complex. It rests, as it must do, on a basic appeal to intuition, and the argument is deductive only from the point at which the beliefs and interests of the notional persons in the "original position" have been stipulated. It is not dependent upon the presumptive findings of an empirical psychology, for we are not to suppose either that there are actual situations corresponding to the original position or that if there were there is a calculable probability that Professor Rawls's two principles of justice would be accepted. On the other hand, there is a presumption of authenticity to the degree that the persons in the original position are conceived as educated, rational, unenvious, morally disinterested heads of households equipped with a knowledge of the normal conditions of cooperation and conflict in human society. The theory, therefore, has to be seen as an aggregation of considerations capable, in the celebrated phrase of Mill which Professor Rawls in fact quotes, of determining the intellect. Definitions and analyses of meaning are only a part of this aggregation, whose ultimate goal is to furnish a "moral geometry" or "grammar of the moral sentiments" which will at the same time relate to the facts of existing social institutions and characterize the structure (here Chomsky is briefly invoked) which underlies our sense of justice as fairness.

It is evident that this enterprise will be beset by some fairly formidable difficulties. But however intractable some of them may prove, there are two fundamental and connected arguments woven into the overall theory which carry strong and immediate conviction. The first of these is Professor Rawls's critique of Utilitarianism. To readers who are already persuaded of its inadequacies, this may seem no great thing: Professor Rawls is not, after all, the first person to feel that the notion of justice can be accommodated only with manifest discomfort within the confines of Utilitarian doctrine. But even those who hold that doctrine to be fatally flawed are bound to admit its refusal to lie down and die. Indeed, it is worth remembering that *The Methods of Ethics* is closely reasoned and eloquently presented, and that Sidgwick had read his Kant at least as diligently as Professor Rawls. The author's critique of Utilitarianism is deep as well as subtle, and does not readily lend itself to a reviewer's summary. But he gives persuasive grounds for the view that the net balance of satisfactions is an inadequate, and under some conditions counter-intuitive, standard for the fairness of the distribution of social goods; that neither classical Utilitarianism nor the average principle of utility would be chosen by persons in the original position; and that despite the appeal of the notion of the impartial, sympathetic spectator, "the fault of the Utilitarian doctrine is that it mistakes impersonality for impartiality".

The second argument is that social justice is to be interpreted not in terms of a particular distribution of social goods but in terms of whatever distribution may result from just institutional procedures. Professor Rawls's aim is neither the construction of a social welfare function from which individual preference profiles can be aggregated into a collective policy decision nor the calculation of a formula for the allocation and distribution of wealth or any other social goods among designated persons or groups. For Professor Rawls, social justice can be shown to be done to the degree that the constitutive rules of an institutional practice are consistent with the principles which would have been agreed in the original position. This approach, with its emphasis on fairness of procedure rather than outcome, circumvents in one step the problems raised by Sidgwick's remark that despite the general agreement on the importance of the virtue of justice, commonsense maxims give no clear decision "when we ask whether primogeniture is just, or the disendowment of corporations, or the determination of the value of services by competition". On Professor Rawls's view, it would be pointless to ask for a yes-or-no answer to such a question as "is primogeniture just?". We should ask instead whether primogeniture can be better defended than some suggested alternative practice by reference to the principles agreed in the original position; and it is not a defect in Professor Rawls's theory, let alone a counter-argument in Sidgwick's favour, if no unique solution to the legislator's immediate problems can be extracted in reply. Justice, in other words, is not necessarily determinate, and should not be expected to be.

Beyond this point, however, difficulties start to arise from the more specific inferences which Professor Rawls seeks to draw from the notion of the original position. Some of these inferences are the same as Kant's own, and others are at least as plausible. Thus, liberty of conscience, universal suffrage, equality of opportunity and provision of a "social minimum" for the indigent are all readily derivable from the notion of the original position, and on some issues Professor Rawls is prepared to be still more specific than this. He argues for example that justice permits the forcible restraint of mutually intolerant sects in the interests of public safety, and that taxes on inheritance and gifts *inter vivos* are just to the degree that unfettered accumulation by some would deny full equality of opportunity to others. Conversely, it is not just to subsidize universities or opera companies at taxpayers' expense on the grounds that they are "intrinsically valuable", but only on the grounds that the least advantaged will also benefit from such subsidy. There are also some interesting remarks about civil disobedience in a democratic society which is already moderately just. But a certain unease none the less pervades the discussion, arising from the difficulty of knowing at any given stage just how far the inferences to be drawn are independent of variations in culture. We are told that the parties in the original position are equipped with a knowledge only of the most general facts about individual psychology and social organization: they do not even know "the stage of civilization" of their society. Yet at a number of significant points, Professor Rawls's suggested inferences depend on psychological and sociological assumptions for which little or no evidence is actually presented.

The most striking instance of this is the interpretation of the second principle of justice. Professor Rawls is quite explicit that it imposes a "maximin" rule—a rule, that is, which in the language of game theory requires players to adopt the strategy whereby their worst possible outcome is made as good as the range of alternatives will allow. In the context of Professor Rawls's argument, this means that justice requires the selection of whatever social policy will most improve the position of the representative member of the least advantaged class. But this leads to an immediate difficulty if we envisage, say, a three-class society, in which the elite are receiving $10,000 per year per head, the technical and clerical class $7,500 and the manual working class $5,000 and we then contrast it with a society in which the corresponding salaries are $10,000, $6,000 and $5,010. On the maximin interpretation of Professor Rawls's second principle, there can be no doubt that the second society is more just. It might, of course, turn out that this choice did accord with the intuitive ideas of fairness of those concerned; or it might be that under no conceivable economic conditions would a society be faced with such alternatives. But there is room for enough uncertainty to cast doubt on the universal applicability of the rule. As has been remarked by A. K. Sen in his book on *Collective Choice and Social Welfare*, to which Professor Rawls makes frequent reference, "Rawls's maximin solution is a very special one, and the assertion that it *must* be chosen in the original position is not altogether convincing".

There is, indeed, a still more fundamental difficulty with the maximin rule, since as Professor Rawls himself concedes there is at least one pay-off matrix for which the "rational" strategy is not the maximin. Consider a matrix in which the first row reads 0, n and the second $1/n$, 1. If n is 2, no doubt it is rational to choose the second row: half a loaf is better than none. But what if n is a million dollars? Would not persons in the original position then choose the first? Professor Rawls's answer is that this is a purely abstract possibility which would be excluded in practice by the levelling effects of universal education and full equality of opportunity. But this is a strong, and not wholly plausible, empirical assumption. In a society with a low but uniform standard of living, an agonistic cultural tradition and a universally popular national pastime—say, bullfighting—everyone might regard it as entirely fair that the best bullfighter should receive a million dollars a year and prefer to risk a negligibly lower income for themselves in order to retain the chance, however slight, of turning out to be Manolete or Dominguín. This might not seem rational to professors of philosophy in New England; but it might to peasants in Andalusía.

It would be a travesty to suggest that Professor Rawls is using the notion of the original position as a device to blind the reader to the surreptitious introduction of his own cultural preferences. He is well aware of the diversity of social institutions in the real world and allows, for example, that either a socialist or a regulated market economy might adequately embody the principles of justice. But it is noticeable that although the book contains numerous references to the literature of economic theory, it is wholly innocent of comparative ethnography. Thus Professor Rawls assumes, much as Mill did in *Representative Government*, that political participation is an unequivocal social good, and that although the size of the polity may impose a limit on its feasible extent, there is nevertheless no warrant for excluding any adult citizen of either sex from an equal chance of it. But what should we say of a society in which a hereditary institution of chiefdom is combined with a powerful ethic of redistribution, strict answerability to elders and people, and decentralization of political authority? Is such a society necessarily less just (leaving aside the inequality of women) than a liberal meritocracy because the office of chief, with its small privileges and heavy duties, is not open to competition?

Professor Rawls might reply that his concern is with large-scale industrial societies in which such an office and the system of social organization of which it is a part are manifestly not feasible. But we have been told that the persons in the original position do not know the stage of civilization of their society; and to exclude consideration of preindustrial society may be to foreclose a legitimate argument to the effect that large-scale industrial societies are necessarily less just than a partly deindustrialized and thoroughly decentralized society might be. Professor Rawls may be right to dismiss the communist utopia of the early Marx as a society in which community of ends is so far assumed that occasions for appeal to the principles of justice have been eliminated. But it is still conceivable that the division of labour might need to be radically modified for social justice to be as fully realized as the basic conditions of human cooperation allow. This line of argument is not explored by Professor Rawls, who merely notes in passing towards the very end of the book that the total abolition of the division of labour is impossible—which no doubt it is.

Professor Rawls does deal more directly with the objection that a beneficent feudal society might satisfy his principles of justice. But again, his dismissal is a little hasty. He acknowledges the point as put to him by Michael Lessnoff in a recent paper in *Political Studies* which is perhaps the most discerning and constructive criticism of Professor Rawls's ideas so far published. But his rejoinder is limited to the observation that a Burkean argument of this kind requires not merely that there is *a* benefit to the least advantaged from certain restrictions on equality of opportunity, but that the least advantaged would be even worse off if the restrictions were eliminated. But this surely is just what some conservative theorists would maintain, and it is a little unsatisfying to have the topic dismissed on the ground that such matters as "whether there are sound arguments overriding the principle of fair equality of opportunity in favour of a hierarchical class structure" are "not part of the theory of justice". Is the reader not entitled to ask whether or not a partially mobile but recognizably feudal system could be squared with the presuppositions of the original position? And is it not relevant to observe, as Mr Lessnoff does, that Professor Rawls himself allows the successful to bequeath some special advantages to their children if the least favoured will come to benefit thereby?

None of these difficulties, however, awkward as they may be, detract from the persuasiveness of Professor Rawls's vision of a just society sustained and regulated by the sense of fairness which it imparts to its members. Professor Rawls's psychology is more explicit and less speculative than his sociology, and his appeal to what we may be presumed to know about human motivations and capacities does give support to his claim that the conception of justice as fairness accords better with the principles of moral psychology than does the Utilitarian alternative. It leads to a distinction between the notions of the right and of the good which takes account at once of the diversity of rational life-plans which justice permits and of their complementarity within the terms of a mutual submission to the constraints of fiduciary obligation and acknowledgment of the value of self-respect. Professor Rawls sees the sense of justice as emerging naturally in a well-ordered society out of the feelings of mutual confidence and respect generated in childhood by the experience of benevolent parental authority and cooperative association with peers. A Kantian kingdom of ends thus becomes a reality by virtue of a common allegiance to the principles of justice and a concomitant recognition that by acting on these principles men express their nature as free and rational equals.

This vision is neither as utopian nor as sentimental as it may sound. It goes without saying that no known society conforms more than sporadically and imperfectly to Professor Rawls's principles. But these principles suggest a way in which the rival claims of admittedly self-interested persons in a world of limited cooperation might be adjudicated without prior commitment to some teleological conception of dominant ends. Professor Rawls is perfectly aware of the impediments to a well-ordered society which result from envy, sectarianism and mutual distrust and the pressures of competition and scarcity. But his case for the good of justice as fairness is argued in a manner consistent with the limitations on human perfectibility of which the parties in the original position are aware. It may be that the idea of the original position will not bear the weight of all the conclusions he seeks to base upon it. But it is possible to question these conclusions while accepting Professor Rawls's claim that it yields a conception of justice more internally coherent and more in accord with our intuitive standards for the assessment of social institutions than its rivals. Whatever the difficulties which it may be shown to raise in their turn, it will exercise a significant and perhaps lasting influence on the central questions of political philosophy with which it deals.

(b) THE EPIC MOULD

WHAT IS justice is a question like what is reality, and the question of the justice of Zeus, which is not impossible to answer since we know so much as well as, in another sense, so curiously little about the ancient Greeks, is also a question about the reality of the world of their poems and the conceptions on which they based their lives. It is a question of vital importance for the understanding of what is most living in the past of Europe, yet it has never been so clearly posed, let alone so powerfully answered, as in the Sather Lectures given at Berkeley in 1969 by Hugh Lloyd-Jones, the Regius Professor of Greek at Oxford.

Of any Regius Professor no doubt much may be expected; when his line of succession is from E. R. Dodds, the author of *The Greeks and the Irrational*, one of the few pieces of work in classical studies in this century which can decently be called great, and from Gilbert Murray, the expectation may be expected to outrun the performance, but by the most stringent standard this book must be regarded as the equal of its great ancestors: it is the crystallization of what is sharpest and deepest in the thoughts of a new generation about Greek reality, and indeed about reality itself. Such a claim will not startle those who have understood the work of Dodds and of Murray; Professor Lloyd-Jones, like them, has produced a paradigm of humanism, and of that peculiar sense of reality as well as that broad and intricate technical scholarship which have characterized Greek studies at their best at least since the days of Wilamowitz. It is a towering and individual achievement, and we may have to wait a long time before we see anything else like it.

The first lecture is a discussion of the *Iliad*. No writer is more real than Homer and no writer more formal. The justice of Zeus in the Homeric poetry is dark, but it is not impenetrable. The just judgment of Zeus is after all part of worldly and human reality, even though Zeus himself may be supernatural; the gods or God are after all part of nature or Nature, and the sense of a just judgment of Zeus is neither unnatural nor bound up with social progress or the development of rationalism. The Homeric poems are by no means primitive, though they used to be thought so: indeed, the entire model of development from the primitive to the rational and complicated must now perhaps be abandoned in the context of Greek society and probably elsewhere; what had been thought of as stages of development in a chronological series must now be seen as levels of consciousness, of behaviour, and of social convention. Homeric society, in any sense in which it ever existed, was not less "civilized" than what followed, but because of the conventions of epic poetry different values and different behaviour hold our attention in it. Conversely, the great rationalist intellectuals and poets and politicians of the fifth century still believed or half-believed in the same Zeus as Homer and the same justice as Zeus, if only because of the overwhelming influence of Homeric epic even in the hundred years after true epic poetry seems to have ceased to be written in Greece.

There is a prima facie difficulty for us of taking Zeus seriously in the *Iliad*, in that like Achilles and Thersites he is simply a character in a poem, described in the same lightly honeyed or checkered and thunderous verses, with the same kind of delicacy and extraordinary strength. It used to be thought he was a heavenly projection of an earthly political system, and indeed it must inevitably be true that the idea of justice and of the free, deliberate will of Zeus is defined from the experience of life, the thoughts and language of a particular people; but Homeric conceptions of justice are subtle as well as simple, and they have evaded analysis until now. The study of individual words and phrases in recent times has been even less productive than the political abstraction, since it has been even more mechanical; dealing with a poem is like dealing with a running stream, it requires contemplative and intuitive, as well as active, powers, and will not succeed without a certain humility and openness to poetry.

The proper audience of an epic poem will not consist of connoisseurs any more than of vapid enthusiasts, still less of mechanical scholars. Professor Lloyd-Jones uncovers Zeus and his justice in a masterly lecture; he diminishes his opponents with authority in that he convicts them of underestimating the *Iliad*. The poem we are shown is not more elaborately contrived than the one we thought we knew, but it is stronger, it has more notes in it, and it is closer to the

archaic age. At this point as at others it would be possible to confirm
or illustrate his findings, which are those of the straightforward
penetration of literature, by the evidence of archaeology and art
history. It is remarkable to see how the scanty visual evidence
coincides with his view of Homeric poetry. The justice of Zeus was
not an invention of moralism or a projection of rationalism, but it
was part of Homer's world before it was part of his poetry, and it
fits everything else we know about that world.

It would be inadequate to give an account of Professor Lloyd-
Jones's line of thought in terms of the adversaries who are routed by
the way, some formally challenged in the text and others impaled in
footnotes, but there is one scholar who is more than an adversary,
rather a *daimon* with whom many of the arguments are a conversation, whose work is always present and in relation to whom Professor
Lloyd-Jones must define himself: the author of *The Greeks and the
Irrational*. Professor Lloyd-Jones's relationship to Professor Dodds
is one of tense and intricate intellectual involvement, but where Dodds
has stressed development, rationality in its emergence and in the
obstacles it confronted, Lloyd-Jones stresses continuity and the
preponderant influence of Homer, who is by no means a savage
theologian. Both aspects of Greek history are objectively present in
undisputed evidence, and the two books are in a way complementary;
but the Homeric idea of the justice of Zeus is terrible, and it is timely
in these years that it should be stressed, just as Professor Dodds's
heroic account of the struggle of reason and the irrational was
timely in the late 1940s (it was published in 1951).

It is curious that at a time when the backbone of modern religions
seems to have melted away, Greek scholarship (of all remote enterprises) and the understanding of Homer presents a conception more
in keeping with the experience of life in this century than the clergy
would dare to entertain.

Human kind, says the bird in Eliot, cannot bear very much reality. The
early Greeks were capable of their unique achievements largely because
they could bear, as their religion shows, very much more reality than most
human beings.

To justify the works of Zeus to man was beyond the scope of even
the most rational Greek poet; it was below the dignity of Zeus and
above the possibilities of man. Whatever of formal justifications has
survived in literature is deeply built into the forms of poetry: it has

entered those forms at a popular, almost a proverbial level, before they became great literature, and has deeply penetrated them.

It will be evident that these are the opinions or preconceptions of the reviewer; Professor Lloyd-Jones's own work is more tightly argued, but it is so stimulating that every reader will wish to break in again and again: it is the privilege or disadvantage of a reviewer much moved by a book that he interjects in marginal annotations and in print. Professor Lloyd-Jones has a happiness of opening and closing and of sudden phrases in common with purely literary writers; for example with the sudden sharp resonances of Gibbon; and like Gibbon he has something indefinable in common with the arts in his own day. In the briskness of Gibbon there were other elements remote from scholarly brooding. The best classical scholars in the past 150 years and no doubt much earlier have had an element of poetry in their talent and vocation; they cannot be called poets manqué since this element in them has been so abundantly fruitful and in verse it would have been less so; it needed for its development the gritty materials and hard intellectual exercise of the scholar's trade, but this is the element which speaks so immediately in their writings, and which separates them so completely from mechanical practitioners. A wide view of ancient literature will not be intoxicating or even acceptable except when it controls details in the well-known manner of the Greek light; wide but uncontrolled views of literature are simply fuzzy, but the genuine breadth of scholarship is a combination of completeness and particularity.

A review of this kind is no place for a profusion of particulars, but a few will be in order. Professor Lloyd-Jones devotes some excellent pages to Hesiod; he points out the ambivalence of Hesiod's social position, his authority as a poet and his lack of standing as a peasant farmer, as being crucial to the poet's conceptions and expectations, and basic to his preoccupation with justice. It was not Hesiod who invented justice, his view of humanity is modest and his hopes in Zeus more natural than personal. Indeed one could reasonably say that if justice is not natural it is nothing. It is obscure in what way Hesiod's conception of a just order is any advance on the *Iliad* or the *Odyssey*; there is a difference of genre certainly, but not one it is possible to explain chronologically with the least assurance. As Professor Lloyd-Jones points out, Homer reveals the world of gods as well as the world of men, both in epic verse, and this difference from later, more numinous writers has many consequences. There were

certainly lyric poets in Homer's day, and the more early lyric poetry
is recovered from papyri, the longer and darker Homer's shadow on
it seems to be; and this includes the nature of Zeus and of justice.
Mimnermus speaks of Zeus in the bleak voice of Achilles, either
because he has read and founded his poetry on Homer or because this
black wisdom was proverbial.

There is room in the intellectual model we are being offered for
development, but not perhaps for fundamental changes. Any
fundamental changes in Greek society seem to have been late in
affecting religion. Not much emphasis is put on the earliest emergence
of the *polis*, because the form in which it emerged was at first aristo-
cratic, and even the philosophers, indeed even the Athenian democracy with its superstitions and its tragedies, departed less far in the
fifth century from a Homeric vision of the justice of Zeus than one
might suppose. Many questions of interpretation central to the study
of the tragic poets are bound up with this view, and they are worked
out in an enthralling way. What altered least in the framework
of poetry, although it did alter in time, was an austere and terrify-
ingly modest understanding of the natural order, an understanding
which to us until now has been as culturally remote as it was unsympathetic. One should remember that the statue of Zeus at
Olympia belonged to the mid-fifth century, but that when the Roman
general Aemilius Paulus saw it he observed at once it was the Zeus
of Homer, and also that Quintilian said of the same statue that it
added something to human religion. The Zeus of Aeschylus is like
that, and yet Aeschylus could hear a footfall of justice neither softer
nor louder than Homer. One of the most important and astonishing
of the phenomena which Professor Lloyd-Jones touches is the position of justice in philosophy and in medicine, where it was vital to
the advance of science, once again in the same period. The normal
condition of a limb was "its just nature", what restored a wrenched
limb was "a just operation", and correct treatment "is established
like a just law". It is as if the very idea of nature followed from that
of justice.

It seems a far cry from "the rudder-stroke of the thunder", but
the justice of Zeus is fundamental to rationality and the unity of
nature. We no longer believe that historical progress is from simple
to complex conceptions; Homer seems younger and more modern.
To Aeschylus as to Homer there is a "grace that comes by violence",
and as Professor Lloyd-Jones well translates: "There is a place where

what is formidable is good and must remain seated to watch over men's minds." Among the tragic poets, and particularly on Aeschylus, he is at his best, brilliantly persuasive, unexpected and original, densely rich in new insights and scholarly arguments. He makes a bewitching suggestion, based partly on the earlier work of Fraenkel, but substantially new and very convincing, that the last play of the Prometheus trilogy was the *Women of Aetna*, and that the whole trilogy was first performed in Sicily on a visit to Hieron. This suggestion is modestly put forward, it is briefly but cogently argued and is essentially conjectural, but it is a conjecture any classical scholar in history, let alone anyone now living, would be proud to have made.

Professor Lloyd-Jones extends his researches as far as Thucydides and the sophists.

Thucydides sees the history of the empire in tragic terms, not necessarily because he has been influenced by tragedy, but more probably because like the tragedians, like Herodotus, like most of his contemporaries his mind was profoundly conditioned by the epic and the whole attitude to human life which it expresses.

One could hardly put more succinctly the central truth of Greek civilization with which this book is concerned. Homer is a dark poet, and there are mysterious evidences in his poems that the world for which he wrote contained darker elements still. The eerie clang of the bird of the goddess during the night raid—no doubt the origin, incidentally, of that line of Milton: "seals and orcs and sea-mews clang"—belongs to a sinister set of beliefs. The ghosts of Aeschylus are not a mere stage convention any more than Hamlet's father's ghost. In the last quarter of the eighth century BC Mycenean tombs were reopened for the purpose of worshipping the dead bodies they contained. The justice of Zeus is not a sunny conception, but the sunny moments of religious fashion never last for long. This book, brilliant and fascinating as it is, will not make relaxed reading for non-specialists, but it is only dusty truths that last.

8

ARCHETYPES AND HEROES
(a) MELVILLE'S MONUMENT

MONUMENTS, those massive piles of cultural accretion, are generally the productions and often the only surviving evidence of empire. Their literary equivalent is the epic, a celebration of the imperial theme; but not all nations have had their territorial ambitions matched by a Homer or a Virgil, and often must settle—as in the case of Tennyson—for a Collected Works in lieu of an *Iliad* or *Aeneid*. America, however, has been doubly blessed in Herman Melville, for as her first great surge of imperial expansion yielded *Moby Dick*, her most recent territorial spasm has produced what

---

(a) *The Writings of Herman Melville*. Edited by Harrison Hayford, Hershel Parker, G. Thomas Tanselle; Volume III: *Mardi: and A Voyage Thither*. 729 pp. $15 (paperback, $3.95); Volume IV: *Redburn: His First Voyage*. 384 pp. $10 (paperback, $2.50); Volume V: *White Jacket: or, The World in a Man-of-War*. 499 pp. $12.50 (paperback, $3.50). Evanston, Illinois: Northwestern University Press.

HOWARD P. VINCENT: *The Tailoring of Melville's "White Jacket"*. 239 pp. Evanston, Illinois: Northwestern University Press. $7.

WILLIAM BYSSHE STEIN: *The Poetry of Melville's Late Years*. Time, History, Myth, and Religion. 275 pp. Albany, NY: State University of New York Press. $7.

MARTIN LEONARD POPS: *The Melville Archetype*. 287 pp. Kent, Ohio: Kent State University Press. $10.

ALAN LEBOWITZ: *Progress into Silence*. A Study of Melville's Heroes. 240 pp. Indiana University Press (American University Publishers Group). £4.25.

GAY WILSON ALLEN: *Melville and his World*. 144 pp. Thames and Hudson. £1.95.

(b) RICARDO AGUILERA: *Intención y silencio en el Quijote*. 199 pp. Madrid: Ayuso.

MIGUEL DE CERVANTES: *Exemplary Stories*. Translated by C. A. Jones. 252 pp. Penguin. Paperback, 40p.

ALBAN K. FORCIONE: *Cervantes' Christian Romance*. 167 pp. Princeton University Press. London: Oxford University Press. £4.

AMÉRICO CASTRO: *El pensamiento de Cervantes*. 410 pp. Barcelona: Noguer. 275 ptas.

MIGUEL DE CERVANTES: *El ingenioso hidalgo Don Quijote de la Mancha*. Introduction by Américo Castro. Part 1: 497 pp. Part 2: 426 pp. Madrid: Magisterio Español. 100 ptas each.

years of neglect denied Melville, a full-dress, monumentally conceived Writings.

The implicit nationalism involved in government support of the ambitious Modern Language Association's Center for Editions of American Authors would seem to be self-evident. A number of authors, from Hawthorne to Howells, are benefiting from the munificent chauvinism of the United States Office of Education, but Melville's is a special case, suiting the temper of the times. For it was during the 1940s and 1950s that the state of Melville studies came to resemble the American whaling industry a century earlier, an epic enterprise reflecting America's optimistic sense of herself and her world mission. Then, with the 1960s, and with the Vietnam debacle, the scope, volume, and buoyancy of Melville scholarship began to fall off noticeably. Some meaning may be found in the tragic history of Professor H. Bruce Franklin, whose *Wake of the Gods*, a study of Melville's use of comparative mythology, appeared in 1963 (a turning-point in American consciousness), and who is at this writing being threatened with dismissal from a tenured post by Stanford University for his advocacy and practice of revolutionary activities.

Equally significant in this connexion is the roster of "contributing scholars" listed by the Northwestern-Newberry Edition of the Writings. Under the captaincy of Professor Harrison Hayford, the roster is almost a roll-call of every scholar who helped to establish Melville's (and his own) reputation during the Golden, or Imperial, Age of Melville studies. The Establishment is in charge here, and though the Writings was initiated during the heady 1960s, it continues a-building, undaunted by national reverses. In a sense, the Writings is less a venture in territorial expansion than evidence of consolidation. Hopefully it will not, like certain sundry pyramids and cathedrals, remain unfinished, for the Writings promises to supply a need long felt by all scholars of American literature—a complete, dependable text of Melville's works.

Melville, of all American authors, has been most unfortunate in his textual as well as his critical posterity. Because of the vagaries of fame, he was by-passed during the first great period of Collected Works, while Longfellow, Holmes, Whittier, and Hawthorne were entombed for the ages by loving friends and relations. And when he did come into his own in the 1920s, he was unlucky in his would-be literary executor, Raymond Weaver. Though a handsome job

of book-design, the Constable edition of Melville's *Works* is notori-
ously corrupt so far as the already published material is concerned,
and inept in its handling of the later, unpublished writings. It has had
the dubious honour of providing a textbook example of editorial
carelessness, the infamous "soiled fish of the sea" for which F. O.
Matthiessen took such an embarrassing dive in his *American
Renaissance*. Equally dubious was the honour accorded the Constable
edition by Edmund Wilson, who, in his bitter and ill-informed attack
on the American Authors project (published in pamphlet form as
The Fruits of the MLA), recommended that it be used as the basis for
a Pléiade-like edition of Melville's works.

One aspect of the Melville boom of the 1940s and 1950s was the
projected Hendricks House edition of the works, an admirable conception with uneven and never-completed results. Though blessed by
astute critical commentary and helpful annotations, the textual
accuracy of at least one of the volumes, *Moby Dick*, was severely
questioned. This will surely not be the case with the Writings at
hand. The financial assistance of the United States Government may,
for those of tender conscience, be an ambivalent blessing, but at
least it ensures the kind of lavish budget necessary to carry out the
textual policy established by Professor Fredson Bowers, who had set
an Olympian standard for the American Authors editions. Like so
much overtaken by the United States, the American Authors project
is an example of over-kill. But Melville at last seems to be assured
of a solid if more than adequate cenotaph. It is therefore with a sigh
of relief that we greet each succeeding volume as it appears from the
Northwestern University Press: heavy, thick, and authoritative.

Professor Hayford and his editorial associates are obviously hew-
ing close to the monumental line in all respects, and the Writings
presents a clean, uncluttered face to the world. The textual apparatus,
the equivalent of air-conditioning and elevator machinery, is kept
clanking and groaning in the rear of the edifice. Moreover, because
of the virtual absence of manuscript versions of Melville's early works,
the textual machinery which often makes such meddlesome gods of
the Bowers of Academe is kept to a minimum so far as the present
volumes are concerned. The Northwestern-Newberry edition further
contributes to cleanliness by acknowledging the temporal nature of
critical introductions and scholarly annotations. Setting its course for
eternity, the Writings is massively bare of all such graffiti, and each
volume is limited to an admirably restrained Historical Note, taste-

fully tucked into the back pages also. "Admirably restrained", because to resist imposing one's critical opinions on posterity is a difficult task for most scholar-teachers. In the present instance, for example, we discover that not all of the eminent authorities are successful at keeping themselves from scribbling in the moist concrete, thus adding a subjective mite to the objective whole.

Though the "historical note" should be limited to the known biographical facts surrounding the writing and publication of the work and its contemporary reception, we find Professor Willard Thorp attempting to have a last word on the implications of structure in *White Jacket*, and Professor Hershel Parker cannot resist the temptation to make a few hurried conjectures concerning the probable composition of *Redburn*. Pardonable violations of editorial decorum, surely, but unconscious tributes as well to the strength of Professor Elizabeth Foster's character, for her Note remains impassive in the face of the baroque rodomontade of *Mardi*—a book which cries out in massive agony for some kind of critical apologia. These are small matters, however. The important thing is that all the advances of scholarship of the past fifty years have created a *Lehrersraum* where none before existed. There is no longer any need to assume a defensive attitude when discussing Herman Melville. He is a world author, and his monument is rising, an imperial pile which makes some acknowledgment of the democratic ethos (and Edmund Wilson's gripe) by its availability in a cheap, paperback version.

Though Melville is now a world author, his fame is largely the result of one book. The epical *Moby Dick* looms large in the corpus, like Tenerife among the Canary Islands. All studies of Melville's work must reckon with that fact of superiority, and seldom question it. As in the case of Shakespeare's will, most of the trouble has been over the second-best. Early on, in the 1930s, *Pierre* had an enthusiastic cult of advocates, "Bartleby" and the other short stories were championed by critics during the 1940s, and the 1950s saw the rise of *The Confidence-Man*. A book appeared recently in America devoted entirely to explicating *Israel Potter*!—and here we have Professor Howard Vincent's admirable study of the sources and structure of *White Jacket*, obviously written under the assumption that it is a book worth a book all by itself. Professor Vincent must be accounted a pioneer in this regard, for he was the first to accord that honour to *Moby Dick*. His G.-Livingston-Loweish *The Trying-Out of Moby*

Dick appeared more than twenty years ago, and was a brilliant and original study of Melville's fusing powers over the many disparate authorities whose work was pillaged for the biblical bulk of his epic. We cannot make quite the same claims for *The Tailoring of White Jacket*, however, largely because the territory has been so thoroughly explored before Professor Vincent arrived with rod and transit.

As Professor Vincent's many acknowledgments make clear, it was Professor Charles R. Anderson's *Melville in the South Seas* which, as early as 1939, demonstrated the extent to which Melville depended on secondary materials, suggesting that the American Shakespeare was himself a plagiarizer (the territorial imperative) on a generous scale. Since that time, Melville scholars have had a field day hunting sources hither and yon, like one of Thoreau's berrying parties. Mostly yon, one might add. If we were to add up the number of volumes which Melville is credited with reading between 1845 and 1856, while he was also at work writing ten books himself, the total would be Munchhausenish. The point is that, whereas in 1949 Professor Vincent had the field to himself, he is now rather inclined to crow like Chanticleer over his own few kernels of discovery. Like Melville's, Professor Vincent's tailoring job is mostly devoted to sewing together the scraps and fragments of other men's work. Where the Writings is evidence of consolidation, Vincent's *Tailoring* is the consolidation of evidence.

As such, it belongs on the shelf next to Professor Thorp's edition of *White Jacket*, for the two are joined by an invisible umbilicus of cooperation. The unique good-naturedness of Melville studies is here testified to by Professor Thorp's and Professor Vincent's mutual generosity, and the net result is that Professor Thorp discusses in small what Professor Vincent enlarges upon at length. And "at length" is surely the word for his technique, for we are treated to page after page of parallel columns of "Melville" and some pilfered "Other", a sort of double-entry book-sweeping that does not make for very exciting reading. Moreover, some of the resemblances between source and finished statement are rather general, acceptable as analogues, perhaps, but one occasionally needs the zeal of the converted to see what Professor Vincent and his fellow scholars have perceived. Indeed, what one admires most about Professor Vincent's book is his enthusiasm for his subject. A man of broad cultural interests and deep aesthetic passions (whose study of Daumier was recently well received in these pages), Professor Vincent's prose sparkles and dances with informed allusions, which float on the tide of his deep certainty, of himself and of his man. There is in him that abiding affection for his great subject which marks the best in Melville scholarship.

One wishes the same could be said about the other most recent studies of Melville's work, which vary from the egregiously self-serving to the ponderously dull. Yet all of these books, like Professor Vincent's, operate from the assumption of Melville's greatness. How else can we account for a study like Professor William Bysshe Stein's, which, while admitting the problems of aesthetics and sensibility raised by Melville's poetry, goes on to devote an entire book to the explication of his later, most obscure verse? It is not *good poetry*, for the most part, claims Professor Stein, yet we must do our best to understand it. Why, if not that Melville is a consummately great artist, whose clumsiest efforts are worth much study? Professor Stein does make some discriminations, the most important of which is the debatable remark that *Battle-Pieces* and *Clarel* are "constricted expressions of [Melville's] poetic talent", a flat statement with nothing to substantiate it but our appreciation of Professor Stein's good opinion, an appreciation that he does little in the succeeding pages to earn. That is, having agreed with Robert Penn Warren that Melville's poetry is a difficult and even painfully tangled thicket to penetrate, Professor Stein is off and running through the underbrush, but few of us will run very far with him.

For there seems to be a certain madness to Professor Stein's method. He declares at the outset that "Melville's late poetry flowers out of the rich soil of emotional and spiritual contentment [and is] written in a mood of quiet exultation". But we must not be lulled into acquiescence by the academic tone of this tired metaphor: the burden of Professor Stein's conclusions, driven home with a self-approving chorus of "certainlys", "of courses", and "plainlys", implies a Melville not far removed from that tenebrific fellow detected by the magic lamp of Lawrance Thompson. Like Professor Thompson, Professor Stein likes to share with *his* Melville "the pleasure of ulteriority", to join in "chortling blasphemies on the absurdity of belief in a supernatural power". Professor Stein's Melville is a bubbling fountain, of chuckles, sniggers, and chortles, which one is to interpret, apparently, as the signs of "quiet exultation" but the net effect of which is to convey the impression of a dirty old man.

For Professor Stein would have us believe that Melville's later

poetry is largely informed by sexual imagery. His approach, therefore, is variously Jungian, Freudian, and, as he admits, "Steinean",
which involves a sort of eclectic union between phallic objects and
Great Mothers, while juggling all manner of mythic analogies.
For his purposes Professor Stein drags along an impressive bag of
symbols, erudition culled from many disparate sources, and his
method is equally various, and subjective to boot. "Helter-skelter" is
the word, and butchery is the result. Surely there is a need for intelligent explication of Melville's very different, extremely difficult
poetry. And there is plenty of evidence that Melville is a cryptic, sly,
ambiguous poet, whose imagery undeniably tends towards sexual,
even perverse, implications. Beyond that, however, most of us are
reluctant to go: we remain behind the Johnsonian stone wall of common sense, listening to Professor Stein yodelling enthusiastically in
the blue distance of absolute conjecture.

The point is not that a psychological study of Melville's work is in
itself ridiculous. Jung himself early recognized that *Moby Dick* was a
rich subject for literary analysis, and Dr Henry A. Murray's introduction to the Hendricks House *Pierre* decorously stressed the
archetypal patterns in that troubled and troublesome novel. But
psychological criticism, whether Jungian or Freudian or whatever,
tends at best to be reductive—an impulse which deadens the very
soul of creative literature—and at worst it allows for the kind of free-
swinging subjectivity which often amounts to a noisy thrashing about
in darkness. The result is likely to be a loud claim for consistency
accompanied by a rather quiet process of special selection. There are,
however, other possibilities, and, if Professor Stein is a glaring example of special pleading, Professor Martin Pops demonstrates the
special limitation of psychological explication when applied to the
corpus of such a writer as Melville throughout.

What Professor Stein has attempted with the late poetry, Professor Pops has essayed with the œuvre, and though he lacks Professor Stein's impressively hindersome erudition, he is well up on the
secondary literature relevant to his own approach, and has written a
better, more controlled study than has Professor Stein. He sticks
fairly close to the business at hand, producing a methodical, chronological explication of Melville's work, using Jungian terminology for
the most part, Freudian when applicable. There is the usual implication endemic to such studies that Melville is chiefly useful as an
illustration of a psychological approach to literature, but more

troublesome, perhaps, is Professor Pops's lack of selectivity—the antithesis of Professor Stein's voice—his insistence on treating *all* of the works, come hell or high water. His main argument, that Melville's life and art record a life-long search for "the Sacred", works reasonably well for the quest romances like *Mardi* and *Moby Dick*, which have deep ties to the mythic past. But it does not have much validity when applied to, say, *The Confidence-Man*. Yet Professor Pops ploughs right along, and when his Jungian terminology fails him he hauls out his battered old New Critical Dictionary and keeps right on analysing.

Indeed, both Professor Stein and Professor Pops serve to illustrate the kinship of the New and the Psychological Criticism. Though they both pay token respect to the fact of Herman Melville, Man and Author, the events of his full, long, and often mysterious life are useful only as they provide grist for the symbolic mill. The burden of attention remains on the works themselves, and a burdensome attention it is, with all the irksome irrelevance of latter-day, decadent New Criticism masking as objective, scientific discourse. Both Jung and Freud were types of poet *manqué* (or perhaps *maudit*), but where their subjectivity yielded insight, what can be said of the following example of Professor Pops's analysis?

A simple elbow in the rib should hardly call forth such retribution as a terrible drubbing, but the [*sic*] Red Whiskers has really done much more: he has elbowed Billy in the sex—in the sir (male) loin (genital), and the genital [*sic*] of prelapsarian Billy may very well be the place from which Eve was born—the rib, not the groin, just as the blow to the side may also suggest the spear Christ Himself ultimately suffers.

From the slight triplet—"Scarce lone these groups, scarce lone and bare/When Theseus roved a Raleigh there,/Each isle a small Virginia fair—/Unravished"—Professor Stein warps and weaves a figure into his own astonishing carpet:

The pun on Virginia (virginity) historically embraces the notorious rape of native female populations by European explorers and settlers, an unholy contrast with Theseus who delivered the island of Crete from the ravaging appetite of the Minotaur.

What is this but a sort of mindless, heedless stuffing of subjective associations into the delicate fabric of Melville's allusory style, with a consequent rending of the veil without an attendant revelation? Under the guise of widening the scope of Melville studies, Professor

Pops and Professor Stein are operating at the same old stand, purveying the second-hand goods of the once-New Criticism, and their accomplishment does not carry us much farther than did the so-called "phenomenological" criticism of the late 1950s, which was the cosmic extension of self-imposed limitations of critical warfare, which is not the same as enlarging the domain of Melville's reputation.

At least Professor Pops and Professor Stein are worthy of some response, and if they seem to wax wrong-headed, at least they wax enthusiastically wrong-headed. Not even this may be said of Professor Alan Lebowitz, and it is difficult to understand why his study was published at all. Professor Lebowitz is concerned with the gradual emergence of "Ishmael" and "Ahab" in Melville's work before the writing of *Moby Dick*, and with their rapid disappearance soon thereafter. This is like selling last year's newspaper. The subject was brilliantly and more thoroughly treated by Professor Merlin Bowen these dozen years since, and much else of what Professor Lebowitz has to say has already been said by Professor Milton Stern and in more exciting ways as well.

Professor Lebowitz acknowledges his predecessors, yet goes right on shining light from a borrowed lantern. While such a rehash might be welcomed by the fabled general reader, Professor Lebowitz's style is so lack-lustre and studded with the usual pedantic load of quotations—the same old quotations, alas!—that one could hardly recommend it to the non-academic enthusiast. Even the bibliography is both dated and tired, and gives out in 1965, as if, having reached a certain point in the sequence of Melville scholarship, Professor Lebowitz was reluctant to read on.

Where it is difficult to understand the intended reader in the case of *Progress into Silence*, a quick glance at *Melville and his World* suffices—it is surely "for the trade". Despite the implications of the title, which, combined with the reputation of Professor Gay Wilson Allen for methodical, encyclopedic scholarship, suggests the wide-ranging, socio-political treatment which Melville greatly deserves, this is for the most part a picture book. What Professor Allen contributes is a rather uninspired commentary, chronologically tracing the main events of Melville's life—a sort of droning lecture accompanying a slide-show. Professors must eat, but considering Professor Allen's reputation as a painstaking and thorough scholar, one is taken aback by his frequent implication that the earlier romances,

despite Anderson's efforts, may be regarded as chapters of autobiography. Nor are the occasional bits of sloppiness, such as calling
the hero of *Redburn* "Redburn Welborne" (even in the index),
or spelling "Tommo" with one "m", much to Professor Allen's
credit.

Well, as Huckleberry Finn would say, that is nothing. Each of these
books is similarly marred by unacceptable scholarly method, rang-
ing from Professor Lebowitz's stunted bibliography to Professor
Vincent's footnote-loose-and-fancy-free system, in which Bantam
paperbacks are cited as references and where "Charles Roberts
Anderson, *Melville in the South Seas* (New York: Columbia University Press, 1939)" is cited in full again and again and again.
Professor Stein seems unaware that Robert Penn Warren's essay on
Melville's poetry has long since been gathered to the bosom of his
Selected Essays, and Professor Pops increases the predictable resistance to his thesis by treating the reader to several demonstrations
of untotal recall regarding certain episodes in Melville's novels. It is
strange that at the very moment when the single most important
contribution to Melville scholarship in America is a definitive,
accurate, scrupulously edited collection of his works, critical studies
of a generally heedless and specifically purposeless nature should be
in such evidence. Still, one of the penalties of becoming a national
monument is that one unavoidably attracts sundry untidy fowl, a
phenomenon which also may be attributed to Melville's new-found
prominence and hopefully enduring fame.

(*b*) CERVANTES'S CONTRADICTIONS

SOME TIME EARLY next year an expensive production of *Don Quixote*
is to be shown on BBC television. After the glutinous sentimentalities
of *Man of La Mancha*, Cervantes's "discreto lector" must be facing
the prospect with some trepidation, unalleviated by the fact that the
principal actor in the television version is particularly remembered
for his roles as Professor Higgins and Dr Doolittle. Moreover,
whereas *War and Peace* gets suitably large-scale treatment on the
media, and novel after nineteenth-century novel is parcelled out for
weekly serial transfer to the small private screen, *Don Quixote*,
which has real possibilities for serialization in film, is periodically
dehydrated for consumption in the theatre or cinema, and sugared

to the taste of about 1870. Such impoverishment may be the inevitable consequence of a transfer of medium, but sentimentalization is not. We have had an astringent, sophisticated *Alice*, but (unless the BBC surprises us) it seems that *Don Quixote* is still conceived, at the most public level, in the retarded Romantic terms of "Dream the Impossible Dream".

There has been no lack of simplified—or of simplistic—readings of *Don Quixote*. And their disparity is the clearest proof of the novel's real complexity. After all, what kind of a character is the protagonist when in one period he is held to be a comic madman, in another a pathetic hero, and sometimes both together? Yet it is so easy to read the *Quixote* in a simple, straightforward way that it can seem absurd to look for ulterior significance. Moreover, Cervantes held out no high ambitions for it, as he did for *Persiles y Sigismunda*, and he made no claim that it contained any hidden mystery, as he did for the *Novelas ejemplares*. All he said he sought to do with *Don Quixote* was give merry entertainment and drive out the books of chivalry. In consequence, the seeming simplicity of the novel has often been transferred to the creative intellect of its author. By Fitzmaurice-Kelly, for instance.

But simplicity is always a challenge to minds that lack that virtue. So *Don Quixote* has also been the frequent victim of esoteric interpretations; and all kinds of secret intentions and doctrines have been imputed to Cervantes. Before the end of the seventeeth century Père Rapin wrote confidingly:

Ce grand homme, ayant esté traité avec quelque mépris par le Duc de Lerme, premier Ministre de Philippe III, qui n'avoit nulle considération pour les sçavans, écrivit le roman de Dom Quichot, qui est une Satyre très-fine de sa nation: parce que toute la Noblesse d'Espagne, qu'il rend ridicule par cet ouvrage, s'estoit entestée de Chevalerie. C'est une tradition que je tiens d'un de mes amis, qui avoit appris ce secret de Dom Lopé à qui Cervantes avoit fait confidence de son ressentiment.

Interpretations of the *Quixote* as a work of more or less disguised social and religious criticism have recurred from age to age. They were particularly common in the later years of the past century and the early years of this. Cervantes as a crypto-Lutheran or a free-thinker was a not unfamiliar figure.

In the past few years there has been something of a revival of esoteric interpretations. A work called *Don Quichotte, prophète d'Israël* was published in 1966, and latterly Cervantes has been conscripted in the cause of social protest. Last year in the United States the message of *Don Quixote* for the campus radical was discovered. Marxist and quasi-Marxist readings, of course, are well established. The most novel and, indeed, heartening fact about the latter is that a few of them have been written and published in Spain recently.

The message of Ricardo Aguilera's *Intención y silencio en el Quijote* is "humanist", in the current political sense of the term. It is studded with quotations picked out of the *Quixote*, like passages of Holy Writ in a fundamentalist tract. The book is quite unhistorical; nevertheless, there is a poignancy in the anachronisms:

La censura es una carga demasiado pesada en el ánimo del hombre de pensamiento. El temor le invade, sumiéndole en la confusión y el desconcierto. Lo más "cómodo" es aceptar las cosas como están y renunciar a toda aventura. Pero el intelectual percibe inevitablemente la voz de su responsabilidad. Es preciso, pues, rodear el peligroso precipicio que se presenta en el camino. No le es posible ya renunciar a su impulso crítico y censor que le invita a contribuir a la destrucción de condicionamientos que impiden el progreso social.

If the reader's mind wanders away from the ostensible subject, Cervantes and the Spain of Philip III, in such passages, the effect is probably not unintended.

It would be idle to deny, however, that *Don Quixote* offers grounds for anti-establishment interpretations. It can plausibly be argued that the clergy are shown to no advantage in the novel. Don Quixote does set free the convicts in the name of a recognizably higher principle than the King's justice. A ducal court does amuse itself frivolously at the expense of Quixote and Sancho. The peasant Sancho does (on the whole) show a surprising talent for governing others.

But critics of the opposite persuasion find it just as easy to come by arguments; and, given the time and place of the *Quixote*'s appearance, it would seem *prima facie* to be easier for them. So we are no less accustomed—indeed, we are more so—to the idea of Don Quixote the perfect Christian gentleman, Don Quixote the Christian saint, as W. H. Auden among others sees him, and Don Quixote the hubristic fool who has to learn Christian humility through disillusionment, as yet others have seen him. We have a "Cervantes reazionario", mirror of conservative orthodoxy and mould of Counter-Reformation form. Quite lately Paul Descouzis has offered us a *Quixote* consciously impregnated with the spirit of the Council

of Trent. With all such views, as with their opposites, the more parti-
san they are, the less they account for, because the evidence brought
in favour of nearly every argument about the novel's "meaning" has
to be weighed against evidence to the contrary.

At the possible risk of another simplification, one might say that
the problem is mainly one of interpreting human behaviour, of
assessing the motives behind the actions of the characters in the novel
and relating them to their consequences. This in turn raises questions
about the role of providence in a world where effects are shown to
spring from causes quite naturally but often incalculably; for the
world of the *Quixote* is not the preordained world of romance (except in some of the "interpolated" episodes) or the picaresque
vision of a world ruled by blind chance. A major reason why *Don
Quixote* offers problems of interpretation to the thoughtful reader
is that the characters themselves are continually confronted with the
same problems. The novel is concerned to an unusual degree with
not merely the events it narrates but the interpretation of them. The
problem of their physical aspect is just the tip of an iceberg that de-
scends to depths of considerable moral and psychological complexity.
The question of whether or not the barber's basin is Mambrino's
helmet is not a real question for the reader, indeed; but that so many
sane characters should insist that it is a helmet is infinitely intriguing.

Some of the deepest ironies in the book lie in the gaps between
intentions and results. One of the few times in his career that the
Knight has a real opportunity to exercise his chivalric profession and
help someone in trouble occurs early on (in chapter four), when he
comes on the farmer Juan Haldudo beating the boy Andrés. Sub-
limely confident of his authority at this stage, he inquires into the
matter, orders the man to desist and rides away. Thanks to Don
Quixote's interference Andrés then receives a more savage thrashing
than he would have done. The victim of Quixote's noble intentions is
not, this time, himself but someone else: a child. The irony here is
something more than comic, and from this point in the novel a whole
new dimension of irony opens up.

The many deceptions perpetrated on Don Quixote by other people
sometimes have consequences alarmingly at variance with the intentions behind them. The largely well-meaning efforts of the Priest
and the Barber to save Quixote from himself by joining in his antics
turn out to be a dubious form of therapy. On the other hand,
paradoxically, the antics at the Duke's castle, indulged in just for the

selfish pleasure of the jokers, seem to do Quixote more good in the end, in so far as they accelerate his disillusionment. The not unmixed motives of the Bachelor Carrasco in going out to bring him home are quickly contaminated by a thirst for revenge after his first failure. When he succeeds in defeating him in combat on the second occasion, the consequences are much graver and more complicated than might have been expected. Don Quixote's growing melancholy is aggravated to the extent that it purges his choler and restores him to sanity. But it also kills him.

For some readers, like Ruskin, the *Quixote* is the most appalling indictment of human ideals. For others it represents the spirit of idealism flying triumphant over the prostrate body of its terrestrial champion. For others it is just *Man of La Mancha*. More than most works of literature, *Don Quixote* is apt to reflect what the reader is predisposed to see in it, for, like all the greatest works, it is a concentrated reflector of life.

Theoretically it is arguable that *Don Quixote* contains intimations of everything else Cervantes ever published. In practice it is foolish to draw general conclusions about him that do not take into account his other works (though people frequently do). Perhaps the two works that best fill out the evidence of his range as a writer are the story "El coloquio de los perros" and his last romance *Persiles y Sigismunda*.

Nowhere does Cervantes present such a bleak picture of man as in his Dogs' Colloquy. Here human predatoriness is unredeemed by heroism and human folly is more abject than funny. At the centre of the story lurks the repellent figure of the witch Cañizares, whom Cervantes shows as morally paralysed by the habit of evil and pathetic in her lucid awareness of the fact. It is a world upside-down, where the two dogs, whatever their faults, have more moral virtues than all but a very few, conspicuously Christian human beings in the story.

The destiny of the dogs is intimately bound up with that of the world, for they will only regain their human form, of which they were allegedly cheated at birth by witchcraft,

> when they see the mighty speedily brought down
> and the humble exalted
> by that hand which has power to perform it.

For some reason, those who attribute something like a modern socialist conscience to Cervantes seem to have passed over this

powerful novella. They would have something less slippery than
Don Quixote to get hold of here, even though the quiet message of
the story is more Christian than political. The "Coloquio de los
perros" has been newly translated for Penguin with five more of
Cervantes's *Exemplary Stories* in a briskly readable version by C. A.
Jones.

A new English translation of the *Persiles* is unlikely at the moment,
although, as Alban K. Forcione reminds us at the beginning of his
admirable new study *Cervantes' Christian Romance*, its immediate
success was comparable to that of *Don Quixote*. It was reprinted ten
times within a few years after 1617, done into French, English and
Italian and imitated by dramatists and fiction writers. If it ever
occurred to anyone at the time how profoundly different this book
was from the *Quixote*, we have no record of the fact; but the "enigma
of the *Persiles*" has bothered modern scholars a good deal. Artistically, it has seemed to upset principles deducible from *Don Quixote*.
Doctrinally, its conformist Catholicism has seemed at variance with
the built-in anti-dogmatism of the other book.

The artistic problems seem less formidable than once they did, but
it has remained for Mr Forcione to produce the most satisfying
rationalization so far made of the apparently disordered riot of
adventure in the *Persiles*. Cervantes's debt to epic theory in the
composition of this romance is now well known, but it only goes so
far. Sixteenth-century Italian and Spanish critical theory explains
little or nothing of the deeper creative structures of either the *Quixote*
or the *Persiles*. For the latter Mr Forcione makes some profitable
use of the modern theories of allegory, myth and romance of Angus
Fletcher, Northrop Frye and others.

As an allegorical "prose epic" built on the framework of the old
Greek romance and recounting a pilgrimage from the wilder shores
of the barbaric North to the centre of Christendom, Tridentine Rome,
the *Persiles* could hardly be more unlike the *Quixote*. The biblical
and other symbolic parallels, which J. Casalduero first pointed out,
make it difficult not to accept that this is, in some sense, a spiritual
history of mankind from the Fall to the Redemption. Mr Forcione
tidies up a good deal in the earlier interpretations along these lines.
In the prolific adventures of the hero and heroine and of the numerous
episodes he discerns a cyclical rhythm of disaster and restoration
symbolically linked to the Christian drama of Fall and Salvation. He
does not quite account for everything, his subtlety is sometimes sus-

pect, and one is left uneasily aware of the deficiency of excessively fluid critical categories. What adventure story, what tale of any kind with a happy ending, does not do a progress through misfortune to salvation?

All the same, even if Cervantes did not execute the grand design quite so neatly as Mr Forcione explains it, this is the best guide to the *Persiles* that there is and one is left marvelling at the way the aged novelist retained his powers right to his deathbed.

The ideological problem is, as Mr Forcione says, that

the *Persiles* and the *Quixote* are about as different as two works of literature could possibly be. In the *Quixote* Cervantes reminds us that the poetic justice which governs the world of fairy tales is sadly lacking in actuality, that human experience is irreducible and infinite in its variety, nuances and gradations, and that it is most valuable precisely because of its irreducibility. In the *Persiles* he prefers to strip away all such gradations and affirm that beneath their teeming surface there is in fact a fundamental pattern which gives life a uniform shape and that there are clear-cut truths which a man can rely on. The ambiguities of experience which fascinated Cervantes from the first paragraph of the *Quixote* to its conclusion are nowhere to be found in the *Persiles*.

If the two books imply such radically different sets of convictions, what kind of a man was Cervantes? There is little besides his writings to go on.

The book that has done more than any other to increase our understanding of Cervantes and his works, and correct ignorant errors about his supposedly untutored and unconscious genius, has now, after almost half a century, gone into its second, revised edition. The appearance of the new and long-awaited *Pensamiento de Cervantes* unhappily preceded Américo Castro's death by only a few months. Don Américo's reluctance to authorize a new edition was well known. It is therefore a relief to find that it is not substantially altered. Complete reorientation in the direction of his later theories would have been a hopeless task anyway. Amendments to the 1925 edition are signalled by square brackets (although this procedure fails to indicate places where something has been simply omitted); new footnotes by the author and by the editor, Rodríguez Puértolas, bring the book up to date with comment on old controversies, new findings, theories and bibliography.

The *Pensamiento* still reads wonderfully well; its clarity of exposition, learning and imaginative criticism are unimpaired. Whatever reservations one may have about Castro's theories on the role of

Nature, harmony and error, or Cervantes's "heroic hypocrisy" (a theory hedged around with more qualifications than his antagonists have generally recognized), the seminal nature of the study is beyond dispute. His perceptions into the influence of Erasmus, Cervantes's literary theory, the novelty of the characterization in *Don Quixote*, its "perspectivism" and other matters have pointed new directions for later criticism, not least Castro's own. He is unrepentant in his view of Cervantes's religious hypocrisy, which is consistent with his later view of Cervantes as an "outsider" of Jewish *converso* descent. Whatever its much-trumpeted faults, this is probably the best book ever written on Cervantes. Its translation into English is long over-due.

El pensamiento de Cervantes roundly situated the author of *Don Quixote* in the tradition of enlightened European Renaissance thought running through Erasmus and Montaigne. Castro's last word on the *Quixote*, "Cómo veo ahora el *Quijote*" (the ninety-four page introduction to the new Magisterio Español edition of *Don Quixote*) assumes a Cervantes of the minority caste of Spanish "new Christians". For all we know, this uniquely Spanish Cervantes, blood-brother of St Teresa, Luis de León, Mateo Alemán, Francisco Suárez and many of the most original minds of the Golden Age, is the historical Cervantes. But we do not know, and Castro here assumes a knowledge he did not have, despite his immense work of scholarship in this area of Spanish life and letters. He has not presented the direct documentary evidence essential to make a certainty out of a hypothesis. Peripheral testimony is no substitute.

This last essay is sad reading. It shows some of the old subtlety and learning and much of the old fighting spirit, but it is prickly, obsessive, ill-organized and out of place as the introduction to a popular edition of the *Quixote*. Without knowing the rest of Castro's later work on Cervantes few will be able to follow it. Nothing is added to the brilliant insights he has offered us into *Don Quixote* in the past by such dubious statements as that Quixote's attack on the windmills is just an excuse for the attack on the friars which follows, that Aldonza Lorenzo is a *morisca*, that Dorotea's main function is to furnish a pretext for an attack on a scion of a family of grandees, or that the finding of the manuscript account of Don Quixote's death (part 1, chapter 52) is a covert allusion to the forged *libros plúmbeos* of the Sacromonte of Granada. In pursuing the image of the subtle anti-establishment Cervantes—a much more plausible one than many, to be sure—Castro has come very close to giving us an implausibly hermetic *Don Quixote*.

El pensamiento de Cervantes offered some kind of explanation for the *Persiles*; Castro's last writings do not. Until we know more about Cervantes the man, if we ever do, we must concur with Mr Forcione that the differences between the *Quixote* and the *Persiles* "should be viewed rather as the differences between two literary genres, each with its own laws and each particularly adjusted to a certain vision or statement about life. Cervantes is not alone among great artists in his capacity to cultivate radically different genres and embrace seemingly contradictory visions of life". Since the composition of *Don Quixote* and the *Persiles* actually overlapped by some years, speculations about the evolution of Cervantes's beliefs do not get us very far. The fact is that the same versatility runs through the whole body of his writings. But *Don Quixote* alone is big enough in its undogmatic open-mindedness to contain the possibility of the dogmatic *Persiles*.

9

DOING WITHOUT
CONSCIOUSNESS

"Behaviourism", wrote J. B. Watson, "is a purely American production." Although widely believed, this is not of course strictly true. In Germany at the turn of the century a group of biologists interested in animal behaviour had strongly criticized the use of terms bearing a subjective connotation. For example, they insisted that the term "vision" should be replaced by "photoreception", which implies only nervous sensitivity to a particular form of stimulation and makes no reference to conscious experience. In Russia, too, a crudely materialistic outlook had overtaken mid-nineteenth-century biology, derived in part from German physiology and in part from a remarkable book by Sechenov, Pavlov's teacher, called *The Reflexes of the Brain*, which appeared as early as 1860.

In this outstanding though now long-forgotten book, Sechenov had endeavoured to show that the concept of reflex action, which had already been accepted as the basic model for the activities of the spinal cord and mid-brain, could be extended to cover the activities of the highest parts of the central nervous system, which he and his pupils regarded as virtually synonymous with behaviour. In addition to Pavlov, Sechenov's pupils included Bechterev, a simple-minded reflexologist whose writings considerably influenced Watson and his early co-worker, Karl Lashley. In some sense, therefore, behaviourism arose in Europe even if it failed to take root there.

None the less, Watson's statement is correct in so far as no other country, not even Russia, has adopted behaviourism as what might be called an accepted academic discipline. Pavlov himself detested psychology, and heartily disapproved of attempts by behaviourists to erect a general theory of learning on the basis of the conditioned reflex. As he saw it, the evolution of speech results in human learning coming to bear a character altogether different from learning

---

B. F. Skinner: *Beyond Freedom and Dignity*. 225 pp. Cape. £2.25.

in animals and considered that his own studies of conditioned reflexes in dogs had little to contribute to our understanding of human behaviour. Largely in consequence of his attitude, there has been no corresponding behaviourist movement in the Soviet Union and Russian psychologists have no scruples about referring to mind and consciousness in the traditional manner.

In America, things went very differently. The style of experimental psychology brought to the United States by E. B. Titchener and others who had studied under Wilhelm Wundt at Leipzig was soon ousted by Watson's behaviourism, which by about 1930 had come almost completely to dominate the psychological scene. Broadly, behaviourism has two main roots, one negative and the other positive. The negative was Watson's rejection of introspective method in psychology, prompted mainly by the failure of experimental psychologists to resolve by introspection the problem of whether or not there is "imageless thought"—i.e. conscious states lacking any discernible trace of sensation or imagery. The positive was the extension of experimental psychology to the study of animal behaviour, largely pioneered in America, and the belief that in the interests of evolutionary continuity, it is essential to employ comparably objective methods in the study of the behaviour of man. Whatever the crudities of early behaviourism and its insistence on excluding all considerations of consciousness from the vocabulary of psychology, at least it brought a healthy biological outlook into the subject and provided the essential intellectual climate for the later work of B. F. Skinner.

Yet it was not long before the limitations of Watson's psychology came to be appreciated. Karl Lashley, from the beginning a strong proponent of behaviourism who later did distinguished work in comparative neurology, was quick to point out that the traditional reflex model simply failed to account for the complexity of nervous integration, even at levels well below that of the cerebral cortex. Further, Watson's early attempts to explain all human learning wholly in terms of Pavlovian conditioning soon came to be regarded as simple-minded and inadequate. Indeed even physiologists began to find the conditioned reflex too simple a model upon which to base the facts of animal learning. For example, J. Konorski, a Polish ex-pupil of Pavlov, felt obliged to speak of "Type Two" conditioning to denote instances of motor learning in dogs which do not strictly conform to the classical model of the conditioned reflex based on studies of salivation. (A homely example would be that of a dog taught to "shake hands" through giving reward when a forepaw is accidentally extended.) Even earlier, learning of this kind had been much studied in America by E. L. Thorndike, whose conception of learning by "trial and error" and of the ways in which reward and punishment respectively strengthen or weaken the links established between situation and response in many ways anticipated Skinner's work. Finally, one may note that Lashley, in a long series of studies, largely failed in his avowed aim of tracing the pathways of conditioned reflexes through the brain.

Born in 1904, B. F. Skinner published his first major work in 1938. It was entitled *The Behaviour of Organisms*, a title some people considered a trifle grandiose in view of the fact that it was concerned exclusively with the behaviour of rats, and under very restricted conditions at that. None the less, it signalled the appearance on the psychological scene of a man with much experimental ingenuity and a powerful analytical mind. First, Skinner argued that the simple reflex, open to conditioning in the manner described by Pavlov, plays very little part in ordinary behaviour. He placed the major stress on what he called *operants*, i.e., motor responses that are emitted spontaneously rather than elicited by particular external stimuli. Like reflexes—or in Skinner's term "respondents"—operants may likewise be conditioned, and for their study Skinner devised an ingenious apparatus known as the Skinner Box, in which the animal learns to press a bar for food reward, which is delivered automatically according to a prearranged schedule. Since most human behaviour is in Skinner's view operant rather than respondent, he believed that work on operant conditioning in animals might throw far more light on human behaviour than the classical conditioning method of Pavlov.

Secondly, Skinner took far more seriously than Pavlov the whole question of *reinforcement*, that is to say the increase in strength or frequency of a response resulting from reward contingent upon its execution. He was able in numerous experiments to show that the relations between reinforcement and performance are a good deal more complicated than Pavlov had supposed, much depending upon the particular programme (or schedule, to use the Skinnerian term) of reinforcement adopted. For instance, animals continue to press a bar much more frequently and for longer periods if the reward is delivered periodically, say after every eight responses, than if it is given after every single response. Indeed what Skinner and his school describe as the contingencies of reinforcement have been elaborately explored in a whole series of experiments with rats and pigeons and are considered by some to have direct relevance to education.

Thirdly, Skinner, unlike some of his contemporary neo-behaviourists such as Clark L. Hull, has never professed great interest in the explanation of learning per se; he is indeed the author of a celebrated paper entitled "Are Theories of Learning Necessary?" His own work has been styled "descriptive behaviourism", its object being to explore the relations between performance and contingencies of reinforcement and thereby to provide the outline of a technology of education.

To assess Skinner's earlier experimental work is not easy. It may, however, be said that his methods do permit a very considerable degree of control over behaviour to be established, at all events in the rat and pigeon. At its most spectacular—as in his famous experiment of teaching pigeons to play ping-pong—such control invites serious comparison with that achieved by professional circus trainers; at its most respectable, it provides a method of quantifying performance useful in studying a wide range of scientific issues, e.g., the effects of brain lesions or drugs upon behaviour. But for the most part, these applications fall within the technical sphere of experimental psychology and would not seem to have immediate relevance to human problems.

Skinner's concern with human behaviour appears to have begun during or soon after the Second World War and to have arisen particularly in connexion with issues of early development, more especially those related to the training of young children. From this he progressed to an interest in educational matters, as witnessed by his pioneer work on teaching machines and programmed instruction. So far, these methods have been limited to what one might call the inculcation of habits or rote learning and their aim seems to be largely the alleviation of educational drudgery. But there are now signs that he is seeking an extension of his methods to education in the wider sense, to what might be called the inculcation of ideals, values and standards of conduct—some might even call it indoctrination.

A clue to Skinner's thinking may be found in a novel called *Walden Two* which he published in 1948. Unlike most novels by scientists, this one is well written and its content closely related to the author's scientific preoccupations. It might indeed be described as a *roman à*

clef. Walden Two is about a fictional community in the tradition of
Erewhon in which conventional methods of child upbringing,
family life and education have been displaced by behavioural
engineering. Unlike most ideal communities, real or fictional,
Walden Two does not represent a retreat from modern industrial
society; rather it presents in microcosm an effectively run small
industrial community. Nor are traditional liberal and humanist
values wanting; Skinner indeed refers to free inquiry, open-mindedness and human dignity as terms which, even if their meaning is
vague, relate to worthwhile goals.

What evidently exasperates him is that so few people who advocate
such goals appear to have the least notion of how to set to work to
attain them. In *Walden Two*, these goals are achieved through carefully planned behaviour training beginning in infancy and carried
through the school years to maturity. The essential principle is that of
reinforcement by reward of behaviour explicitly accepted by the
community as desirable—little use being made of "aversive" training
through the use of punishment. This regime is alleged to produce a
totally planned upbringing with consequent withering away of the
arbitrary and often inconsistent patterns of discipline ordinarily in-
culcated by parents and teachers. Far from suppressing spontaneity
and freedom, Skinner believes that behavioural engineering will in
fact enhance them. Further, he argues cleverly that training in coping
with negative and frustrating emotional states will actually liberate
children from the constraints of neurosis. As the fictional founder of
Walden Two remarks: "We control adversity to build strength."

Is it in fact possible to envisage such a community? Provided that it
is kept small and agreement can be reached as to the values and codes
of conduct that are to be embodied in it, there seems no particular
reason why *Walden Two* should not exist in fact. Indeed there are
said to be a number of communities in the United States based upon
this particular model. In several respects, too, it resembles some of the
Israeli kibbutzim, in which collective child-rearing has greatly
weakened family structure and a tremendous sense of purpose has
been generated by the acceptance of a common ethic.

Beyond Freedom and Dignity could almost be described as a sequel
to *Walden Two*, though it takes the form of a serious contribution to
modern thought. Skinner deals in successive chapters with the technology of behaviour, freedom and dignity, punishment and its alternatives, values and culture, and the nature of man. Although he has

interesting and often highly provocative things to say about all these large and difficult questions, it is perhaps best to limit consideration to the discussion of the technology of behaviour. For it is this, after all, which the author considers to justify his excursion into regions "beyond" traditional ethics.

Broadly speaking, the technology of behaviour advocated by Skinner in this book is essentially that evolved in his animal studies and applied in his work on programmed instruction. It might be envisaged as an attempt to impose upon the real world the kind of behavioural engineering adumbrated in fictional form in *Walden Two*.

What is Skinner attacking? In psychology, one of the commonest gambits used by the proponent of a new theory is to erect a straw man—a caricature of an existing theory—which is then cleverly demolished. Skinner's straw man is what he calls "autonomous man". By this he appears to mean the view of man that holds that his behaviour can be explained by reference to "personalities, states of mind, feelings, traits of character, purposes and intentions". By dispossessing "autonomous man" and replacing him by the planned effects of environmental manipulation, Skinner believes that psychology will achieve scientific status comparable to that of Newtonian physics. But is Skinner truly the Newton of psychology?

One might have supposed that "autonomous man" died with J. B. Watson, though even Watson admitted the existence of hereditary patterns of behaviour and his work stimulated the study of behavioural genetics no less than that of learning. Skinner, on the other hand, seems to have very little interest in genetics or, indeed, in biology generally. Given the magnitude of his claim, this might seem a pity. From G. T. Fechner onwards, many attempts have been made to establish experimental psychology on the model of physics but none of these has had lasting success. Indeed the most solid parts of modern psychology would seem to be those securely anchored in the structure and function of the nervous system. But it is precisely these aspects of psychology that Skinner disregards. His behavioural technology owes nothing to the neurological sciences and it is indeed quite as remote from them as is Freud's psychoanalytical method. Is it not likely that behavioural technology, like psychoanalysis before it, will be overtaken by advances in our understanding of the physical basis of behaviour?

But let us be fair. There is no question that Skinner has given us a method of studying animal learning of considerable scientific and practical value. It has also found limited, but none the less highly useful, applications to certain relatively limited aspects of human behaviour. Skinner's reinforcement theory can satisfactorily explain some aspects of social learning in childhood and after, though its application to the acquisition of language has proved altogether less happy. But what it has not done—and what it is doubtful whether it ever can do—is to explain those aspects of human behaviour which are ordinarily said to display intelligence and judgment, and are ordinarily ascribed to "autonomous man" simply because science does not know enough to provide a better explanation. True, it is doubtful whether terms such as "freedom" or "dignity" will have any place in a scientific explanation of behaviour—and here one may agree with Skinner—but as no such explanation at present exists it is difficult to see why they should be debarred from our psychological vocabulary.

Although *Beyond Freedom and Dignity* is well-written, provocative and thoughtful, it is marred by the fact that the author suffers from a well-known occupational disease of psychologists, namely premature generalization from limited evidence. A fellow-sufferer was Freud. Pavlov, on the other hand, strongly resisted this disease, or at the worst was only a very mild case of it. Again and again he trounced psychologists for going beyond their evidence and until they should learn not to do so refused to accept psychology as a natural science. Skinner's claim to be a natural scientist cannot be disputed, but this is not a scientific book.

Why should a book rather narrow in scholarship, philosophically naive and scientifically almost worthless attract such wide notice, both here and in the United States? Certainly it is well written but there must be more to it than this. One reason may be the curiously ambivalent attitude which many people hold towards human engineering. On the one hand, the enormous success of science and technology has given hope that human and social problems will likewise yield to scientific method. On the other hand, the possibility of control over behaviour which the application of scientific method may bring strikes terror into many a humanist heart. People fear, not wholly without justification, for the values embodied in our culture which Skinner seems to reject along with all the rest of "autonomous man". This ambivalence appears to have prompted the hostile reception accorded in many quarters to Skinner's latest work.

Yet just as the hopes vested in the capacity of science to solve human and social problems have been so largely disappointed, so are the fears associated with human engineering proving grossly exaggerated. Skinner's principles embody little more than is already known to parents, teachers and, for that matter, trainers of performing animals; all he has done is to formulate our knowledge more adequately and to provide experimental techniques designed to make it more precise. He has also proposed that it should be applied in more consistent and systematic a fashion. There is, further, no reason to believe that Skinner himself fails to uphold the traditional values of our culture. He is an enemy only to empty and spineless humanism, with its endless repetition of well-meaning precepts without any thought as to their translation into practice.

In conclusion, perhaps Watson was after all right in speaking of behaviourism as a purely American production. Masked by a powerful intelligence and sophisticated experimental acumen, one senses in Skinner the naive idealism of the author of *Walden* (One) and the characteristic American belief in human goodness and perfectibility, given only the creation of a benign environment. Skinner embodies not only the formidable technocracy of mid-twentieth-century America but also the simplicity and optimism—one might almost say innocence—of an earlier generation of American intellectuals, happily far from extinct.

IO

CORRIDORS OF POWER
(a) MORISON AND *THE TIMES*

THE BIOGRAPHY OF Stanley Morison offers an exacting challenge to the biographer and to the biographer's reviewer. To start with the platitudes. Morison was a man of many parts and many careers. He enjoyed, thanks partly to this, an exceptionally wide variety of friendships, which he tended to keep in watertight compartments, presenting to each acquaintance a large area of genial warmth and an area of impenetrable reserve. He was in essence a lonely man, leading a solitary life. How can one tie up all this in one bundle? How can one writer encompass the diversity of the theme?

The variety of careers is the most obvious, though not the most formidable, difficulty. Morison was, first and foremost, a typographer. This was the function which he exercised at the Monotype Corporation, at the Cambridge University Press, and—initially—at *The Times*. His scholarly researches, originally directed to the improvement of the prevailing state of printing, and never wholly divorced from that pragmatic aim, broadened out into the history of the subject from its beginnings, and into the kindred topic of calligraphy, so that the field of his professional interest embraced every form of the presentation of the written word to the reader. Throughout this field Morison became a master, and in many parts of it the unique master.

Such was the foundation of the immense reputation which Morison acquired with astonishing rapidity. It was appropriate that his biographer should be an expert in the field; indeed the blurb describes Nicolas Barker's work as not only "the definitive life of Stanley Morison" but also "the authoritative account of typography in the twentieth century". Morison came on the scene at the crucial moment of a vast expansion of the printed word, and of a reaction in every

---

(*a*) NICOLAS BARKER: *Stanley Morison*. 566 pp. Macmillan. £10.

(*b*) A. J. P. TAYLOR: *Beaverbrook*. 712 pp. plus unnumbered plates. Hamish Hamilton. £6.50.

(*c*) CHRISTOPHER SYKES: *Nancy*. 543 pp. Collins. £3.95.

sphere of art against what were now felt as the narrow and constricting conventions of Victorian society. He was at the centre of the great explosion. There is no reason to doubt that his fame, specialized but secure, will endure as a great typographical reformer and innovator. Innovation, particularly in this country, likes to masquerade as the restoration of an ancient tradition. Here too Morison was in good company.

Mr Barker does full justice, not unmixed with the touch of adulation permissible in an official biography, to these achievements. He occasionally travels a little too briskly for the layman, throwing out names and technical details in bewildering profusion. But the untutored reader cannot really complain; the total picture is not blurred. On the other hand, a reviewer in the journal which Morison once edited, under the shadow of the parent newspaper to which he devoted a major part of his thought and activity over a period of thirty years, may be conscious of a certain perfunctoriness in the treatment of these years and of some lacunae which, perhaps necessarily, remain unfilled. But once again, the essentials are there. Mr Barker quotes an entirely private and personal letter in which Morison describes "the change from Dawson to B^n-Ward" in the editorial chair of *The Times* as "a worthwhile contribution to the war effort", and speaks frankly of himself as "invested with much 'occult influence' so that little is done without prior knowledge".

A word should be said here of Morison's *History of The Times*, the four volumes of which absorbed him off and on—and rather more "on" than "off"—for upwards of fifteen years. They constitute the most solid, though probably not the most impressive, product of his meticulous scholarship, and are, like all his work, a phenomenal achievement by one who had no formal education after the age of fourteen. Some of the chapters were originally drafted for him by others—further research would reveal more about the processes of composition—but it is doubtful how much of these tentative drafts survived in the final version, almost every line of which bore the imprint of Morison's dominant personality.

The main personal assessments in the history—the elevation of Barnes, the demotion of Delane, the total eclipse of Buckle, the fascination and tragedy of Northcliffe—seem likely to survive. A few hobby-horses are ridden rather hard. A somewhat capricious selectivity is sometimes at work. The last volume occasionally threatens to diverge into an excursus on European diplomacy or

British foreign policy; and there is some special pleading motivated by Morison's personal loyalty and devotion to R. M. Barrington-Ward. But no future historian will ignore it. Mr Barker goes to the root of the matter when he says that for Morison "history was the art, not of recording, but of explaining, the past". Morison understood more about history than some of our currently practising professionals.

The real problems of Morison's biographer are, however, the paradoxes of his opinions and of his personal life—both, no doubt, connected and intertwined. Barrington-Ward, in the early days of their acquaintance, described him as having "a good mind, which is yet an odd jumble of beliefs and prejudices continually in contradiction", and found the contradiction in a clash between "traditionalism in religion and radicalism in everything else". This was a superficial diagnosis. Morison's radicalism preceded his Catholicism, and his Marxism followed close on its heels. Religion for Morison was a movement of revolt, and meant no acceptance of any establishment. A reference to the Catholic Church as "this bunch of macaroni-merchants" could certainly be paralleled in utterances about the high priests of Marxist orthodoxy. Neither would imply any uncertainty about what he regarded as the fundamental doctrines of Christianity or of Marxism. The puzzling contradictions were not between the two but within both of them.

Mr Barker pays more attention to Morison's Catholicism than to his Marxism, partly perhaps from personal inclination, but mainly because he knew Morison only in the last years, when old age had tamed the rebellious vigour of his youth and maturity, and reconciled him to things he no longer had the strength to anathematize. But he very fairly provides the evidence to redress the balance. Exactly when Morison first heard of Marx is not clear; Mr Barker names the British Socialist Party, a sect of the extreme Left, as a channel, but quotes no evidence. What is certain is that, when in prison as a conscientious objector in the First World War, he met Palme Dutt, Page Arnot, and other future founders and leaders of the British Communist Party. Prison has often been a breeding-ground for revolutionaries. In 1923 he applied unsuccessfully for party membership; and in 1929 he addressed his friend Graham Pollard, a party member, as "Dear Comrade", apologizing in jest for the fact that he was "not technically a comrade".

Barrington-Ward in the verdict just quoted noticed Morison's "insistence on class". Contemptuous references to "the boss class", or more briefly to "the narks", often decorated his conversation. What changed after 1931 was his assumption that the Labour Party was an effective spearhead of the campaign against capitalism. He now perceived that "the capitalist system is still strong, too strong for the idealists who have been for so long the support of the socialist"; the Labour Party was dead for thirty years, and the Liberal Party would revive. But the basis of his opinions did not change. In the last decade of his life he continued to denounce "many rich people in the West End and some pettifogging investors in Surbiton, all profiting by things of which they know nothing", and he thought that the word profit "should stink in the nostrils of any decent man".

But here too there were contradictions. Morison did not spurn the amenities, and even some of the luxuries, of West End club life. If profit stank in his nostrils, he none the less worked hard to earn profits for *The Times* and rejoiced at the results. He said sometimes that, having been placed through no choice of his own in this repulsive society, he felt free to play the game by its rules so long as it lasted. He bargained sturdily with the Monotype Corporation and *The Times* for pensions sufficient to provide the comforts of old age. The *Encyclopaedia Britannica*, to which he came too late to render much service, contributed substantially to the affluence of his last years. Morison had no capital; but he did better for himself, as the phrase goes, than many capitalists.

Paradoxes of character and behaviour go deeper than paradoxical opinions. "I was born a rationalist", declared Morison on a solemn occasion, "and a rationalist born is a rationalist for life; I see what I see and have seen less by the eye of faith than by the eye of reason." One hesitates whether to call this a classic example of self-misunderstanding or an unconscious cover-up for things he could not bear to contemplate. In 1908, at the age of nineteen, brought up as an agnostic, he was received into the Catholic Church, which he never left. On September 10, 1912, he lighted on the Printing Supplement published that day by *The Times*. It kindled a flame of excitement and enthusiasm which determined his vocation and the whole course of his career, and which burnt on, unextinguished and undimmed, till his dying day.

In 1916, still untried and inexperienced, in the throes of a struggle to assert his faith as a conscientious objector to the war, he married a wife more than sixteen years his senior; the unfortunate woman apparently understated her age by ten years. In 1924 the marriage was on the rocks; its history can probably never be written, but Mrs Morison seems to have been sensitive to what was in store. The same year saw the beginning of an intimate friendship between Morison and a young American woman named Beatrice Warde, who shared his interests in typography and whose husband, after two years of strain and stress, left her on his account; this passionate, though platonic, relation endured for the rest of his days. None of these landmarks in Morison's career bore notable witness to a rational way of life.

The same thing may be said of the mounting enthusiasm which caused Morison to give long years of devoted service to that ancient monument of the British traditional establishment, *The Times*, and of the infatuation—the word is scarcely too strong—for Beaverbrook which overtook him in 1948. None of these events can be explained, or could have been predicted, in rational terms. Had his actions been governed by the dictates of reason, Morison's achievement and Morison's personality would probably have been far less impressive. What drove him forward was a succession of violent eruptions of powerful and powerfully controlled emotion, which imparted a unique force and vividness to everything that he did.

Morison's letters and reported speech offer problems of interpretation. His utterances, written and spoken, were often tricked out in a dazzling Shavian display of wit, panache, and self-dramatization. A generation of excavators has failed to unearth from the records of Shaw's life much of that genial warmth that radiated from Morison over the circle of his friends. But for both men the sparkling epigram, the odd mixture of self-mockery and ostentatious self-assurance, the outrageous paradox, served as a façade for a hidden hollowness and emptiness at the core.

Morison himself has left clues. Two categories of his letters stand out as wholly free from this extraneous ornament, and entirely simple and sincere: those dealing with questions of professional scholarship, and those addressed to Beatrice Warde. In an odd little disquisition written for Beatrice in the early days of their association, Morison toyed with the word "reality":

Unless human relationships were founded upon reality, there could not be any permanence in them. And, when reality exists, a certain fire bursts forth spontaneous combustion if you like. . . . There is a specific real nature . . . and that is real which helps that nature to ascend from the implicit to the explicit.

Morison at that time could not define reality further—even to himself. But more than thirty years later, in a spoken tribute to Eric Gill after Gill's death, he reverted to the word:

He believed in certain things—what? The fundamental basic things. The man, the woman, the child, the family, all of which he bore out. It's a very different thing for me. No wife, no child, no family, my golly, I mean I can see at once, without any further argument, I mean, how remote I am from the realities he faced and did. There's no doubt about it. I've felt it continually—continually.

Morison was by destiny, not by choice, a solitary.

The paradox of personal relations was the ultimate paradox in Morison's life. His present biographer has opened up much that he chose and strove to conceal; at a time when none of those closely concerned is still alive, this was legitimate and inevitable. He writes of Morison's "distinct if courteous misogyny, due to shyness and to fear of the strength of his own emotions". To call Morison a misogynist would be misleading to the point of perversity. His early relations with his mother can presumably never be documented. But she was a strong and able woman with a feckless and drunken husband who eventually deserted her; and everything points to the strong influences under which her only son (he had two sisters) grew up. The limited selections printed in the book from Morison's correspondence with Beatrice Warde testify to the unique role of that intimate and frustrated relationship in his later life.

Morison liked to say when moralizing about himself—often in contexts with a specifically sexual application—that he would have been a very wicked man if he had not submitted to the discipline of the church; and he commonly spoke of his religion not as a thing of joy but as a "hair-shirt". It was psychologically an important resource for him to externalize his deep-seated inhibitions by debiting them to the injunctions of the church. The assertion of his own potential wickedness is as significant as it is unconvincing. It is tempting to trace in this hidden and tragic conflict between powerful passions and the powerful inhibitions which held them in check the dynamic force which filled his towering personality, with its inexhaustible intellectual fervour embracing both the broadest syntheses and the minutiae of scholarship.

One compensation found by Morison is particularly relevant to his service for *The Times*—his preoccupation with what he once called in another context "the reality of power". Morison had none of the gifts of the politician; his political judgments were frequently wrong. But his qualities were peculiarly suited to the role of *éminence grise*, the exercise of known but publicly unavowed power. His enthusiasm for Northcliffe and Beaverbrook, both failures on the political stage who sought to exercise power from the wings, falls into this pattern. Mr Barker does not exaggerate when he describes Morison's role at *The Times* as "the unofficial adviser to successive editors"; indeed on some points he seems to underrate the extent of his influence. What, however, can hardly be overstated are the benefits which *The Times* derived from that influence at a crucial period of history. The re-organization of *The Times Literary Supplement* after the war falls into place as a supplementary benefit.

Mr Barker does however perhaps give less than due weight to the other side of the picture. He rightly dissents from Donald Mc-Lachlan's estimate of Morison in his recent biography of Barrington-Ward. But McLachlan reflects the view of those members of the editorial staff who resented Morison's intrusion and the position which he acquired; and one cannot feel that this reaction was surprising or wholly unreasonable. Morison was capable of a certain ruthlessness and asperity towards those whom he did not suffer gladly. When Sir William Haley succeeded to the chair, Morison's reign was over. He was deeply hurt by the chillier climate of a changed Printing House Square, especially as he had promoted the new editor's candidature. But that was not a reason; and his hopes that things would go on as before were hardly realistic.

Morison's place in the history of the printed word is secure. But how much will remain of the impact which he produced beyond this technical sphere on a far wider circle of his contemporaries, and which made so many of them feel that they were dealing not merely with an expert typographer or a meticulous scholar but with a great man? Much of the record must rest on oral tradition, which is already fading; and perhaps the opportunity for a great biography which would have recaptured the fire and drive of his personality in his most creative years is already past.

Meanwhile we shall remain lastingly grateful to Mr Barker for a book which does full and expert justice to his technical achievements, and assembles every scrap of information available about him in the printed or written record. Occasionally, indeed, one may feel that he tried too hard—does one care about the exact address of the tobacconist's shop kept at one time by Mrs Morison senior in Holloway? But the whole work has been done with affectionate care and masterly precision. In a volume of nearly 600 pages the present reviewer has spotted only two tiny specimens of what Morison once gleefully called "the flotsam and jetsam of our illiteracy": Melk is not in Czechoslovakia; and the indexer has conferred on Schramm, an obscure German librarian of the early 1920s, the initials of an historian of the same name who flourished in the Nazi epoch.

(b) BEAVERBROOK THE FIXER

BETWEEN his startling entry into British politics and society in 1910 and his death in 1964, Max Aitken, Lord Beaverbrook, astounded, amused, enraged, disgusted, and entranced his contemporaries. Judgments upon him are invariably vigorous. To some he was a sinister *éminence grise*, an evil man who delighted in mischievous intrigue, was wholly unprincipled, and used his newspapers and money for disreputable purposes. To others he was an interesting lightweight, who overrated himself and has been overrated by others, who easily became bored, who flitted irresponsibly from one scene to another, and whose impact on the history of his times was not of serious importance. And there were those by whom he was profoundly admired, deeply respected, and even loved. The commentator, viewing these extreme estimates, may be forgiven for wondering where the truth really lies.

In some respects A. J. P. Taylor is the perfect biographer of this strange and fascinating man. Mr Taylor's outstanding qualifications as an historian and sardonic commentator on modern British and European history hardly require mention. He remains one of the few really original intellects in contemporary historiography—often idiosyncratic, frequently iconoclastic, sometimes wrong-headed, occasionally very wrong indeed, but always interesting, always provocative and always exciting. On the other side of the coin there are Mr Taylor's prejudices which are formidable, and there is the factor of his complete devotion to Beaverbrook. Some observers of this warm and profound friendship found it puzzling, but no one who knew both men found it at all surprising. Thus the nagging question is whether the friend and companion of the late years could be a fair and objective biographer.

How are we to test these apprehensions against the unfolding narrative of Beaverbrook's extraordinary career and the development of the portrait of his perplexing personality?

Beaverbrook was a child of the Manse, and no understanding of his complex character can begin without appreciation of the importance of this fact. For always, beneath the surface, there lay apprehension and feelings of guilt. His literary style was heavily dominated by the Old Testament, but this was not the only consequence of early influences. Two other characteristics appeared more dominant at the time, an innate love of mischief and an enjoyment of making money —but with the latter went a rigorous integrity. In his rapid early rise to considerable wealth he made many enemies, but in the fiercely competitive world of Canadian finance his implacable sense of business rectitude was as important in his survival and success as his quickness of eye and movement. "I did not make situations", he once remarked, "I turned them to account". This was a somewhat overmodest assessment, as Mr Taylor amply demonstrates.

Then, in 1910, the young Max Aitken arrived in England, already a millionaire: he quickly became a close friend of Bonar Law, and entered Parliament. Eyebrows rose sharply, but in reality Aitken's friendship with Law was absolutely complete. Mr Taylor handles their friendship perfectly, and emphasizes both its obviousness and its complexities.

Having entered Parliament, Aitken's interest in the House of Commons ended. He was not a man much given to hearing others talk, nor greatly interested in making prepared speeches to such an audience. "I am not at all interested in wasting time in futile opposition to Radical measures in the House of Commons", he wrote bluntly to the Party Chairman. His passion was for political "fixing", and no eye was more penetratingly turned upon the leading personalities in the political maelstrom.

The first coup, and it was a devastating one, was his role in the unexpected accession of Bonar Law to the party leadership in 1911. This role was characteristic. He was the man who, above all others, propelled Law firmly into the vacuum created by the animosity between those groups in the party who favoured either Austen Chamberlain or Walter Long. Perhaps Law would have taken his stand if Aitken had not been there to stiffen and steady him, but it seems unlikely. In the tangled story of the Irish Question between 1912 and 1914 he acted as intermediary, as the go-between who attempted to achieve compromise, and it was he who brought Law and Asquith together at his home for three meetings. The attempt failed, but the episode gives a sharp insight into the real calibre of "the little Canadian adventurer". At the time, very few people knew of this; they saw the façade, and the majority were repelled.

Already the principal aspects of his personality could be discerned. His quick intellect made him soon bored, and he was constantly embarking upon new ventures, or thinking of doing so; he was essentially solitary and self-reliant although sharp and determined, he was in reality not a hard or ruthless man, but peculiarly vulnerable, often hesitant and unsure of his course; he was generous to all who were in difficulties, a real foul-weather friend, but less interested in the successful and eminent; and he took much glee in his role of go-between, intermediary, and "fixer". He was a highly erratic husband. And, virtually by accident, he had entered into the world of newspapers.

In the letters, writings, and actions of the young Max Aitken in 1914 we see the essential character of the subsequent Lord Beaverbrook. Yet he was, and was always to be, an elusive man, an enigma even to those who had come to appreciate his qualities; only his enemies found him a simple man to categorize, and they did so to their subsequent profound misfortune.

Then, the war. Aitken became the virtually self-appointed voice of Canada in Britain and Aitken the natural publicist and appreciator of propaganda had emerged. But he remained also the fixer, the go-between, and the one-man liaison team between the Canadian Government and London.

The formation of the First Coalition in May 1915 owed very little to Aitken, who was in France at the time, but Asquith's downfall in December 1916 was another matter. It was, he later claimed, "the biggest thing" he had done, and has been related in *Politicians and the War*. Mr Taylor's description of how this extraordinary book was prepared, and why parts of it should be approached with caution, cannot be faulted. Mr Taylor is right in his more modest estimate of Aitken's importance in the crisis than that which Beaverbrook subsequently claimed. "If Aitken triumphed, this was due to the mistakes of his adversary, not to his own skill. This often happens in life."

One result of the crisis was the most strange of all; Aitken found himself in the House of Lords. His own version portrays him as a helpless victim of a series of misunderstandings; his biographer is unimpressed with his version, and the documents fully justify his scepticism.

Aitken went very willingly to the Lords, despite the King's displeasure. He was already embarked upon his career as newspaper proprietor, having just acquired control of the *Daily Express*. And all this within six years of arriving in England!

In the Lloyd George Coalition Beaverbrook's role was initially that of conciliator and middle-man, and perhaps his persuasion of Law to accept Churchill as Minister of Munitions was his most difficult, although the reconciliation—not of long duration—between Lloyd George and Northcliffe was another major achievement. But it was in this period that Beaverbrook was beginning to take journalism and newspaper ownership—and, with him, the two were really synonymous—seriously, and R. D. Blumenfeld, the editor of the *Daily Express*, began to receive the kind of instructions and requests couched in menacing language with which he and his successors were to become very familiar. By 1917 he was being publicly numbered among the Press Lords, and a new phase in his life had begun.

To treat any of Beaverbrook's spheres of action in isolation would be to miss the real point of the man, and it is one of the many outstanding features of Mr Taylor's book that he eschews such an approach. As he comments: "Even when he was busiest with his papers, he was also half a dozen other men at the same time: politician, historian, financier, racehorse-owner, cinema promoter, and general entertainer." But, although it would be dangerous to divide Beaverbrook's life into periods, there is definite justification in regarding the acquisition of the *Daily Express* as a turning-point.

He was a natural journalist, but he was something more. His concept of the *Daily Express*—and subsequently the *Sunday Express* —as a family newspaper "with an enormous and infinitely varied circulation" was there from the outset, and remained to the end. The *Evening Standard*, however, was marked for another audience, and was given remarkable latitude in supervision. Opinions have varied, of course, about the qualities of these newspapers throughout their existence, but it can hardly be challenged that the Beaverbrook newspapers had a unique character which was the direct result of the views of their proprietor (despite his reiterated complaints that he was no such thing). The early days were very difficult indeed, but the papers survived and prospered greatly. The *Express* journalist, asked for whom he wrote and who replied "one little old reader", had hit upon a very fundamental truth. For good or bad, the Beaverbrook newspapers became an extension of Beaverbrook's complex personality; when seen in this light, the fact that Tom Driberg, Michael Foot, David Low, and "Vicky" worked for the Beaverbrook newspapers as well as R. D. Blumenfeld, John Gordon, Arthur Christiansen, Dean Inge, James Douglas, and the deeply-loved Castlerosse, was not at all strange.

Meanwhile, Beaverbrook's political interests—"career" would hardly be the appropriate term—varied. He became the first Minister of Information in the Lloyd George Coalition, and his method of working was a foretaste of what was to come in 1940. Beaverbrook was an improvisor, with a scorn of neat organization, of elaborate structures, of hierarchies, of committees, or other boring paraphernalia. The results were mixed, but on balance they justified his approach, and were an effective response to the wails of anguish from Whitehall. Anyone familiar with the operations of the Ministry of Aircraft Production in 1940 will read Mr Taylor's account of the work of the Ministry of Information in 1918 with deep recognition. The episode demonstrated, as Mr Taylor remarks, that "Beaverbrook was ill-suited to be a Minister except in abnormal circumstances".

This brings us, with a gigantic leap, to 1940. In the meanwhile, Beaverbrook had played a role—perhaps a major one, although this is arguable—in the downfall of the Lloyd George Coalition in 1922 and in the subsequent elevation of Bonar Law to the Premiership. His actions when Law resigned in the following May are not so clear, and Mr Taylor is somewhat cavalier in dismissing Lord Davidson's account of Beaverbrook's support for Curzon against Baldwin, particularly as he later admits that Beaverbrook later destroyed a large part of his papers for 1923. The Empire Crusade of the early 1930s, most fairly and perceptively related by Mr Taylor, was destroyed by one devastating phrase by Baldwin in the St George's by-election of March 1931; but its root cause of failure was its imprecision of political objectives. The alliance with Rothermere was at best uneasy, and the Crusade was in reality Beaverbrook. The Crusade, after riveting political attention for over a year, in Mr Taylor's words, "trailed away into obscurity".

This, it appeared, would be the fate of its leader. Beaverbrook was still fascinated by politics, but at a distance. His intervention in the Abdication Crisis is related somewhat briefly by Mr Taylor, and some commentators might question his emphatic denial that Beaverbrook's objective had not been to damage Baldwin. But, despite occasional forays into politics, Beaverbrook was a minor political figure in the 1930s, and many of his comments on contemporary events—particularly international events—are rightly rebuked by his biographer. He was, like Churchill, a "busted flush", with his wealth, his companions, his houses, his newspapers, but with little real influence.

When Churchill made him Minister of Aircraft Production in May, 1940, it would be incorrect to say that Beaverbrook was a forgotten man, but the public had lost sight of him for a considerable period, and he himself commented gloomily on the passing of the years and harped forlornly upon the need for reconciliation with the approaching darkness before him.

Then, the transformation! The improvisations, the buccaneering, the piratical commandeering of materials, the passionate exhortations, the furious telephone calls, the melodramatic propaganda stunts—of which the most notorious was the "saucepans for Spitfires" episode—the threats of resignation, the rows with colleagues and the rest of Whitehall! David Farrer has described this so well that Mr Taylor could hardly do better, but he adds the solid matter. Beaverbrook did not win the Battle of Britain. He had not ordered the Spitfire or the Hurricane off the drawing-board, nor created the radar chain, nor trained the pilots; these were Lord Swinton's creations. What Beaverbrook did do was to keep this small but magnificent force in operation and to demand priority for Fighter Command.

Beaverbrook's conduct at the Ministry of Aircraft Production remains intensely controversial, and some readers will not be convinced that Mr Taylor has written the last word on the subject. But to this reviewer, at least, Mr Taylor's advocacy is fair and convincing.

After this, was not the rest anticlimax? The split with Churchill, the advocacy of the Second Front, the passionate flirtation with Russia? He eventually returned to Government, but not on the same terms as in the glorious days of 1940. Mr Taylor defends him from the oft-repeated charge that he was responsible for Churchill's notorious "Gestapo" speech in the 1945 general election, but his influence was a significant one in the 1945 Conservative fiasco.

Although the shadows now gathered, there was more light to come, including a very happy second marriage. His interest in his newspapers was unabated, and his return to writing won him a new position, which was perhaps exaggerated but which enchanted him, as a serious historian of the First World War and its immediate aftermath.

The old mischievousness was never quenched, and, despite declining health, he was mentally alert to the end. The famous—perhaps dangerous—charm still exercised its extraordinary potency. He remained elusive, difficult to track down, delighted to see his friends, but relieved to see them go. He had always been a very complex mixture of good and bad, of warm kindness and of occasional harshness, and thus it was to the end. He died, as he had lived, a mysterious man. Law's dying words to him had been: "You are a curious fellow."

It is in Mr Taylor's recognition of this fact, in his refusal to offer simple solutions, and in his determination to cover all aspects of his subject's life and personality with thoroughness and sympathy, that the true quality of this biography lies. Perhaps, on occasion, the handling of certain episodes and aspects might have been sharper and more critical. There are several incidents over which historians will take issue with Mr Taylor's accounts. The illumination he brings to his subject is often too benign. The prejudices to which this review referred to at the outset are evident enough. But, what matter? Beaverbrook's life, for all its unevenness, was in its strange way a work of art. So, also, is this biography.

(c) CLIVEDEN'S CRACKER

THE FIRST WOMAN to sit in the British House of Commons was an American who got there only because her husband had been unwillingly elevated to the House of Lords. That was an odd twist, but with Nancy, Lady Astor, odd things were happening all the time. It is as an oddity—a "caution" in the North-country phrase—that a biography of her is justified. On a serious political level there is little to report about Lady Astor except that she was a Member of Parliament for twenty-six years. She did something to promote nursery schools. She retarded a relaxation of the divorce laws—a perverse achievement considering that her own first marriage had been dissolved. She raised the age at which young people could be served with alcohol in a public house from sixteen to eighteen. Having been a fervent supporter of Chamberlain she was one of the honourable forty who wrought his downfall in May, 1940. During the Blitz she was courageous and indefatigable in Plymouth, the city which she represented and of which her husband was Lord Mayor throughout the Second World War. That is about the lot—hardly enough to cover a memorial tablet, let alone to fill a book.

The most important event in Nancy Astor's life was her marriage to Waldorf Astor and not her election to Parliament, which was indeed a consequence of the marriage. Before then Nancy Langhorne was a somewhat wild Virginian girl, much given to rushing her fences, a character all right but with no public significance. She made an unfortunate first marriage, got out of it, and came to Europe to recover. She certainly knew how to follow the dictum, "Do not marry money, but go where money is." On her first visit she captured the affections of Lord Revelstoke, the banker, and imagined that she was in love with him. She soon wearied of his overriding concern with business affairs. On her second visit to Europe she won the more welcome attentions of Waldorf Astor and married him in 1906. Waldorf's father, William Waldorf Astor, was a fantastically rich American expatriate who gave Cliveden to Waldorf and Nancy as a wedding present. A little later he acquired *The Observer*, also an attractive inheritance. Waldorf was less pleased when his father alleviated the boredom of the First World War by buying a title. It was this which consigned Waldorf to the House of Lords in 1919, when the first Viscount died, and so propelled Nancy into the House of Commons.

The Astors lived on a grand scale. They had Cliveden for the weekends, a big house in London, another at Sandwich for the golf, and yet another in Scotland. They often gave dinner parties in London for fifty or sixty guests and at Cliveden had fifty gardeners, to say nothing of a chef with five assistants. Waldorf and Nancy were for many years a happy couple—she impulsive and unpredictable, he cautious, restrained and yet devoted. Nancy liked other men to be in love with her, though at a respectful distance. No guest at Cliveden went padding back from his hostess's bedroom in the early morning, as they did at other Edwardian houses. Some of these lovers had, however, a profound effect on Nancy, more indeed than

Waldorf had. Philip Kerr, later Lord Lothian, converted himself from Roman Catholicism to Christian Science and then converted Nancy also. From Kerr Nancy learnt, too, her passionate and unreasoning hostility towards "RCs"—an obsession enshrined for many years in *The Observer*'s trust deed.

Christopher Sykes suggests another paradoxical source for this obsession. Hilaire Belloc was a friend of Nancy's, as many unbalanced letters in this book show. His obsessions were against the rich and the Jews, obsessions that Nancy did not share. But she picked up the trick of obsessions from Belloc and switched it against Belloc's own religion. This was a characteristically wrong-headed performance. Later Bernard Shaw replaced Belloc as the chief literary lion of Cliveden. He and the Astors visited the Soviet Union in 1931, one of the great comic episodes of our time. Shaw claimed to have been a Marxist socialist for sixty years, though it is clear that he did not have much idea what this meant. Having praised Stalin, he went on to praise Mussolini and Hitler, in the latter of whom he discovered "the greatest living Tory" with *Mein Kampf* as "really one of the world's bibles". Though Shaw was a vegetarian and a teetotaller, he liked the good things of life. No doubt Nancy's principal attraction for him was that she was a very rich woman.

Wealth was not of course Nancy's only asset, though it enabled her to use her other gifts. Shaw said after a visit to Cliveden that he had spent Sunday with a volcano. Nancy Astor was not big enough to be a volcano. She was a Chinese cracker, discharging sparks in all directions. Some of them were dazzling, some merely painful. When she proposed to write her autobiography, one of her sons suggested that it should be called *Guilty but Insane*. The remark was not spoken altogether in jest. In public, rudeness was Nancy's principal stock-in-trade. At election meetings she could shout down and silence the most persistent heckler. In Parliament she maintained a stream of interruptions, some of them relevant. Mr Sykes prints from Hansard Nancy's silly interruptions which almost wrecked the great speech that Churchill delivered after the Munich conference. Her own speeches were, for the most part, rambling and ineffective and became worse as she grew older.

When Nancy first ran for Parliament she declared: "I am not standing before you as a sex candidate." But she knew now to play on her sex once she arrived. Her first prank was to steal the seat traditionally reserved for Sir William Joynson-Hicks, and there is nothing in the book funnier than the bumbling old gentleman solemnly drawing the attention of the House to this outrage. During the 1920s she carried the concerns of women and children almost alone. In 1929 the women MPs rose to fourteen. Nancy invited the nine Labour women to lunch and proposed that they should drop their Labour allegiance in favour of a Women's Party under her leadership. One of them remarked: "If only she did not have to boss us!" Thereafter Nancy ran down. She was never happy except in opposition, and yet had to support the National government. She became a nuisance, a figure of fun.

Though her husband owned *The Observer* and her brother-in-law owned *The Times*, Nancy often had a bad press. In her early days, Horatio Bottomley discovered that she was described in *Who's Who* as "the widow of Robert Gould Shaw", though Shaw was in fact still alive. This was meat for Bottomley, who ran a campaign headed: "A Hypocrite of the First Water—The Poor and the Rich". Later Bobby Shaw, the only son of her first marriage, caused her further trouble. He was convicted of a homosexual offence. Beaverbrook, though not acquainted with the family, ensured that the story was not mentioned in any newspaper. For his act of disinterested charity he earned no thanks but instead persistent abuse in *The Observer* for his manipulations of the press. Mr Sykes passes over this episode in a single embarrassed sentence.

The worst trouble came in the later 1930s, when Claud Cockburn, editor of *The Week*, discovered a nest of appeasers in "The Cliveden Set". Mr Sykes shows painstakingly that there was not much in the story. There were appeasers at Cliveden such as Tom Jones or for that matter Lothian. There were many guests of an entirely opposite conviction. Nancy had not the persistence to be a conspirator. But she was often rash. She gave a lunch for Neville Chamberlain to meet overseas correspondents, and he revealed his plans for betraying Czechoslovakia. When the news leaked out, Nancy denied that the lunch had ever taken place. The next day she retreated and explained that she had only meant to say that Chamberlain had not given any official interview.

Her last years were sad. Though she did much to inspire the citizens of Plymouth, she also sought advantages for herself. When a consignment of chocolates arrived from America for the Plymouth women and children, she wanted some. Waldorf refused and, when she flew into a temper, withdrew into another room where he had a heart attack. After the war their relations grew worse. Nancy wished to run again for Plymouth; Waldorf prevented her doing so, and she never forgave him. The final blow came when Waldorf allowed *The Observer* to go left. He and Nancy became virtual strangers, meeting only for occasional weekends. As compensation for abandoning Plymouth, Nancy wished to be made a peeress in her own right. James Stuart, the Tory Chief Whip, put the idea to Churchill; there was no answer. Mr Sykes later protested to Stuart that there must have been an answer of some sort. Stuart replied: "Oh, well, if you call an embarrassingly long silence followed by an angry grunt an answer, there was." The mutual dislike between Nancy and Churchill was always intense. She once said to him: "If I were your wife, I'd put poison in your coffee." Churchill replied: "And if you were my wife, I'd drink it."

In her last years she still fired off sparks, but increasingly at random. There were also flashes of kindness. During the Profumo case some of the dirt washed on to her son Bill, then the third Viscount Astor. The news was kept from her. The newspapers were cut before they reached her, and some friend always rang up just before the six o'clock news. One morning she collected the papers herself and read the story. She said: "We must go to Bill at once." On the way there she forgot what had happened and asked: "Why are we going to see Bill?" Her last words were: "Am I dying or is it my birthday?"

Mr Sykes has drawn a beautiful portrait of this strange, difficult woman. For her early years he has used the autobiography that Nancy began. He has built up a fund of reminiscences, his own and also those of others. He has skilfully worked in material from other books. This is a most winning biography, sympathetic and almost convincing. Nancy Astor was a fascinating woman. She was brave and stimulating. She certainly stirred things up. But she was also a spoiled child of fortune. She captivated men and then tormented them. Despite her kindness, she was indiscriminately cruel, a bully who knew that her great riches made it impossible for most others to hit back. Many of those who knew her, including some who suffered from her, loved her. The detached reader, however, who did not know her, is left with an enormous sense of relief that he escaped this ordeal.

II

THE POSITIVIST PROGRAMME

PETER MEDAWAR has brought together some recent essays and lectures in which he looks at general problems of philosophy and civilization from his standpoint as one of the most distinguished living biologists. *The Hope of Progress* begins and ends with two principal pieces—"Science and Literature" and "On 'the Effecting of All Things Possible' ". In between there are shorter essays on psychoanalysis; on the work of the National Institute for Medical Research, of which he was for so long a distinguished director; two mainly concerned with the genetic improvement of man; and a review of J. D. Watson's well-known book *The Double Helix* about the discovery of the structure of DNA. They all have that elegance and lucidity which we have come to expect from Sir Peter. He is one of the few scientists of today with a technical competence in handling the written word which earns his essays a claim to be literature in their own right. The sense of a personal style is very strong; perhaps a somewhat swashbuckling style—an eighteenth-century elegance not without a hint of the Rake. "Anyone who thinks otherwise [about an interpretation of Blake's views on the relations between the imaginative faculty and reason] is a fool or a knave": do people describable as fools or knaves really have any views on this topic, one way or the other?

The essays must also, of course, be judged on their content, as science or as philosophy. As science they are, as would be expected from someone of Sir Peter's authority, almost faultless. It might perhaps be argued that in the discussion of the possibilities for the genetic improvement of man he presses his arguments farther than is wholly justified. He argues that the case for "positive eugenics"— that is for constructive rather than merely remedial eugenics—is based on the model of stock breeding. If horses, dogs and cattle can be improved by selective breeding, it is argued, why cannot human beings? Besides giving the moral and political reasons for rejecting

---

P. B. MEDAWAR: *The Hope of Progress.* 133 pp. Methuen. £2.

140

this suggestion, Sir Peter provides a scientific argument against it. This is based on the fact that stockbreeders nowadays realize that they are dealing with populations of animals and that all populations of animals must, under natural circumstances, contain a wide range of different hereditary factors. If they wish to aim at uniformity in such desirable characters as rapid-growth-rate in broiler poultry or pigs, they may achieve this by producing uniform cross-breds, which are hybrid and would, if allowed to breed further among themselves, produce very varied offspring, many of them having little economic value. The whole rationale for any attempt to improve the genetic endowment of mankind has therefore, Sir Peter claims, disappeared along with the out-of-date theory of stock breeding on which it was originally founded.

However, against this it might be urged that breeders of the most important type of stock, dairy cattle, do not use the methods Sir Peter describes. The improvement of these animals involves keeping in being a heterogeneous gene pool, and trying to inject into it in every generation useful rather than harmful genes. There is no obvious reason, at the level of genetic mechanisms, why one could not keep adding useful genes to a human gene pool. The biological weakness of such a suggestion does not arise mainly, as Sir Peter argues, from misunderstanding about the nature of the genetic processes involved; it comes from the practical impossibility of deciding what one could mean by good genes, and even if one could decide this, the difficulty of discovering them.

The two major pieces in the book are not science in the same sense as the questions we have just been discussing; they belong rather to philosophy. In the second of these, Sir Peter appears as a defender of science against the attacks which have been made on it in recent years, when a mood of pessimism and disillusionment has led many to repudiate the notion of progress and to advocate casting out science along with it. Sir Peter answers robustly: "To deride the hope of progress is the ultimate fatuity, the last word in poverty of spirit and meanness of mind." And to set the tone of his counter-attack, he chooses as the title of his essay a gallant phrase from Francis Bacon, perhaps the main founder of the belief in the value of material improvements obtained by the application of science—"The Effecting of All Things Possible".

Sir Peter's opponents are unlikely to be convinced if the matter is left there. Effecting of all things possible? Nuclear weapons, the automated battlefield against South-East Asian peasants. Concorde? Is this the progress which it is the ultimate fatuity to deride? Certainly Sir Peter would not argue that it is. But it is necessary to ask what is the origin of his blindness to the real nature of the challenge to science, which is a claim that the essential method of scientific thought inevitably leads to a rejection of much that is of most value in human experience, to a denial of values, of beauty, of humane qualities in general.

Sir Peter's own view of the nature of science would probably be difficult to defend against such an attack. He is a positivist, committed to the view that science works according to a "hypothetico-deductive" scheme, which he calls "the most important methodological discovery of modern thought". According to this, the essential procedure is, first, to formulate, by means of imagination, a hypothesis from which certain conclusions can be deduced about how things should operate in the real world.

Originally, when the scheme was first propounded, the second stage was to perform experiments to see if they did so operate; and if the deductions were confirmed, the hypothesis would be said to be proved. Later, logical analysis rendered the notion of positive proof less acceptable, and Sir Peter claims to be a follower of Karl Popper, who modified the scheme by suggesting that, even if we cannot definitely prove a hypothesis, at least we disprove it if things do not operate as we deduced they should. But, whether we lay more stress on agreement or disagreement between deductions and experimental observations, what we are supposed to be doing, according to this view, is discovering the "truth". And of this, Sir Peter writes: "When the word is used in a scientific context, *truth* means, of course, correspondence with reality. Something is true which is 'actually' true, is indeed the case." There lies the nub; if something "corresponds with reality", or "is indeed the case", does it necessarily comprehend the *whole* of the reality in question, is it *all* of the case?

Sir Peter's views on this come closest to explicit expression in the first essay, his Romanes Lecture on "Science and Literature". He explains his purpose thus:

If I had to choose a motto for this lecture, I should turn a remark of Lowes Dickinson's upside down. "When science arrives", said Lowes Dickinson, "it expels literature." . . . The case I shall find evidence for is that when literature arrives, it expels science.

Sir Peter argues that literature expels science by a willingness to accept a criterion of truth less rigorous than that which he has defined for science:

> In this second conception of truth, a structure of imaginative thought—for example, a myth, especially if it appeals to magical agencies—will be judged true if it is all of one piece, hangs together, doesn't contradict itself, leaves no loose ends, and can cope with the unexpected. . . . All scientific theories must make sense, of course, but in addition they are expected to conform to reality, to be empirically true.

It is the relaxation of this condition, or the failure to enforce it, which Sir Peter sees as the characteristic of literature.

Sir Peter prints a reply to his Romanes Lecture by John Holloway, who questions rather sharply, and considerably more thoroughly than one can hope to suggest here, not only the validity of Sir Peter's particular comparisons between scientific and literary truth but the general framework of thought within which these comparisons can be made:

> If I am right, then the "telling stories" metaphor is no good for either the preliminary or the definitive stage of scientific theorizing. . . . Professor Medawar sometimes asserts, and sometimes implies, that literature is not "about" anything at all; but at the same time constantly speaks as if it were either about the same reality as science . . . or about another, wider, but perfectly genuine reality.

The hypothetico-deductive scheme, in its positivist form, seems to suggest that science is like a piece of fiction that has turned out to be a narration of actual happenings. Dr Holloway claims, surely rightly, that it is not like a piece of fiction at all; and adds the point, very revealing about the real nature of literature, that the best fiction "corresponds to reality" a good deal more completely than photographically exact reportage of quotidian banalities. He does not, perhaps for lack of space, develop this point. But there is certainly much to be said for the contention that, while the aim of science is to analyse the causal structure of reality, that of literature is to create an instance of "reality"—imagined, of course—in which at least some aspects of that structure are buried less deeply under trivialities than usual—though remaining unanalysed: "The cases of Anna and Vronsky, or Clarissa and Lovelace or Birkin and Ursula . . . bear on life more sharply than just to count as 'what might be true'." The relevant criterion of "truth" is implicit in that phrase "bear on life more sharply"; and it by no means implies that if the hypothesis

"Anna and Vronsky" is true, that of Birkin and Ursula cannot be so also.

Among the philosophers of science who accept that its fundamental method is based on some sort of hypothetico-deductive, rather than purely inductive, scheme, there has been a movement, in post-Popperian times, which would see the criterion of scientific truth as not very far removed from the criterion of truth in literature just adumbrated. The best known, but by no means impregnable, citadel of the thesis is T. S. Kuhn's *The Structure of Scientific Revolutions.* The hypothesis which a scientist formulates and tests are, it is claimed, cast within a certain framework of thought, a paradigm; and the degree of their correspondence with reality is assessed within this context. But the paradigm may change, and then a new *type* of correspondence with reality will be looked for. Science on this view is like a painter trying to draw a decent "likeness" of a sitter. There is no doubt that the sitter has definite characteristics; some likenesses are "truer" than others.

This is a mode of thought which has a traditional background almost as long as that which leads to the positivist confidence that we can definitely state what "is indeed the case"; thus Blake's "Everything possible to be believed is an image of truth", and Whitehead, for whom reality consisted of "events", each of which "prehended" some relationship with every other in the universe. These are of course extreme examples, chosen to bolster the plausibility of Sir Peter's rejection of the whole notion. In the words of Dr Holloway:

Of "the concept of truthfulness which belongs essentially to the imaginative literature, that in which the opposite of a truth is not a falsehood but ... another truth", he says, with a touch of scorn which one cannot but detect not infrequently when literature and its values are at issue—"*We are back in* [*Blake's*] *Beulah.*" But I do not believe that "real life" is Beulah at all.

This is an argument, from a professional in the field of literature, which some scientists may feel is not fully met by Sir Peter's "Rejoinder", where he narrows the issue down to the question, "Did Coleridge really grasp the idea of a synergism between reason and imagination?" (in the sense that this synergism has been formulated by Popper and Medawar himself); and proceeds to the claim, which, on the material presented to us, he triumphantly justifies, that "I do not wish to appear arrogant, but on this technical and rather specialised subject I am probably the better informed and the better read."

The possibility which Sir Peter does not seem ready to contemplate is that Coleridge's poetry may have penetrated more deeply than Popper's logic into this so-simple-seeming thing, what "is indeed the case". And he might then have felt it desirable to attach some indication of direction to the final phrases of his book, an endorsement of Hobbes: " 'there can be no contentment but in proceeding'. I agree" —*Doch, aber wohin*?

12

POETRY OF 1972

(a) SEAMUS HEANEY

Wintering Out

and ALAN BROWNJOHN

Warrior's Career

SEAMUS HEANEY'S earlier books, *Death of a Naturalist* and *Door into the Dark*, were better received than all but a few during the past ten years. What almost everyone has commented on has been the sharpness and immediacy of his physical images, and the fastidious precision of his language. The actual substance of his first book—the sights and smells of a remembered childhood on an Irish farm—seemed to have something of the appeal of Laurie Lee: not cider with Rosie, exactly, but taties with Paddy. Nostalgically earthy emotions were appealed to, redolent of days behind the plough, shooting snipe, digging peat, lifting potatoes, peering down wells. And all these activities (not, one would have thought, the stuff of which metropolitan literary critics are made) were summoned up and transmitted with a sensuousness so neat that it was almost dandified.

Mr Heaney's second book had plenty of bogs, bulls and buckets, but it was remarked that human beings were getting a bit more of a

(a) SEAMUS HEANEY: *Wintering Out*. 80 pp. Faber and Faber. Paperback, £1. ALAN BROWNJOHN: *Warrior's Career*. 56 pp. Macmillan. £2.

(b) DONALD DAVIE: *Collected Poems 1950–1970*. 316 pp. Routledge and Kegan Paul. £3.75.

(c) JOHN FULLER: *Cannibals and Missionaries*. 63 pp. £1.50 (paperback, 95p). JAMES FENTON: *Terminal Moraine*. 63 pp. £1.50 (paperback, 95p). Secker and Warburg.

(d) RANDALL JARRELL: *The Complete Poems*. 507 pp. Faber and Faber. £4.

(e) YANNIS RITSOS: *Gestures and other poems 1968–1970*. Translated by Nikos Stangos. 88 pp. Cape Goliard. £2.20 (paperback, £1.10).

(f) PETER PORTER: *Preaching to the Converted*. 61 pp. *After Martial*. 48 pp. Oxford University Press. Paperback, £1 each.

showing; and the thatchers and eel-fishermen, though less lovingly re-created than the thatch and the eels, gave promise that his marvellously apt mimetic skills were going to be used in ways that might stretch the mind as well as the senses. As the grim situation in Mr Heaney's native Ulster became grimmer, a different kind of poem began appearing above his name in the periodicals—recognizably by the same man, but speaking from the centre of a bitter, and bitterly present, conflict; for example, one that looks at an Orange band, and ends:

> Training the note of hate on the ear's greed,
> His battered signature subscribes "No Pope".
> The pigskin's scourged until his knuckles bleed.
> The air is pounding like a stethoscope.

But what has happened to these harsh and compassionate new poems? *Wintering Out* carries such a piece as a preface or dedication ("This morning from a dewy motorway/I saw the new camp for the internees"), but much of the rest of the book is "Thigh-deep in sedge and marigolds", to use one of Mr Heaney's lines. Though the blurb seems to suggest that a year recently spent by Mr Heaney in California is reflected "in a noticeable widening of his poetic landscapes", there is really not much sign of this; and though the tone is starker and bleaker (the "Fishermen at Ballyshannon/Netted an infant last night/Along with the salmon"), the bog oak, turf-banks and cobbles prevail, and no one is plucking up the latter to throw them at anyone. What *is* new, and interestingly so, is a desolate sense of the remote past, conveyed through such images as flints and Tollund Man:

> His last gruel of winter seeds
> Caked in his stomach,
>
> Naked except for
> The cap, noose and girdle,
> I will stand a long time . . .

Mediated through such apprehensions of a cruel prehistory, even the sedge and marigolds appear to be blighted: disease, deprivation, "the semaphores of hurt" signal below the habitual rural surfaces. All this may be Mr Heaney's way of distancing immediate emotional concerns; perhaps he thinks the uncollected poems are too rawly topical and don't deserve preservation. Lacking them, *Wintering Out* gives the slightly unsatisfactory impression of being a transitional book, skirting round themes he is reluctant to tackle head on.

Careful distancing is part of the spirit of Alan Brownjohn's new book too; but there all resemblances end. Mr Brownjohn's development has been much slower and more hesitant than Mr Heaney's. This is his fourth book, and by far his best. The air of slightly fussy prosing, as of an Oxford logical-positivist muttering over his next article in *Mind*, has almost disappeared, and there is a confident variousness about *Warrior's Career*, moving with ease from an ironical ballad on the shrine at Walsingham to a remorseless and devastating "Ode to Centre Point", and from sad urban vignettes to a sardonic and broadly comic calypso on King Arthur, Sir Bedivere and that celebrated sword. There are developments of the oblique, highly circumstantial fictions he began to use in his last book, in which invented characters (James Carra, Elizabeth Pender) perform their Jamesian manœuvres, and a frightening reduction of this ploy in "The Packet". Most bizarre of all, "Pastoral" presents a fox-hunt on the moon:

> In all these men and women pride was burning
> To have this ceremony in such a place:
> The air-locked air smelt grand, the beasts were sprightly,
> The clothes were filled with arrogance and grace.
>
> The faces, just as furious and paltry
> As were their ancestors' before their births,
> Joyed at the springy touch of lunar pastures
> As had those solid forebears' on the earth's . . .

In Mr Brownjohn's new poems, the concepts of science-fiction, modish chat about pollution and technology, liberal commonplaces about charity, are all steadily and wittily probed; the manner is dry and circumspect, but not at all unfeeling. They search out hypocrisies, evasions, the complexities of human relationships and the oddities of change almost in a spirit of social hygiene. What they have to say is troubled and humane; the means by which they say it reflective and steady:

> We used to be some self-absorbed people living
> In a compromised age, about twenty years ago. We hated
> it, it
> Was a terrible age, and underneath we liked it in a way, it
> Was because it gave us the chance to feel like that.
>
> Now it has all changed, and we are older,
> And we hate the age completely, not nearly so

Entranced with our hatred. But now there are lots of younger
People entranced with hatred of this terrible age,

While underneath they like it in a way, because
It gives them the chance to feel like that. We ourselves feel
lost
Because we can't tell them they are compromised like us,
That being hard for the self-absorbed to see.

And all the time the ages are getting worse and worse.

(b) DONALD DAVIE

Collected Poems 1950–1970

IN DONALD DAVIE'S WORK the relation of the critic to the poet seems deeply ironical. We can enjoy the vitality of the newest experimenters in verse without denying the strength of Mr Davie's warnings against them. For, when all restrictions are lifted on the materials available for poetry, the poet suffers a frightening pull to use the most violent of them. One may win awards for bravery simply by handling certain mixtures of lethal emotions, or by giving first-hand accounts of life at the poles of behaviour. At last, it seems, verse can compete with the novel or even the film; and grateful armchair explorers can visit the fierce tribes of darkest Paranoia by opening a thin octavo.

At the same time, high-minded critics feel an urge to act as outriders to the hero of literature. They observe the general neglect of poetry. They admire the self-sacrifice of unpaid, uncheered genius. The least they can do, they may think, is to interpret the artist sympathetically to an ill-informed audience, and to avoid blaming the poet for defects of art. One can praise the moral conscience where one cannot praise its expression; one can expound the esoteric learning of a writer whose rhythms—however significant—grate on the ear.

By taking his stand at the poet's side, the critic defeats only the expectations of the literary reader. This is the man with seductive memories of great or charming poems, who looks in new verse for a mastery of speech. It is the reader who wants a fresh disentanglement of wisdom from the web of need and instinct, a sudden coherence revealed in hunks of existence that looked shapeless.

But there is another reader, the groping apprentice. Precisely what

attracts some talents to the writing of poetry is the availability of
material; and to them the art involved seems spontaneous. Under the
united pressure of inarticulate bards and kind reviewers, poetry
receives an odd kind of appraisal. The measure of accomplishment
becomes not the constantly renewed satisfaction of literary readers
but the establishment of undemanding models for unlearned authors.
Those poets who exploit their most secret sensations, like those who
celebrate the crises of public opinion, are often too brisk to shape
their work. They want pretexts for delivering it raw; and they are
numerous enough to supply a loud chorus of praise for teachers who
excuse them. Ezra Pound, William Carlos Williams, and Charles
Olson have been made into apologists for irresponsibility. What
hasty poets look for, and what good-natured critics often endorse, is
just a quick method of binding together some ill-assorted intensities.

It is to Mr Davie's merit that he has always resisted the confusion of
achievement with excitement. Whoever recalls the notorious dispute
with Al Alvarez will appreciate Mr Davie's wish to support literary
values:

> The practise of an art
> is to convert all terms
> into the terms of art.
>   ("July, 1964")

Against him push the many who believe that a violence within us
must fight the violence without, by means which transcend literary
judgment. But with him stand some formidable powers, not least the
witness of writers surviving under the stifling regimes of Eastern
Europe but confirmed in the virtue of the poetic act.

Mr Davie has not been afraid to recommend and use models painfully created by the forebears of our poetry. He has pleaded for
aesthetic control and praised moral principles even when they suited
the fixed order of society. He has distrusted easy motions and in-
fringed on no legitimate privacies. At the same time, he has utterly
rejected provincialism and studied poets who live in regions or speak
languages ignored by many of his contemporaries. He has willingly
experimented with the styles and structures of three centuries. He has
maintained a record of conscious integrity, misrepresenting his
character neither to himself nor to others. So he has admitted
tergiversations and failures to meet his own requirements.

Yet turning from Mr Davie's programme to his poems, one feels troubled. After all the distaste he shows in "Pentecost" for self-indulgent "self-communers"—

> They see and hear with the thorax
> They are eloquent in pidgin

—Mr Davie still places the rights of the audience below those of the poet. He comes to terms with his own experience when he embodies it in verse—"the chart/I keep, of my own sea-changes" ("Resolutions"). But any reader who stands between him and the world he responds to is moved on. Mr Davie's very integrity prevents him from violating the purity of an impression in order to reward the attendance of an onlooker. To his own nature and to nothing else—he implies—the poet must be true.

Since Mr Davie's candour is matched by his discretion, he has few startling communications on the subject of himself or his intimates. This is to be regretted. Two quatrains from "Autumn Imagined" indicate how delicately he can deal with married love:

> The shuffle and shudder of Autumn
> Are in our love.
> Those last thin garments, come
> Let's have them off!

> Drop them about your knees.
> The beech-tree rains its gold.
> We are deciduous trees,
> And our year grows old.

Elsewhere he suggests poignantly but with dignity the tension that strains a secure partnership ("Across the Bay").

Very seldom does Mr Davie choose themes like these, which appeal to normal curiosity. More often he delivers his views on moral principles, or the writing of poetry, or various anti-heroic figures from British imperial history. These have to be genuine views, never modified so as to draw and hold the mere reader of the poem. So again Mr Davie examines his inner character, its origins and development, but with so much self-respect, so much restraint, and so little humour that one feels finally less edified than subdued:

> My strongest feeling all
> My life has been,
> I recognize, revulsion
> From the obscene;
> That more than anything
> My life-consuming passion.   ('Revulsion')

Take me or leave me, says the flat, declarative tone.

It is a fair question whether a poet can be loyal to Candour without betraying Art. Can one properly define "art" in terms that exclude the audience? Or if one's first aim is to record the precise shape of experience, can it be more than chance that makes the shape please anybody else? Too many of Mr Davie's poems advance erratically toward capricious goals; too many trail off in a defiant bathos, as if to say: It happened so, and so you must take it.

Therefore, while the metrical or stanzaic forms may be clear enough, the craftsmanship is rarely meticulous; and if the forms do not obstruct the underlying movement, they often seem irrelevant to it. When Mr Davie sets up a pentasyllabic line and then violates it, as in "Christmas Syllabics for a Wife", one hardly knows whether the irregularity expresses anger or is an oversight. To add the principle of rational control to the other demands is to limit the range of the poems not merely in tone but in subject. It is also to create a number of irresoluble dilemmas when the poet is distinguishing his own character from that of more visceral talents but voicing sentiments as extreme as theirs, as in "To Helen Keller". The paucity of living persons in Mr Davie's poems is not compensated for by the number of characters rescued from history; these are too plainly projections or anti-masks of the poet; and one sometimes feels locked into his obsessions.

So it is unfortunate that Mr Davie should have decided to publish an unsifted collection of virtually all his work. A book one-quarter the size would still have had space for experimental pieces and Hudibrastics; but it would also have displayed more visibly the elements that literary readers want: the interesting versification of "Dudwood", the wit of "Obiter Dicta", the psychological insight of "Vying", the refinement of "Time Passing, Beloved", the pathos of "Heigh-ho on a Winter Afternoon", the wisdom of "The Hardness of Light".

(c) JOHN FULLER
Cannibals and Missionaries

and JAMES FENTON
Terminal Moraine

WHEN a famous imprint returns to publishing poetry there is joy in Heaven, and when its first batch includes poems as good as John

Fuller's and James Fenton's the joy is accompanied by gratitude for the judgment involved. Mr Fuller and Mr Fenton can, and no doubt will, be represented as crusaders in the War for Standards—troops raised by Wit in its campaign against neophile Dullness. This is part of the story, but not the most important part. Each poet is as much an innovator as any English experimenter looking Westward. Mr Fuller's poem "Ghost Village" is new to all classifications, the spirit of Auden inhabiting but not possessing it: Mr Fenton's "The King-fisher's Boxing Gloves" is original enough to baffle the intelligence while delighting the imagination.

Of course, the ingredients of these books are familiar, even traditional, but they are arranged in highly personal patterns. Mr Fuller is as skilled as an Old Master—there is not a flawed poem in his book, though there are some which tread water instead of getting anywhere. Mr Fenton can be dull (most of his Newdigate poem "Our Western Furniture" is indeed prize-winning stuff, startled here and there by a dark truth among the iambics), but he has reaches of audacity which mark him out among the young poets of Britain. Both books breathe the air of the 1970s. Contemporaneity may not be worth boasting about, but it is a very different thing from fashion.

Mr Fuller has one poem where his technical address is self-defeating. "The Labours of Hercules" is a sonnet-sequence in a progressive Hungarian form which recently overwhelmed George MacBeth. (It consists of fifteen sonnets, Nos 2 to 14 each beginning with the last line of its predecessor, the last line of No 14 also being the opening line of all, and the final sonnet made up of all fourteen repeated lines. Needless to say, No 15 has to be specially constructed and tends to get written first.) Mr Fuller follows the twelve labours dutifully if cloudily and fits them out with some amusing anachronisms (of the labour concerning the carnivorous Stymphalides, he writes, "the sixth was for the birds"), but there is nothing in the sequence to take it beyond a technical exercise. Imagination should know what to refuse when sheer skill comes to tempt it. But this is the one failure: there are many successes. "Scenario for a Walk-On Part" has an ease of movement which supports its theatrical self-awareness perfectly. Most of us are aware of an alter ego who is as rusty as he is superfluous. In the last stanza, the dramatis personae leave this stooge to his fate.

> The sexy minister reclaims his scarf,
> A girl in denim runs to meet a train,
> Mrs Jocasta bastes the fatted calf,

> The guests have taken to their beds again:
> I hold the floor but nobody will laugh,
> Nobody is there to kiss if I complain.
> I enter only in the second half,
> Unwilling, underwritten, used to pain.

"Aberporth" is accomplished but also warmly human. It is a landscape with figures, the sort of descriptive poem which opens inwards with a series of fine rhetorical flourishes. Above all, the musical handling of the language is eminently satisfying:

> The sea is much visited here, whose colours are cooler
> And life uncertain as well it might be in
> The earth's tears. Gulls on the sand look sharp.
> Without anxiety the jellyfish is
>   hideously still,
> And the same could be
>   said of the cliffs where wind carries
> The loves of freewheeling crickets across a haze
> of sun-baked blackberries.

The strangest poem is "The Two Sisters", whose Mary and Martha polarity gives Mr Fuller the chance to compose a chain of hard aphorisms. The story is baffling, but the atmosphere grows more oppressive as you read. To create so sombre an effect in such stately verse is a real achievement. The songs and pieces for music are much simpler. "London Songs" succeed where so many urban song-cycles fail—they put their place names and Betjemany details into a convincing metrical harness. The slightly Surreal tone of much of "Cannibals and Missionaries" suggests that Mr Fuller is changing his poetical stance. The perfect technique now reflects a disturbed world, making these his most impressive poems to date.

Mr Fenton's fondness for nonce words, mineralogy, and Light Verse have earned him a place among the Sons of Auden. This is true enough, if it implies that his Pleasure Principle is in good shape, but it doesn't describe his special flavour as a poet. "The Pitt-Rivers Museum, Oxford" is a survey of man's atavistic and imperial past disguised as Oxonian whimsy about anthropology. It is one of his most brilliant assumptions, a serious and compendious poem linking the study of science with the ends of action. Like many of his best poems, it is really political in aim. The last stanza makes its point succinctly—the reader adds his own QED:

> All day
> Watching the groundsman breaking the ice

From the stone trough,
The sun slanting across the lawns, the grass
Thawing, the stable-boy blowing on his fingers,
He had known what tortures the savages had prepared
For him there, as he calmly pushed open the gate
And entered the wood near the placard: "TAKE NOTICE
MEN-TRAPS AND SPRING-GUNS ARE SET ON
                                    THESE PREMISES"
For his father had protected his good estate.

There is as much Lewis Carroll as Auden in Mr Fenton. The last
two poems in the book, "Lollipops of the Pomeranian Baroque" and
"The Kingfisher's Boxing Gloves" are examples of his lunatic logic,
his perfectly judged sewing-machine rhetoric. To have your own voice
at twenty-two is remarkable—for it to be pre-Freudian and pre-
Modernist and yet audaciously right might seem only a gift from
Oxford. But "The Kingfisher's Boxing Gloves" is a poem like a self-
sealing tank: puncture it with questions about its meaning and
nothing of it leaks away. Stanza by stanza it grows more oracular, as
if the priests of Delphi had tried their hands at Victorian Light Verse.
Here is part of its Snarky progress:

His LEM is waiting at the station
To take him to the mountains of the moon.
On board he hears the countdown with elation,
Is horrified to see his mother swoon
And turn into a dim distant relation
He sees his world become a macaroon.
"Quite a small step for our civilization—
Not at all bad for a legless baboon."

Mr Fenton may go in almost any direction from *Terminal Moraine*,
but six dazzling poems in the book show that he is already far up on
the glacier.

(d) RANDALL JARRELL

The Complete Poems

RANDALL JARRELL'S best poems are those that do not evade his
despondency but employ it. Employment of this sort was rare
because he did not like to convey such a feeling as his own—no
doubt for fear of sounding sloppy. In most of his work Jarrell

shunned personal subjectivity and felt bound to start from observed life, fact, real experience. "Real" normally meant disappointing experience, which he then countered with ironic insights or with dreams. The shield of the dramatic monologue always attracted him, though he seldom gave convincing expression to people unlike himself.

In the poems he wrote about the Second World War, Jarrell tried to mask his native despair as an emotion created by the war. The strategy did not work. This theme became the wastefulness of war. But he seldom dealt with the carefully shaped, irreplaceable persons the world had lost. Instead, he wrote about the possible life the men had missed. This vanished futurity could hardly be concrete or particular, and the soldier therefore was too often a case rather than a person.

If one judges from Jarrell's poems, one must suppose that he himself longed for a past he never owned. The immediate present could not satisfy his hunger for a sense of life because it was not authentic. His immersion in aesthetic or intellectual experience—poetry, criticism, music, museums, gifted friends and brilliant conversation—seemed detached from the inner self, the "other", that his painful childhood nourished and that he hunted in mirrors. "An English Garden in Austria", dense with *Kulturgeschichte*, offers to the reader a speaker who exists only as a collage of civilized allusions, footnotes to a suppressed book.

To supply the absent life, Jarrell used dreams. In his dramatic monologues, defeated women and troubled children—the fathers do not count—keep trying to distinguish between sleep and waking, the life they never had and the life they cannot understand. But where Jarrell intends to give them character, he can only provide them with references—ideas and quotations they should have known if they were as bright as he. The poet cannot separate his creatures from himself.

The dreams in Jarrell's poems often have a perverse relation to reality. A hideously wounded soldier thinks his condition must be a nightmare but wakes to find it fact ("A Field Hospital"). Other soldiers, safely in a hospital in their own country, dream they are overseas, yearning to be home ("A Ward in the States"). In such poems sleeping and waking are no longer escapes from one another. The polarities dissolve, and the man is trapped in his pain. Finally, death seems equivalent to life.

This dissolution of polarities is the source of Jarrell's wit. He utters (in irony) a commonplace, then negates the commonplace, and finds both statements are true:

> ... she says, 'Life
> Is life.' 'See how it sounds to say it isn't.'
> ... 'Life is not life,'
> She says. It sounds the same. ("Woman")

There is no escape from triteness. Life, propositions about life, and the denials of the propositions—all are bathetic.

Sometimes, in his late poems, Jarrell tries simply to recapture the short period when his childhood was serene. He does not convince. The particulars are neither rich nor seductive; the tone is either conventional or sentimental. Finally, one infers that there was no halcyon period but that as Jarrell lost the hope of advancing into serenity, he magically transformed a childhood year into the happy time he needed somehow, somewhere.

In a few poems Jarrell does bring himself to meet his despair head on, and finds the words that it requires. In "90 North" he compares a boyhood dream of heroic achievement (ending usefully in death) with adulthood's sour taste of success:

> Here where North, the night, the berg of death
> Crowd me out of the ignorant darkness,
> I see at last that all the knowledge
> I wrung from the darkness—that the darkness flung me—
> Is worthless as ignorance: nothing comes from nothing,
> The darkness from the darkness. Pain comes from the
> > darkness
> And we call it wisdom. It is pain.

Towards the end, in late works like "Hope" and "Woman", Jarrell gives up trying to frame the poem in fact. The dreams surrender to a glorious comic fantasy as the despair flowers in wit—for if living is indeed a kind of dying, one may as well live (or write) wholly to please oneself. In "Hope" a forlorn husband dreams a new version of the Sleeping Beauty:

> ... when the Prince kissed her on the lips
> She wiped her lips
> And with a little *moue*—in the dream, a little mouse—
> Turned over and went back to sleep.
> I woke, and went to tell my wife the story;
> And had she not resembled
> My mother as she slept, I had done it.

(e) YANNIS RITSOS

Gestures and Other Poems 1968–1970

YANNIS RITSOS has always been a poet of some promise and interest; he has now become more important. For years he has been heroized by the left, and the tendency of his critics to see some immediate relation between a politically desirable attitude in poems and the more lasting virtues of poetry has confused the issue. He has now emerged after many bitter experiences as a stronger poet than ever before, strong by anyone's standards. There was a time when he shared with Éluard, to name a poet of comparable importance, the temptation to draw his passion larger than life-size, but his poems were always alive at the core, and now they are like small, bitter trees that have flowered.

> Sometimes words come almost by themselves, like leaves of
> trees—
> the invisible roots, the soil, the sun, the water have helped,
> old rotten leaves have also helped.

The poems end terribly; they are as concentrated as walnuts, and like much modern European poetry they translate excellently into English. Each poem is dated, so that one can see three or four short poems, all of them white-hot metal which will cool into strength, all of them written on one day. The English is inevitably a further cooling process, but the drawings by Ritsos with which the poems are illustrated recapture white heat almost unbearably, so that the book becomes too moving to assimilate just as a literary exercise. The difference between literary exercises and the kind of poetry which we cannot do without has to do with form, in the deep sense of a "marrow of form" of which Lorca wrote. It is something technical, objectively present in certain poems; it cannot be pretended or imitated. It is not the same as psychological seriousness or sincerity; it is or includes an objective element of passion in the texture of language which we recognize instinctively. It is not a principle that can be isolated by academic criticism or easily demonstrated in a book-review but its presence will easily be detected by an open-minded reader of these poems. Ritsos has fulfilled the hopes of his friends and confounded his lukewarm admirers.

These are not poems on an enormous scale; they are more like the

Three Secret Poems of George Seferis. One has the impression that they were similarly difficult to translate, since at certain moments they seem to swivel on a sixpence, the tone suddenly closes or opens or becomes thunderous, images are sensed and then thrust forward in the scope of very few words. Ritsos is unusually lucky in the skill of his translator; one could wish only that he had been equally lucky in the generosity of his publisher, and that we had the Greek text of the poems on facing pages. Not that the edition is less than handsome, though it is careless in places, but one must assume it will circulate clandestinely in Greece. People are hungry for poetry in such circumstances, and anyone hungry for a poet in his own language does deserve access to the text. The poems are not propaganda: it is simply that they could not have been written by anyone else, or anywhere else, and they convey a powerful, rather black courage. It may be that the prisoners of a police state can save the honour of their country, but poets like Ritsos can in some sense save its soul: certainly in retrospect, but immediately only if they are read.

> the dancers would jump lightly
> on the ship imitating rough action with improper grace, the
> motion
> of non-existent oars, sweat, blood.
> Then an old sailor
> spat at their feet and walked away to the small woods to piss.

A poem is human language after all, and language is behaviour; the "Gestures" of these poems have a resonance and a reality. From the series "Stones" in 1968 they have a tension and a life like that of violin strings hardly stroked; later in the concentration-camp on Leros and on Samos there is a dark, articulate flowering, everything is said openly, and set against a vivid recreation of ancient history. In "Gestures", the principal subsection of this book, something has dropped away, the poems are about ten lines long, but there is a terrible, ragged eloquence, the sense of a winter leaf held together only by its veins, and the starting-points of poems are obscure and sinister; some of the strongest poems are in this section, so far as one can judge without seeing the originals; they are quite direct and cut to the bone from unexpected directions. The last section, written in 1970, is the blackest and bitterest; these poems are painful to read, but always with the same strength. It seems no exaggeration to acknowledge that in these years Yannis Ritsos has become at last a great poet.

(f) PETER PORTER

Preaching to the Converted and *After Martial*

ONE THING that has become increasingly obvious in Peter Porter's work is that he is not primarily a satirist but an elegiac poet. Death broods above and behind his poems with a suffocating presence, and it is the horror of this that seems to determine his pessimistic, blackly humorous attitude to the things of this world. Whenever he appears to be speaking in his own person (and he used to be a great one for making direct references to himself—*A Porter Folio*, "Porter" rhyming with "aorta", and so forth) the distancing is ironic: there is a deliberate, chilling gap between the maker and the thing made. The gap can, in *Preaching to the Converted*, be seen as that which lies between the gaze of eternity and our mortal existence.

Mr Porter is thus a very serious poet, for all his skill as an entertainer:

> Really, he's more frivolous who thinks poetry
> demands portentousness, that some subjects
> are proper to the Muse and others aren't.

This is the voice of Martial as mediated by Mr Porter in one of the fifty transmogrified epigrams in *After Martial*; and it is a voice that often closely matches Porter's own—sardonic, wryly humorous, full of the names of things, often scabrous, always unseriously serious. Here too death is the measure of all things:

> Small and select, the restaurant called *The Mouthful*
> Overlooks Caesar's tomb and you may view
> The sacred domes with garlic on your breath.
>   Wine and dine there if you've got the pull,
> See and be seen, for even as you chew,
>   The God Augustus welcomes you to death.

It is a happy chance that has brought these two learned and lively poets together. Mr Porter is at great pains to call them versions, rewritings and remodellings, but one is in fact seldom in doubt what he is up to. The anachronisms (at random, Fortnum's, *The Sunday Times*, postwar credit, Kama Sutra birds, Black Mountain lyrics) put Martial's world in focus rather than distracting from it. The absurdities of fashion, sexual behaviour, boasting, meanness, hypochondria

are constants; the only variables are the names and faces. And underneath it all is the realization that

> death
> has the best of ever-bearing crops.

In both books the range of manner is very wide, from cryptic and
oblique free verse to formal and even stately structures. *Preaching to
the Converted* develops an oracular and riddling tone which has
always been Porterish but which now moves in a more grandly
stately way (in "Between Two Texts" and "A Hint from Ariosto", for
example), and sometimes the stateliness sheds its runic quality and
becomes straightforwardly sententious and poignant, as in "Fossil
Gathering", which moves towards this exalted conclusion:

> *A Little Guide in Colour* tells us how
> These creatures sank in their unconscious time,
> That life in going leaves a husk the plough
> Or amateur collector can displace,
> That every feeling thing ascends from slime
> To selfhood and in dying finds a face.

All that survives this *Totenreich*, this Kingdom of Death, is whatever
is well made on "the Isle of Ink", or in the canvases or compositions
of artists, "the cold immortals". The sordid, the showy, the modish,
the anarchic, the senselessly liberated are reduced to plaintive footnotes; only the favoured artist—Stravinsky, Scarlatti, Hardy, all
celebrated here—manages to outstare death.

In the margins of this overriding concern are lighter essays, in
which the high style has deliberately lost weight and is trim, nimble
and smart. Twelve "Postcard Poems" are examples of this—imaginative notations to go with well-known paintings—and, more exuberant-
ly comical, "Mort aux chats":

> Cats smell, they can't help it,
> you notice it going upstairs.
> Cats watch too much television,
> they can sleep through storms,
> they stabbed us in the back
> last time. There have never been
> any great artists who were cats.
> They don't deserve a capital C
> except at the beginning of a sentence.

Here again there are parallels with the Porter/Martial poems—mini-
malist squibs ("Instant Fish/ by Phidias!/ Add water/ and they

swim"), and such joke exercises as the monologue put in the mouth of a statue of Priapus.

These two books show a strongly-flavoured yet subtle poet at the height of his powers. Martial arrived in Rome from his native Spain at twenty or so; Porter came to London from his native Australia at about the same age. Does our present-day deracinated colonial see a congenial foreshadowing there? Whatever the answer, we can endorse—and underline with greater warmth—the sentiment with which Martial/Porter ends his first epigram:

> My pleasure
> is to please myself and if the Muses listen
> I may find an ear or two to echo in.

13

GERMANY'S JOYCE

ARNO SCHMIDT'S *Leviathan*, published in 1949, was awarded a Grosser Literaturpreis by the West German Academy of Sciences and Literature; yet it took until well into the 1960s for his name to become at all well known outside a narrow circle of admirers. There is little excuse for this; hardly a year has gone by without a new work from his pen. Between 1951 and 1953 Schmidt published three short novels—*Aus dem Leben eines Fauns, Brand's Haide, Schwarze Spiegel* —which together made up the trilogy *Nobodaddy's Kinder*. This was followed by many short stories, critical essays and radio features; two longer critical/biographical studies (*Fouqué und einige seiner Zeitgenossen* and *Sitara und der Weg dahin*); experiments in mixed media with the painter Eberhard Schlotter and a group of actors; and, above all, a further series of novels (*Das steinerne Herz; Die Gelehrtenrepublik; KAFF, auch Mare Crisium*) which culminated in the book that will ever remain the firmest pillar of Schmidt's fame; *Zettels Traum* (1970). *Zettels Traum* is so long and complicated, and written in so difficult a post-Joycean idiom, that a "decipherers' syndicate" has been founded in Germany to trace its many allusions, unscramble its polybrid vocabulary, and eventually—one hopes—produce something akin to the *Skeleton Key to Finnegans Wake* by Campbell and Robinson. In this country the London University Institute of Germanic Studies plans to publish a modest preliminary survey of the foothills of *Zettels Traum* before the end of this year.

But here, less than two years after *Zettels Traum* burst upon us, we have yet another work of fiction, in the same large format (10 inches by 12 inches), like the earlier work reproduced by offset from the author's own typescript, though with fewer marginal comments and fewer hand-written corrections. Its main title, *Die Schule der Atheisten*, deliberately recalls comedies of the seventeenth and eighteenth centuries and suggests, at the same time, one of the guiding

---

ARNO SCHMIDT: *Die Schule der Atheisten*. Novellen-Comödie in 6 Aufzeügn. 271 pp. Frankfurt: S. Fischer. DM 64 (paperback, DM 42).

themes of Schmidt's fiction since *Leviathan* and *Nobodaddy's Kinder*: the contradiction between being a thinking man and subscribing to any religious doctrine: the contradiction, above all, between what we see, hear, smell and know of the world around us and the very idea of a just and benevolent God. This is only the first of many links with Schmidt's earlier novels, short stories and essays. In fact, it would be hard to find any work, other than the much longer and much more difficult *Zettels Traum*, which affords so good an introduction to the world of this obsessed and fascinating writer.

The subtitle "Novellen-Comödie" prepares the reader for a mingling of the epic and the dramatic: a comfortable form which allows the author to construct an interestingly differentiated typographical picture and, at the same time, to play an intricate game with his narrative perspectives. Characters and topographies are introduced in elaborate stage-directions, inset towards the middle of the page; when the characters speak (and they are, for the most part, exceedingly communicative), their name appears, in capitals and underlined, on the left hand side of the page, and the speech that follows each such appearance is punctuated by further, bracketed stage-directions and authorial comments. Other comments, quotations, documents, even pictorial illustrations, appear at frequent intervals in the margins. This fusion of the epic and the dramatic recalls, at times, the experiments of Arno Holz and Johannes Schlaf in the early days of German Naturalism; as does also Schmidt's effort to reproduce the nuances of spoken language (with its regional inflections, hummings and hawings, omissions and repetitions) and his fascinated dwelling on details not usually mentioned in polite literature.

The scene is laid in Tellingstedt, "story-town". The very name prepares us for fantasy—the kind of fantasy Schmidt has called "sustained mental games", *Längeres Gedankenspiel*, a deliberate exploitation of day-dreaming which challenges the intelligent reader to reconstruct for himself the "reality" that induces men to have recourse to such fancies. However, like Gottfried Keller's Seldwyla, this dreamt-up little town, whose very name labels it fiction, is given an exact geographical location: on the river Eider, within a North German townscape and landscape whose features are evoked with an economy and a precision that would do credit to any nineteenth-century realist. Schmidt prides himself on his exactitude: he is very hard on fellow-writers who fail to check whether the bright moonlight they describe on a verifiable date does in fact tally with the planetary and meteorological facts. Goethe's *Werther*, for one, fails to pass this and other tests—but then Arno Schmidt's "Goethe, bleib bei deiner Lyrik!" has already achieved almost proverbial status in Germany.

As in *Schwarze Spiegel* and as in *Die Gelehrtenrepublik*, the main action of *Die Schule der Atheisten* takes place in a future divided from our own time by an atomic war. The year is 2014; only two super-powers, the United States and China, are left to confront each other, with a few protectorates and "reservations" in between. One of these reservations, deliberately preserved as a tourist attraction, is Tellingstedt and its surrounding countryside—a North German setting which is to Arno Schmidt's fiction what Wessex is to Hardy's. A good deal of the action takes place in and around a house attractively crammed with old books and prints which belongs to a man of seventy-five called William T. Kolderup. Kolderup's attitudes and ideas, of which we learn a good deal, are all but indistinguishable from those put forward or implied, from time to time, in stage-directions and incidental comments. His perspective therefore becomes that of the reader—though he is also reflected, and not always in a favourable light, in the consciousness of the other characters.

Like most of the central reflectors in Schmidt's novels, Kolderup is a *Sonderling*, a man apart, divided from those around him by his age, his intellectual interests, his collector's instincts (not as maniacal here as in *Das steinerne Herz*!), and his partly Danish ancestry. He is also a man of very decided views and prejudices (against "popular" art, against any kind of idealization of countryfolk, against the principle of collective authorship, against Christianity, against Marxism . . .) which he shares with most of the positive characters in Schmidt's earlier fiction, with the raisonneurs of his radio-essays, and with whatever persona Schmidt has constructed to articulate his literary views and criticisms. Unlike the earlier characters, however, Kolderup is a man of some consequence in his region: a man of substance, a Justice of the Peace of almost Solomonic wisdom (or rather, "a Daniel come to judgment", a further development of Daniel Pagenstecher, the hero of *Zettels Traum*), and, when need arises, a politician who can deal effectively with the foreign ministers of the super-powers.

Behind this fantasy, this *Längeres Gedankenspiel*, the reader is clearly invited to surmise the impotence of such intellectuals as Kolderup in the *real* society of contemporary Germany. Kolderup lives with his granddaughter Suse, who is in love with a young journalist and druggist (APOtheker—a wry grimace at a younger generation) and who has taken under her wing a much put-upon young woman always known as "Nipperchen". Into their idyll irrupts a party from the United States, headed by the formidable ISIS, a female Foreign Secretary; it includes also her hardly less formidable female bodyguards, her "court-poet" Cosmo Schweighäuser, and one Tim Hackensack, who has the unenviable task of assuaging, on demand, the Foreign Secretary's apparently limitless sexual needs. No sooner has this party arrived in Tellingstedt than it is joined by a similar delegation from China—all males this time except for one subordinate of indeterminate sex (the only pronoun which can effectively cope is *es*). There have been, it appears, some alarming landings from other planets, and it is advisable for the two earthly superpowers to sign a Treaty of Mutual Toleration.

From then onwards a number of plot-strands are skilfully and intricately intertwined: an intrigue to allow Cosmo and Nipperchen, who have fallen in love, to live together despite laws forbidding inter-marriage between United States citizens and inmates of the reservations; a plot to relieve Tim Hackensack of his burdensome duties by substituting a rustic whose sexual equipment and prowess are matched only by his stupidity; a judicial comedy centring on a drunken sea-captain and identical female twins (both of whom he is, in the end, allowed to marry); a sea-journey to the island of Fanö, where Kolderup retrieves from his old home a number of curios of great interest to the visiting dignitaries from the superpowers—and, inci-dentally, some copies of *Zettels Traum*, which seems to be as hard to get hold of in 2014 as it is in 1972. During this sea-voyage Kolderup begins to tell of an earlier one, supposed to have taken place in 1969, and continues his story in snatches and at intervals until the end of the book, so that two time-schemes and two sets of adventures become subtly entwined.

The earlier sea-voyage brought together three professed atheists: Kolderup himself (then a young man), a Marxist professor from East Germany, and Cosmo's father Gottfehd Schweighäuser. When their ship runs into difficulties, they find themselves thrown on to an inhospitable desert island in the company of a missionary, who re-joices in the name of Chadband, and who has brought along his delectable wife—a fact, it turns out, of great interest to the visiting Foreign Secretary from the United States, for Mrs Chadband was later to become her mother. On the desert island hunger, hallucinations and deliberate mystifications test the atheists' steadfastness. The Marxist fails his test miserably (if you can believe *that* doctrine, you can believe anything), but Kolderup emerges a wiser as well as a sadder man, ready to grow into the sage sceptic who tells the story in 2014. In good *Comödie* fashion—the archaic spelling is, of course, deliberate and pointed—*Die Schule der Atheisten* ends with the conclusion of a treaty, with rewards, decorations and titles handed out all round, and with a triple wedding.

This is a strange amalgam indeed: deliberate reminiscences of older comedies, from Shakespeare and Fletcher to Ferdinand Raimund, merge with pungent critiques of social and cultural phenomena of our own time and an immensely detailed presentation of the thoughts, sensations and apprehensions of a modern intellectual. The mixture works, however, and makes—for the most part—delightful reading. Arno Schmidt has here given us a refreshingly funny book, whose high and low comedy derives from many sources. The reader finds himself constantly challenged to hold Schmidt's fantastic elaborations against the literary originals they derive from and parody—Shakespeare's *Tempest*, Schnabel's *Insel Felsenburg*, Jules Verne, Poe and many others provide grist for Schmidt's fast-grinding mill.

We are asked to recognize, in the fantastic world of the future, heightenings of our own present and immediate past. Schmidt turns a jaundiced eye on Women's Lib and American Matriarchy—and, hey presto! the United States of 2014 is entirely dominated by women (her President, we learn with little surprise, is one Joan Cunnydy); American men are reduced to a subjection whose ludicrous and scabrous details are unsparingly unfolded. Male-dominated literature has, of course, to be re-written—there is a hilarious account of Goethe's *Faust* in which all the characters have changed their sex while retaining their function in the plot. Modern journalism, advertising and tourist industries also have been projected into the future and now look twice as large as life and just as horrible—the whole population in Kolderup's "reservation", under the direction of a professional Guide, racks such brains as it has to invent ever-new "archaic" customs, superstitions and saws for the delectation of tourists from the super-powers.

These anti-utopian fantasies are deliberately played against what we are to take as more positively utopian *Denkspiele*. Within the "reservation", the churches are disestablished; the right to vote depends on an educational test; and effective power is wielded by precisely the kind of intellectual whom earlier stories (notably the powerful and justly famous "Caliban über Setebos") had presented as impotent and covertly snarling outsiders. Much amusement may be derived too from Schmidt's juxtaposition of incompatibles: brilliantly caricatured television programmes from East and West Germany unrolling themselves in one typed column while a parallel column gives us Kolderup's spoken and unspoken comments; or allusions to pastoral idyll while we are invited to watch some particularly unappetizing and grotesque aspect of rural life.

Many of Schmidt's finest comic effects inhere, as will have been realized, in the way he structures his tale: in the counterpointing and interlacing of different narrative time-sequences; in different apprehensions of the same phenomenon presented side by side in parallel columns or divided horizontally like a mathematical fraction; in familiar works of literature prefiguring the action of the book or peeping out beneath parody and contrafacture; in fantasies designed to conjure up in the reader's mind an image of the reality that may have given rise to them.

No less important, however, is the texture of Schmidt's language. Following the lead of Joyce and Lewis Carroll (who, with Sterne, head his literary pantheon and to whom he has devoted excellent critical essays), Schmidt abandons Duden rules of spelling and punctuation to produce typographical "estrangements" (*Verfremdungen*) capable of rendering regional peculiarities of speech and the inflections of the speaking voice with marvellous accuracy. They introduce, at the same time, a multitude of ulterior meanings through complex puns which involve, as the book progresses, all the major European languages. It takes a page or two to get into this style—but the puns come less thick and fast here than they do in *Zettels Traum*, and it is not long before the adventurous reader is able to unpack with surprising ease such portmanteaus as: *Sünd-Tax; phällitschissima Nutte, gnäj Frau; GeleerSamcoit & PollynHistörie; manuell de Phall'ja* and *grosse PolyTück*.

Arno Schmidt had first tried out his liberated orthography, and a typographical layout which counterpoints reality and fantasy, in a work which we can see, in retrospect, as the watershed of his art: *KAFF, auch Mare Crisium*. There the central protagonist had seen life as a progress from weeping to a rattle in the throat, with farce and dissonance in between, and had summed up that Beckettian insight in operatic terms: "Die Uhwertüre ist Wein'n; Röcheln das Fienale; dazwischn Possn & höllische Dissonantzn!" That tells us something of the dark background against which Schmidt's comedy must be seen. In the fantasy-world of *Die Schule der Atheisten,* Kolderup is given more of a chance to fulfil himself than other, similarly endowed and handicapped characters in Schmidt's writings; yet he too is made to reflect that his autobiography could have no title but ACCURSED TIMES: " 'VERFLUCHTE ZEITN!'—d's wär *Mein*—Titl! (Für Meine Selbst-Bio.))."

Not surprisingly, traces of the "accursed times" through which Arno Schmidt has himself passed are never far away. Ovens, in this imaginary world of the future, are known as "Eichmanns". Only Kolderup remembers why, and the macabre jest whose origin has been forgotten twists the knife once more. What is the foul and prurient *Furchenalmanach für 2015* but another crest of that wave of pornography that swept over the permissive 1970s? Kolderup's own dwelling on the details of the sexual act is anti-pornographic; like many of Schmidt's heroes he is obsessed with the pathos of the aging body and the black comedy of the struggles between the mind's high aspirations and the body's earthy desires. And that world made uninhabitable by atomic radiation which we must imagine not too far from the reservation of which Tellingstedt forms part—what is it but the consequence of the policies and events of our own world, the 1969 of Kolderup's flashback narrative, the 1972 in which we are ourselves reading the book? Even in Tellingstedt, the "story-town" in which Kolderup makes his corner of sane living—even there everything he encounters in his progress from immobility to silence only confirms the necessity of atheism. Would it not lead to blackest despair if we thought that the world had actually been planned to turn out as it did by an all-wise, all-foreseeing God? The title of Schmidt's early trilogy, *Nobodaddy's Kinder,* is as appropriate for Kolderup and his crew, superficially the happiest and most "fulfilled" of Schmidt's creations, as it ever was for the outcast voyeurs who appeared in some of his most memorable earlier fictions.

With their monomaniacal insistence on a series of constantly recurring views and prejudices, their horrified fascination by the sexual and excretory functions of the human body, their failure to observe the verbal taboos polite society imposes on most of us, Arno Schmidt's central intelligences resemble all too often those pathetic old men one sometimes sees in our city streets, arguing loudly with absent enemies, shaking their fists and shouting abuse into emptiness. But then—Schmidt's work is an indictment of the very conditions that make such men what they are and then prove incapable of providing help for them. His criticism of "Blut-und-Boden" romanticism, of resurgent militarism and nationalism, of telly culture and pornography, is usually just and almost invariably effective—not least because made with so much humour and self-persiflage. He has an unfailing ear for the nuances of living speech. He has a rare feeling for literary form, coupled with a Stakhanovite capacity for taking pains, which makes it an exciting adventure to unravel his narrative strands, follow his ingenious involutions and listen for the subtle and constant play of echo and counterpoint.

In two indispensable essays, "Berechnungen I" and "Berechnungen II", Schmidt has himself provided a guide to many of his procedures and explained their rationale. He has created a number of interrelated, complex central characters—Georg Düsterhenn in "Caliban über Setebos", Daniel Pagenstecher in *Zettels Traum* and William T. Kolderup in *Die Schule der Atheisten*—and has surrounded these with mostly grotesque minor characters in a distinctive world evoked with a wealth of cunningly selected detail. He has devised actions, sometimes minimal and sometimes complex, sometimes realistic and sometimes fantastic, enabling his central protagonists to exhibit fully their quirks, their obsessions and their potentialities. He has conjured up a fictional ambience in which all the sympathetically presented characters care deeply about literature, in which literature is of central importance, in which literary knowledge and literary taste function as an index of civilization.

A school for atheists? Perhaps—though at times it seems more a school of Manicheans, or for those who believe that some evil demiurge is amusing himself at man's expense. But in reading *Die Schule der Atheisten* we undoubtedly enter a school in which we may usefully learn to question accepted values and conceive some respect for lonely, odd, usually underpaid and socially powerless intellectuals of a literary turn of mind—a respect which may yet prove a not unwelcome antidote to the self-hatred and self-doubt that afflicts so many of us who answer, at least in part, to that description. We may learn rather more scatology than most of us would like (that does get rather tiresome at times); but as a school of often grotesque verbal wit and fancy *Die Schule der Atheisten* is so enjoyable that many of its alumni will inevitably be drawn to that higher academy represented by *Zettels Traum*. But even if they go no farther they will never forget the distinctive if sometimes irritating voice of the story-teller and raisonneur who has been their teacher—the voice of Arno Schmidt, whose combination of the provincial with the experimental (a "productive misalliance" rightly praised by Peter Demetz) is proving for many one of the pleasures they would least like to miss in the literature of postwar Germany.

I4

FICTION OF I972

(f) DAVID STOREY

Pasmore

Pasmore is a simple story, though not always simply told. A London college lecturer, the son of a coalminer, suddenly suffers from unaccountable fits of depression. His historical work seems meaningless, and he cannot bear to touch or be touched by his wife. He stumbles, or sleepwalks, into an affair with another woman. In spite of her quite superhuman blankness, his joy in life is briefly restored. (So is his feeling for his wife: a syndrome for which there should be some regular paramedical title, like Zeno's Complaint.) But things cannot last. He tells his wife, moves out, gets done over by a strong-arm man sent by a jealous husband. It seems time for the ritual journey North, for explanations to indignant parents and uncomprehending sisters. Pasmore is always polite, taciturn, apt to agree with those who find his behaviour impossible either to understand or to excuse. But he never budges from the notion that his passions are both above and beyond his control.

Back in a London flat, he sinks into a total and slovenly apathy, punctuated by the humiliating misery of weekly visits to his children. His wife leaves the house whenever he comes in. Soon he discovers, more to his surprise than the reader's, that she has taken up with another man. It seems time for the ritual tragicomedy of drunken desperation: in Pasmore's case being arrested for loitering outside his own house with a pocketful of threatening telegrams. ("I challenge

---

(*f*) DAVID STOREY: *Pasmore*. 201 pp. Longman. £2.

(*g*) C. P. SNOW: *The Malcontents*. 237 pp. Macmillan. £2.25.

(*h*) SUSAN HILL: *The Bird of Night*. 185 pp. Hamish Hamilton. £1.95.

(*i*) ALFRED DUGGAN: *Knight with Armour*. 306 pp. £2.40; *The Lady for Ransom*. 280 pp. £2.25. Peter Davies.

(*j*) NATHALIE SARRAUTE: *Vous les entendez?* 222 pp. Paris: Gallimard. 17fr.

you to meet me at dawn stop fishing rods at thirty paces.") His collapse is total. After a visit, and a punch in the face, from his father, he takes to his bed. When he leaves it, he hardly makes sense to anyone. There is nowhere to go but home. Since the lover has moved on, that is where he goes.

All this is described in Mr Storey's most obstinate and obsessive prose. Sometimes the pared-down style is plain to the point of pretentiousness. "It was the first meal he had had for several days. He drank some wine. He felt happy." That is the Hemingway of *Across the River and Into the Trees*, more self-parodying than self-effacing. There is nothing glib about the dialogue, either.

"D'you come here often?"
"No", he said.
She nodded, took her drink, sipped it then put it down again.
A moment later she picked it up again and finished it completely.
"Let me get you another", he said.
"I'll get it."

The deliberate staccato suggests not only a nervous meeting faithfully transcribed, but the meretricious brevity of a Pinter film-script. (The visit to Pasmore's parents also seems to be written with the camera in mind.) Mr Storey is right to strive for economy, but a few of these 200 pages are bald rather than bold.

And the boldness is only one character's friend. *Pasmore* is entirely Pasmore's property: the central figure is allowed not only an all-consuming passionate inconsistency, but a total blindness to anyone else's moods. After a violent scene with his wife (and much smashed crockery) Pasmore "could do nothing at all except stare at the wall, appalled that anyone, not least someone who knew him so well, could be so immune to his suffering". *Her* suffering merely gets up his nose. "The thought of her sickened him: the distress, the demands." "He began secretly to despise her: someone who could so easily be deceived. Her naivety irritated him." His fits of remorse are as egocentric as the actions which provoke them. That he should injure what he loves is supremely his tragedy, not theirs. When he takes his children on their disastrous outings, he feels "a sort of terror ... at their incapacity to be reassured". Not, of course, at his incapacity to reassure them.

There's a wide streak of male chauvinism here, for those who like it. (A common condition among the hypergamic working-class, also known as Porter's Complaint.) Pasmore will get few cheers from sexual egalitarians for passages like this:

He couldn't rid himself of that image: another man, in public, in possession of his wife. . . . He held his head, trembling and crying. What on earth could any man want with her?

The last sentence is particularly fine. But it should be set against another piece of Pasmore's mental furniture:

that instinct which had told him from the very beginning that women were superior to men. . . . What came out of their wholeness, this sense of life, was something which men could only compose for themselves by edict, that moral order which they fitted onto life like a suit of armour, hoping to contain from the outside what could only be directed from within. So it seemed to him that women were little less than gods, drawn here to love and be loved, to praise and be praised, the sole illumination of men's struggle to exist.

It's Gravesian rather than Lawrentian, and a fine piece of theory. Pasmore's wife, silly cow, can't understand a word of it. Perhaps it feels a lot less godlike to lie awake masturbating beside a husband who has lost all desire. Pasmore's behaviour suggests not gods but mothers, whose adult self-sufficiency is an object of resentment as well as admiration. "All he had ever wanted was wholeness." But when things are going well, who is to admire the fact that he can ride without hands? "Whatever qualification he placed upon it, his life was full of richness; yet there was no one to appreciate it but himself." No one good enough, perhaps.

But *Pasmore* is far from a silly book, and its ravenous demands cannot merely be met with a few pieties about the importance of developing moral relationships based on tender feelings for the sovereignty of others. It is a fine piece of masculine subjectivism, a bawl from the heart well worth setting opposite *The Pumpkin Eater* or *The Love Object*. Its settings and trappings are conventional: Mr Storey is interested in inner life, not interior decoration. If he sometimes abuses his talent, it can stand the strain; and the overworked adjective "powerful", in his case, does not merely mean writing in a loud voice.

(g) C. P. SNOW

The Malcontents

TWO YEARS AGO C. P. SNOW completed the sequence of eleven novels,

Strangers and Brothers, on which his literary reputation will ultimately rest. In the later volumes there was evident a concern with
what is happening to English society in the widest cultural sense. The
penultimate book, *The Sleep of Reason*, dealt with a murder case
based in part on the Moors murders, and the failure or refusal of the
young to accept the materialistic standards of their society is one of
the principal themes. The completion of a work like *Strangers and
Brothers* must have left any writer pondering what to do next. A
lengthy pause might have been expected, but Snow's appetite for the
complexities of modern life and his zest for the act of writing remain
undiminished, and *The Malcontents* carries on the arguments about
youth and society conducted in *The Sleep of Reason*, except that
where the young people in that book viciously rejected the power of
reason, those in this one virtuously accept it.

The Malcontents thus reads very much like a twelfth volume in the
series, with Lewis Eliot left out. Without being one of the major
novels, it has throughout a powerful storyteller's grip, and it contains
some of those passages of insight into the ways in which human beings
react to each other which stand out so surprisingly in the efficient,
even flow of Snow's writing. Such a passage occurs when Stephen, the
principal character, tells his mother of the scandal in which he is
involved, in the certainty that he will get support from her. He is
astonished by the wholly personal, unsympathetic quality of her
response. "This is unspeakable", she cries. "How do you expect us
to get through this?":

The cry, high-pitched, was angry; so, when he turned to her, in disappointment that was emptier than disappointment, was the expression on her
face. The fine features were ravaged: her mouth was open, she might have
been a football fan shouting at the referee: the remoteness, the coolness,
had gone, all gone.

The shock is as much the reader's as Stephen's, yet the hysterical
egoism of this generally calm, capable woman seems to be just right.

The affair in which Stephen and six of his friends are concerned is
the centre of the book. The seven, who call themselves "the core", are
students at the university attached to an orderly cathedral city, and
some of them live in the locality. They have come across a bit of local
Rachmanism, which leads through an agent to an influential Tory
MP, and they are preparing to expose it. Suddenly they learn that the
details of their whole operation are known and, more than this, that
they must have been made known by a member of the core. The

group turn in on themselves, and by argument and discussion try to discover the traitor's identity. Then one of them walks out of a window at a party, perhaps as a result of being given LSD. He dies, an inquiry follows, all their plans are ruined.

It would be wrong to give more details of the developments in a tale which has something of the puzzle interest of a detective story. A similar creation of suspense can be found in *The Masters*, and here as there it is splendidly maintained. Yet it must be said that, as an engine for ordering the action, this exposure of Rachmanism is far from satisfactory. It is treated with the deliberate vagueness used by Henry James in dealing with the operations of revolutionary conspirators, but one is still left asking questions. Why did it have to be "two weeks and three days" before "the balloon" was "ready to go up", how did the core hope to make the attack stick when so many similar exposures have failed for lack of hard evidence, why should the exposure have been affected by the death of one member of the core and the trial of others on drug charges? To these questions one attentive reader found no answer, except that all this did not really interest the author. The Rachmanism is machinery used to get the story going, and it is not meant to be investigated too closely.

It is particularly because of this structural weakness that *The Malcontents* cannot be regarded as one of the more important novels, but the characterization of the seven young people also lacks the suppleness and subtlety of Snow's finest creations among dons, scientists and civil servants. The middle-aged or old tend to create the young in their own image, and it is difficult to accept the more intellectual of these young people. The working-class radical contemptuous of student politics and regarding ideas of revolution as "a blink in a middle-class eye" is very convincing, and the Jewish Marxist, the drug-taker who remains throughout on the fringe of the group, and the sexy daughter of a rich surgeon, are acceptable minor figures. It is Stephen, his girl Tess, and their friend Mark, whose purity of motive often seems pure priggishness, and whose conversation is surely not that of any young people anywhere, whether Tess is crying out, "It's a pretty dark tunnel to be in", when referring to their situation, or Mark is advising Stephen, "Whatever you do, you must do it in your freedom."

Yet it is possible to make too much of this. It seems likely that Snow knew the chances he was taking in creating such figures of a generation far removed from his own, as James understood the improbabilities he was letting himself in for in putting down on paper the revolutionaries of *The Princess Casamassima*. And James's eloquent defence against the "probable ironic reflexions on the full licence for sketchiness and vagueness and dimness taken indeed by my picture", might be made in a slightly different form by Snow. He began, it is clear, from the point that the malcontents of his title had to be moved by the attempt to do something good, something that would in a small way improve society, rather than by any personal or purely political motive. Their motivation had to be intellectually reasonable, because in the terms of their creator the use of reason is identifiable with goodness. Grant these assumptions, and characters like Stephen, Tess and Mark are inevitable. One may find them unacceptable, but it should not be thought that they were conceived in a spirit of literal realism, any more than was James's much-derided Hyacinth Robinson. Novelists learn to accept, and to try to use, their own limitations, and that is what Snow has done here.

With this said, it remains true that the finest things in the book are not the pictures of youth, but the relationships of the young and their parents, like that of Stephen and his inhibited, periphrastical father; or the hostility built up between Stephen and the conventionally-minded solicitor Hotchkinson, to whom he goes for advice. The brief portrait of Hotchkinson is done with casual brilliance:

Hotchkinson was wearing a suit of heavy ginger tweeds. He was a very big man, heavy-shouldered, thick through the chest. In a doughy small-featured face the eyes were shallowly set with full flesh or underlids beneath them, which gave him an expression assertive and surreptitiously salacious. His voice was strangulated, husky, and high, such as one sometimes hears in star games players or other massively muscular men.

Scenes like this interview between Hotchkinson and Stephen, or those in which Stephen tries desperately to come to terms with his parents, have a subtlety and depth not excelled by anything to be found in *Strangers and Brothers*.

(*h*) SUSAN HILL

The Bird of Night

THERE HAVE BEEN clues here and there in her previous books that Susan Hill was, like many of the rest of us today, troubled and fascinated by the apparently arbitrary way in which human beings are dismissed as "mad", by the possibility that the so-called insane are saner than the world cares to admit. But even considering the wide range she has so far covered, it would have been a rare guess that hit on the subject of Miss Hill's new and strange novel. *The Bird of Night* is in the form of an old scholar's ruminative memoir, a last tribute to the only relationship that has in eighty years really counted, his painful, patient, generous love for the mad poet Francis Croft. We are to accept that Francis, a survivor of the Somme, has now been recognized as a genius, as the major English poet of the 1930s; young men plague his crippled, solitary friend with their tape-recorders and impertinent questions, begging for "papers", letters, anecdotes. But Harvey, now a recluse on a wind-swept Suffolk estuary, is still obstinately loyal—there are no papers, he will say nothing about the great man, he will only record, haphazardly, some incidents of the friendship he embarked on, little knowing how it would devastate his life.

At no point does Miss Hill refer, even obliquely, to any sexual expression of the love between Francis and Harvey. At no point does any woman appear in the story, and the two men—one already something of a literary lion, the other a meticulous academic—are scarcely ever shown except in each other's company. When, at one of his earlier mental crises, Francis is committed to hospital in Battersea, his dour Scots father visits, deeply embarrassed by the "odd" ménage and by the disgrace which, in his eyes, Francis's manic behaviour has brought on the family. There is a publisher, a doctor, a silent peasant family in Venice (for whom Francis insists on buying lavishly unsuitable presents)—otherwise, the memoir consists entirely of the old man's efforts to tell the truth about the poet and his madness.

Miss Hill has tried hard, without too obviously avoiding the odd few lines "quoted" from Francis's work, not to give us too much evidence on which we might so easily disbelieve that genius was displayed. She relies on occasional references to public recognition of Francis as a great poet, on extracts from Francis's diary describing the pain of a poem's gestation, and on an assumption that the reader will spot how a midnight walk in a wood in deep snow became the "well-known" poem about the owl. It is a large assumption and a daring one for any novelist, and one is uneasily conscious throughout this book that Francis is under half-conscious scrutiny—would a genius babble so emptily about the delights of London society, about

Harvey being his big brother, about being on the train to Venice? Is his petulant childish behaviour—a Hamlet telling Horatio he does not understand what life is about—intended to show us the genius or the madman? Francis is, indeed, very much a Hamlet figure, portrayed as lonely, manic-depressive, increasingly paranoid, given to sudden whimsical escapades. In his worst periods, when Harvey is nearly murdered or driven insane himself by incessant piano-thumping and alarming truculence, the poet is forgotten and the relationship between a man and his friend, the long despairing days and womblike existence endured for love, dominates the book. Here Miss Hill is very good indeed, suggesting the nightmare with amazing restraint, allowing us to see just how loyalty is capable of suffering, without a trace of self-pity appearing in the old man's account.

Of her own talent there can now be no doubt—Miss Hill has established in a remarkably short time that she writes with very considerable control and power, using the minimum of stylistic elaboration yet suggesting a strongly poetic instinct for precise images; she has also now shown that she is ready to tackle possibly the most risky and unlikely material open to a woman novelist—a depiction of genius, insanity, a tale of two men who loved each other many decades ago, a tale with no sex, no politics, no topicality. Even if we are not wholly convinced of the poet's greatness, this remains a brave and moving novel about madness, and the speculation it raises about the value we put on unbalanced lives is not to be lightly forgotten.

(i) ALFRED DUGGAN

Knight with Armour and *The Lady for Ransom*

ALFRED DUGGAN was one of the best historical novelists of this century. A reissue of his works is both welcome and overdue. It is to be hoped that the dour and stodgy jackets enshrouding this first couple will not put off new readers.

He is a prime example of the symbiotic relationship between the historian and his fictional interpreter. Research being a full-time job, some of its most distinguished practitioners have been unable to fit into their crowded schedule many, or even any, experiences of human action, of the kind whose records they amass. Scholar-adventurers have nearly always been archaeologists: Myres, Lawrence, Pendlebury. Historians are more inclined to remain in the study, when they give thoughtful pronouncements upon the motives of men of action, like celibate popes upon marriage. (Alexander the Great has attracted a lion's share.) Grote never set foot in Greece on account of bandits, had but the vaguest idea that its geography had formed its history, and went to his grave unaware that Demosthenes was the kind of man who would have been an embarrassment at the Liberal Club.

One lifetime is not long enough both for the facts and the truth. Duggan, whose first book, *Knight with Armour*, would have been happily accepted by many sound writers as their crowning achievement, had spent his preceding forty-five years in qualifying himself to extract the truth from the facts.

Of Argentinian-Irish and American descent, he became Lord Curzon's stepson; had an Oxford career which might have come straight out of *Zuleika Dobson*; passed, and saw, rapidly through Marxist atheism, returning to his Catholic faith; enlisted in 1939, as a ranker, in a special force which was a kind of commando prototype; and, on being invalided out after the Norway operation, went into a munitions factory, where he finished the war years at a bench.

Between Oxford and the war, he had studied, like Lawrence, the Crusader castles of the Middle East (perhaps, like Lawrence, with Malory in his rucksack), and became absorbed in Byzantine history. At home he rode, and knew thoroughly the horse both in health and sickness. The importance of this lore to medieval history emerges from his work like a revelation.

One of his best books, *Conscience of the King*, is set in the Dark Ages, with Cerdic, a ruthless opportunist, helping along for profit the descent of barbarism, and offering a snake's-eye view of his betters. Ambrosius, the last Count of Britain, is in 470 still a Roman general, competent in discipline and strategy; but his scratch infantry, half trained, half barbarous, crumbles around him in battle. Forty years on, the infamous Cerdic just gets away with his life at Mount Badon from Arthur's cavalry. Artorius, a pure-bred but adaptable Roman, has been to Constantinople, brought back a herd of the big horses still unknown in Britain, and trained his riders in the techniques of the fully-mailed Byzantine cataphract, with war-saddle, stirrups, lance and sword. His comitatus vanishes into a western sunset; the big horses (a brilliant insight this) keep mating with the native ponies, so that the breed dies out and cavalry tactics with it.

But in one lifetime, the day of the legions is over, and the medieval knight has cast his first shadow over north-west Europe.

It is roughly five centuries after this watershed that *Knight with Armour* opens, and Roger de Bodeham, landless cadet of a minor English manor, expends the last three years of his young life among the travails, squalors and miseries of the First Crusade.

Evelyn Waugh, obituarizing Duggan, wrote: "Though in his working years entirely happy in his private life, he surveyed contemporary history with nothing but calm despair." It must have been the despair of a Stoic soldier-philosopher. No one has better transmitted the sight, smell and feel of those ages in which things fell apart and the centre could not hold. Eternal verities are defined mostly by their absence, like the setting of a wrenched-out jewel; but definition remains. The secret of his enduring vitality lies in this, and in the astonishingly detailed follow-through of his historical imagination.

He knew not just war, but specific war; the feel of sunheated armour on unwashed skin in the stinking slum of the siege-lines; the cruel lives of the horses; their desperate importance to the knight who, his one mount dead, can slide down out of knighthood in a single hard campaign and find himself a mere man-at-arms. Roger is middling poor, middling brave, middling quick on the uptake. As the muddled, corrupt, inefficient war drags on he grows hungry, thirsty, dirty, armour-sore; loses his ambitious young wife, picked up along the way, to a knight with a better eye for main chances; feels the simple vision he set out with fade into a stubborn, pedestrian honesty. He just manages to die within the Holy City—flung down into its streets from the fighting on the walls—unshriven, because that morning the confessors had had too many calls upon their time, and without communion because he has been so sick with dysentry that he was afraid of throwing up the Host. It is told as it was, without a sermon, without a sneer.

It is a war fought among the ruins of civilization. All that is left of Rome is its mighty fortresses; the Roman skills are dead. Ramshackle siege-towers collapse before the attackers mount them; not a man has drilled in his whole life under arms; they cannot even march without blundering into each other. Into a forgotten past has vanished the day when Alexander, running his eye over the phalanx before battle, saw a single man fiddling with an unready javelin-strap, and shoved him by hand out of the line.

The chief character of Duggan's second book, *The Lady for Ransom*, is called Roger, like that of his first. (Perhaps he was even so diffident as to suppose *Knight with Armour* would sink without a trace.) We are here a few decades back; the Crusade has not yet begun, unravaged fields bear vines and olives, straight Roman roads pass intact temples and marble tombs. The Emperor in Constantinople is hiring Norman mercenaries to repel the infidel; among them Roussel de Balliol, the Red Fox, essentially a landless pirate, nevertheless a nobleman leading his own band of knights and soldiers. His obligations to Christendom sit lightly on him; his urgent concern is to find himself a fief, if possible with a serviceable castle. Land gives wealth and status, but the owner of a castle can, if need be, defy his overlord.

With this novel the real Duggan style emerges. First-person narration plants the story *in medias res*, and deploys a double humour of hindsight and insight, touched with bitterness, as the goggle-eyed Normans encounter the ancient sophistications so soon to disappear. Duggan was never beguiled by the devil in sheep's clothing who urges writers to equip the past with a modern anachronistic conscience. His people have the morals of their time.

The Red Fox never gets his fief; but *Lord Geoffrey's Fancy* is a delightful jaunt among the fiefs of Frankish Greece; a happy interlude of *amour courtois*, chivalrous little wars fought in silk surcoats, decent overlords doing their best by their schismatic Greek tenants, bearing up pretty well under small trials like excommunication; a midsummer knight's dream, with Dukes of Athens living on the Acropolis, and old gods smiling in the woods.

This book was a return to the Middle Ages from a splendid foray into ancient Greece and Rome. *Elephants and Castles* makes sense (in itself no mean feat) and entertainment from the wars of Alexander's successors; and Duggan never wrote anything better than *Three's Company*, a masterly account of poor old Lepidus, the obtuse angle of the triumvirate, stuck helplessly between the brilliant rake Antonius, and Octavius the clever prig, winner of the end-game. (Michael Ayrton's wickedly witty jacket should be preserved; it won't be bettered.)

With this very last book, *Count Bohemond*, Duggan returned to the scenes of *Knight with Armour*, this time from the standpoint of the high command. We get the aspirations, ambitions (fiefs and castles, of course), intrigues; the deep-felt unassailable obligations of the good vassal, sometimes victorious over those of the Christian pilgrim; devout vows dashingly kept or quibblingly evaded; savageries which seem explicable, between religious fanaticism and the pressures of war. The formidable Bohemond is left in mid-career; the sequel which would have completed his story Duggan did not live to write.

His few faults were mainly defects of virtues. Nearly all his books are too short; not just in that one would like more, but that dialogue often has to carry too heavy a load of information. But the pill is well coated in a crisp, easy style, steered neatly between false archaisms and grating modernisms. A certain scent of the medieval, which is retrieved by Zoë Oldenbourg, does get lost; but the essential matter is never falsified. He creates few stereotypes, though his belief that all eunuchs were obese and mentally warped suggests he never read Dr Burney's journal upon the singer Farinelli. These are trivia in the context of a high and consistent standard. He is an irreparable loss to the historical novel, and it is well that what he gave it should be preserved.

(*j*) NATHALIE SARRAUTE

Vous les entendez?

IN *Vous les entendez?* Nathalie Sarraute resumes her vocation as a registrar of the unutterable. With effortless malevolence, she puts a match to the dead wood of polite conversation and shows it up as an alibi, a cover-story for the "sous-conversations" which are socially inadmissible except in fictions. Just below the affable traffic in clichés by which most of us survive, sentiments of a more hurtful kind are continually lobbying for air-space; in Mme Sarraute's cruel and exact novels they get it. Like Ivy Compton-Burnett, she colloquializes human encounters down to their roots and strips all authenticity from the blameless tip of them which is all we usually see. There could be no better method for pillorying the vacuity of conventional dialogue, in life or in books.

Her victim in *Vous les entendez?* is not an entirely new one: it is the connoisseur. In *Les fruits d'or*, Mme Sarraute took her knout to the pet phraseology of the literary pseuds; this time it is the "art-lovers". As in that earlier novel, the ado is, very pointedly, about nothing. Before it was a novel, also called "Les fruits d'or", which was the non-existent excuse for much critical posturing and bickering; now it is another art-object, a rough stone sculpture of an animal from some pre-Columbian source. This creature (and no English word can preserve the unkind ambivalence of the French *bête*) belongs to no namable zoological species but is a cross between several. It is a metaphor and not a straight imitation of the natural world.

Its owner sits admiring it, and himself for owning it, in the company of an old friend. The living is gracious and he is, judging by the words he actually speaks, the unflappable aesthete; smug, appropriative and fiercely watchful of the cultural decencies. But he has his worries, and under his own roof too. Upstairs there are his children and they are frighteningly far from sharing his own reverence for his possessions. Instead, the acoustics of *Vous les entendez?* are dominated by the sound of their uncontrollable laughter. The young generation are neither numbered nor named, but as *ils* they wield great power, and their collective iconoclasm towards the idol on their father's table dislocates utterly the ease and security in which he habitually lives. There is anguish, therefore, in the question which the father puts to his quiet, uncommitted friend: "Vous les entendez?" But the friend is not much help, so studiously balanced and reasonable is he; the only consolation he can rise to is of the "we were young too, once" kind.

Downstairs, then, we have Art and upstairs Nature scoffing at Art's pretensions, and *Vous les entendez?* comes into being as the trouble-shooter in this intractable dispute. It is a series of fantasies of reconciliation, coming and going in the imagination (*the* imagination rather than any particular imagination) and, in the end, by the repeated failure of its efforts, widening the fissure it had set out to plug. The father oscillates between postures (or fables) of tyranny and abjection, but there is no way he can free himself from the grim situation in which he has been put. For his difficulties are not familial ones at all, he is a man abruptly deprived of his protection against the realities of life itself.

His art-collection, and the stone animal in particular, are his security. He may fancy that he picks up choice pieces in order to rescue them from decay and restore them by their solitary confinement in his house. Actually, however, it is they which have shielded him against the acknowledgment of his own decay and mortality.

The orderliness of art is an illusion which has sustained him, but it cannot stand up to the spontaneous, anarchic laughter that it has now provoked. Spontaneity is what the art-lover has fought perversely to amortize, and for him Nature is sufficiently and safely available in his stone animal. But the worst of it is that he has made a fetish not only of art but of his language, whose dead forms also have to be measured against the healthily communal peals of laughter, the "cascades de candeur" which threaten him with an unwanted immersion in common humanity.

Vous les entendez? wrecks the art-lover's standing in every way. He is unmasked psychologically, aesthetically and even politically— since the language that he uses is that of the master class of connoisseurs and any usurpation of it by underlings, i.e. his children, is a grave transgression. But Mme Sarraute's novel is not an opportunistic tract, riding on the back of the youth movement. It cuts much deeper, by demonstrating, with chilling intelligence and brevity, the falsehoods of all resort to words and the vanity of supposing that language has any lasting hold on reality. Its one small consolation is to show that if all language is false, some languages are falser than others.

15

DISPOSSESSED AMERICANS

CURRENTLY, the Indian is as American as organic food. Whereas a few years ago, at a time when size and colour determined the quality of fruit and vegetables, few volumes, with a handful of honourable exceptions such as those published by the University of Oklahoma Press, occupied the middle ground between anthropological monographs and pulp fiction, the situation is today vastly different. Dee Brown's *Bury My Heart At Wounded Knee*, for many months high on the American best-seller list, represents the most successful publication in a renewed outburst of enthusiasm for literature on the Indian, which has seen a development of Red Studies along the lines of Black Studies, and has encouraged the reprinting of many titles. The first Americans are no longer the last to receive attention.

Numbers and distribution apart, there are good reasons for distinguishing between Black Power and Red Power. Historically, servitude must be compared with subjugation, depersonalization with dispossession. Culturally, the relationship of Indian and European

---

DEE BROWN: *Bury My Heart at Wounded Knee*. An Indian History of the American West. 487 pp. Barrie and Jenkins. £3.50.

VIRGINIA IRVING ARMSTRONG (Compiler): *I Have Spoken*. American History through the voices of the Indians. Introduction by Frederick W. Turner III. 206 pp. Chicago: Swallow Press. $6.00 (paperback, $2.95).

ODIE B. FAULK: *The Geronimo Campaign*. 245 pp. Oxford University Press. £2.60.

CIYÉ "NIÑO" COCHISE and A. KINNEY GRIFFITH: *The First Hundred Years of Niño Cochise*. The Untold Story of an Apache Indian Chief. 346 pp. Abelard-Schuman. £2.50.

VINE DELORIA, JR.: *Custer Died For Your Sins*. 256 pp. Collier-Macmillan. £2.75.

STEPHEN LONGSTREET: *War Cries on Horseback*. The Story of the Indian Wars of the Great Plains. 335 pp. W. H. Allen. £2.50.

WILLIAM L. McDOWELL, Jr. (Editor): *Documents relating to Indian Affairs 1754–1765*. 657 pp. University of South Carolina Press for the South Carolina Department of Archives and History. $20.

HARRISON BIRD: *War For The West 1790–1813*. 278 pp. Oxford University Press. £3.45.

W. McKEE EVANS: *To Die Game*. The Story of the Lowry Band, Indian Guerrillas of Reconstruction. 282 pp. Baton Rouge: Louisiana State University Press. $8.95.

involves a multitude of contrasts and connexions, which at various stages of American history have been invoked to justify or condemn national attitudes. The stereotype and, to a degree, the response of the Indian have excluded solutions by assimilation or equalization: even the most intransigent liberal would hesitate to propose bussing Indian children, and to the extent that alumni of the Carlisle Indian school are no longer prominent in the world of sports it could be argued that reservation life has grown more, rather than less, central to communal recognition by American society at large.

From the earliest days of colonial settlement, fascination, conscience and self-interest have shaped opinions and attitudes towards the American Indian. Illusion and reality have compounded the widest possible variety of views, from those depicting the Indian as the Noble Savage to those urging that North America be rid of its native vermin. Missionaries, traders, soldiers, and frontiersmen adopted more strikingly different opinions of the significance and standing of Indians than did, at a greater distance, literary and liberal observers. From afar, cults have been formed to celebrate an exotic nobility, render homage to military prowess in campaigns whose outcome was all too predictable, and at the present day, to honour societies which neither polluted nor ravaged their environment. If the Indian had not existed, Americans would have had to have invented him in order to define the indigenous limits of their new society: as it was, the United States extended from where Europe stopped to where the Indian began, and its quality and achievement could be gauged in relation both to feudal restraints and to aboriginal anarchy. In this sense, primitive and dispersed though the Indians were, their presence provided an essential yardstick of comparison and the means by which the achievements and failures of White American civilization could be assessed. The reputations of Nature and the Indian rise and fall sympathetically, so that an age of flight from urban decay and high-rise living (even though the steel of the structure may well have been erected by Mohawks) to the rural simplicity of communal life and "fresh" foodstuffs is prepared to appreciate the availability of a paperback edition of the American Indian Cookbook.

The advance of American civilization into Indian territory unites symbolic qualities, frontier experience and dramatic adventure. The line of descent from Ned Buntline to John Wayne is clear and complete; the greater subtleties to be found in literature at the level of

Last of the Mohicans and *Little Big Man* may depend parasitically upon the same basic themes, manipulated against the conventional form. The liberal guilt of the undoubted conqueror seems reflected in the choice of events given emphasis: Custer's last stand, whatever it may prove, hardly reflects credit on the United States Army, but has been recounted time and again in tones not used to describe the disasters at Cawnpore and Isandlwhana. Some savages, it appears, are nobler than others. And, despite the growth of psychological complexity in the delineation of conflicts between Whites and Indians, it would seem improbable that the essential element of dramatic development will be abandoned so long as a canyon, a skyline and an Indian capable of a death-defying leap upon an unsuspecting horseman remain available. Social outcasts the Indians may have remained but their role in the concept of the West is secure.

Frontier experience overwhelmingly discounted Indian virtues: fear and contempt were, at best, glossed over by irritation at the savages' refusal to conform to the conventions of White society. Throughout the eighteenth and much of the nineteenth centuries the trading frontier encouraged the worst elements of both civilizations to display themselves in the least favourable light. Documents describing their contacts and relations make for grim and monotonous reading. *The Colonial Records of South Carolina* have reduced to scholarly proportions a series of episodes centred upon trade disputes, war parties, scalp deliveries and fatal brawls between settlers and Indians. Circumstances admitted of no lasting agreements: as one officer interrupted his chronicle of events to remark:

The Savages are an odd Kind of People; as there is no Law nor Subjection amongst them, they can't be compelled to do any Thing nor oblige them to embrace any Party except they please. The very lowest of them thinks himself as great and as high as any of the Rest, every one of them must be courted for their Friendship, with some Kind of a Feeling, and made much of. So what is called great and leading Men amongst them, are commonly old and middle-aged People, who know how to give a Talk in Favour of whom they have a Fancy for, and that same may influence the Minds of the young Fellows for a Time, but every one is his own Master.

What was observed in 1757 was to hold good for more than a century after: delegates of a system of political democracy resting on the principle of representation could not accept—though it would admittedly have conflicted with their own material interests to have done so—that Indian chiefs had no right to surrender lands which were not merely tribal property but, literally, the gift of God. If Indians broke treaties the cause was not simply that, judged by the tests of Western civilization, their terms constituted acts of fraud; it was rather that the surrender of land was unthinkable within an Indian cosmology.

Throughout the centuries of progressive dispossession a constant theme recurs in which custodianship and natural dependence form the Indian case for resistance. From Pontiac's declaration that

These lakes, these woods, and mountains were left us by our ancestors. They are our inheritance; and we will part with them to none. Your nation supposes that we, like the white people, cannot live without bread and pork and beer. But you ought to know that He, the Great Spirit and Master of Life, has provided food for us in these spacious lakes, and on these woody mountains. . . .

there are direct links, irrespective of time and tribe, to Crazy Horse's blunt assertion that "One does not sell the earth upon which the people walk", and the Supreme Court testimony in 1915 of a Yakima Indian Chief that

God created this Indian country and it was like He spread out a big blanket. He put the Indians on it. They were created here in this country, truly and honestly, and that was the time this river started to run. Then God created fish in this river and put deer in these mountains. . . . For the women God made roots and berries to gather, and the Indians grew and multiplied as a people. . . . My strength is from the fish; my blood is from the fish, from the roots and the berries. The Fish and the game are the essence of my life. I was not brought from a foreign country and did not come here. I was put here by the creator. . . .

If one views the Indians as practising ecology before the White man, having destroyed the buffalo, turned the Great Plains into a dust bowl, stripped the forests and polluted the rivers and lakes, found it necessary to devise the term and propose belated palliatives, then the shift from an attitude of contempt to one of respect becomes more understandable. Nature was conserved by the Indian and destroyed by the White.

It cannot be pretended, however, that dignified and moving statements such as appear in Virginia Armstrong's *I Have Spoken* represent more than an aspect of Indian reactions to White incursions. It was always possible to obtain Indian signatures to treaties; from the beginning to the end of the Indian wars their warriors fought on both sides. An alliance with the White man, credible enough when the

Indian position lay in maintaining a balance between French and English or British and American, becomes a matter of mercenary gain when Apache scouts provide essential assistance in tracking down their own nations in the desolate South-West. Despite the firmness with which Indian spokesmen held to their basic beliefs, most Indians would make any sacrifice to secure alcohol, arms and ammunition. If they obtained too little of the last two items, they secured all too much of the first: British rum, French brandy, and American whisky proved more effective than military might in destroying Indian resistance.

The survival of tribes as societies required isolation from trade and settlers, and this was provided by the establishment of reservations in remote and impoverished regions. The consequence was existence in name rather than in fact: tribes which had come to terms with their environment, however forbidding, were moved hundreds of miles to become abject dependents of an impotent and graft-ridden government agency. The outcome was decay rather than preservation and, in the immediate aftermath of the post-Civil War years, mass escapes and widespread death and destruction before the roving bands were destroyed, forced to surrender, or broken up. The trans-Mississippi West after 1865 provides the closing, and most spectacular, phase of Indian warfare, in which the opposing forces were so unequally matched that White defeats seemed not only testimony to the invaders' incompetence but proof of Indian military prowess. Perhaps the campaigns were distinguished rather by a more neutral quality: the savagery with which both sides conducted themselves.

Narratives such as *Bury My Heart At Wounded Knee* and anthologies such as *I Have Spoken* stress the cruelties and massacres involved in the repression of the Indian and the dignity with which White arguments were refuted. There is ample evidence to sustain these views. Against them, however, must be set the parallel course of Indian atrocities, which even if excused by Dee Brown as imitative of prior acts against them, still create a record of torture, death and destruction from whose details one is glad to be excused. The quantification of competing acts of extinction is rarely enlightening, and in the case of Indian wars such a quantification must be set against the imbalance of military resources and the implication that massacres conducted by Whites are proof of duplicity whereas Indian killings were at best reactions and at worst "natural". Such views have led to sharply differing estimates of Indian leaders. Odie B. Faulk concludes his study of *The Geronimo Campaign* by praising his subject's "dignity, his heroism against overwhelming odds, and his knowledge of that bravery . . .: these enabled him to survive as a great American".

On the other hand, Geronimo's nephew, Niño Cochise, held his uncle in considerably lower esteem: he declared him to be "not the world's smartest man, not even by Apache tribal standards. When he was drunk or suffering with a hang-over which was frequently the case, he was either an absolute dullard or a ferocious beast. When cold sober, he was a bombastic speaker. . . ." Whichever opinion seems the more acceptable—and the language in which Cochise's memoirs are presented seems on occasion somewhat odd—prominence in war did not guarantee nobility in character. Few leaders can be accorded the undoubted respect due to Chief Joseph of the Nez Percés. Their feats were often as wantonly cruel as they were physically re-markable.

A similar assessment could be made of their military opponents. So long as conflict occurred east of the Mississippi the Indians consti-tuted formidable allies or opponents in campaigns conducted on foot in heavily wooded areas under conditions of primitive firepower: their allegiance could tip the balance between rival White detachments. After the mid-nineteenth century the Indian problem overlapped that of Western expansion. The Eastern tribes had either been expelled, like the "civilized tribes" of Georgia, were suffered to exist in still in-accessible regions, as was the case with the Seminoles of Florida, re-tained a distinct but detribalized existence in remote rural areas, colour and local knowledge preserving the identity of groups such as the Lumber River Indians of North Carolina, or were relegated to restricted and stagnant reservations from which an occasional and exceptional individual such as Ely Parker, the Seneca Indian who became Grant's secretary during the Civil War, would emerge.

The struggle west of the Mississippi assumed very different forms: the horse rendered it more mobile and the existence of overland routes to the Pacific provided a constant reminder, except in the most in-accessible and generally least habitable areas, of the growing promi-nence of White interests. Plains Indians, with a way of life dependent on access to the buffalo herds, found their basic resource destroyed for pleasure and fashion and their migratory movements brought forcibly to an end; mining rushes took no account of Indian sensibili-ties. So the Black Hills of Dakota, a sacred place of the Sioux and granted to them in perpetuity by the Federal government, became, in the wake of gold discoveries, the scene of warfare which would culminate in Custer's disaster at the Little Bighorn. The Nez Percés, who had lived on amicable terms with the White man throughout the century, were driven into flight and violence in the 1870s by orders to quit their remaining lands so that prospectors could extend still further the search for gold. Only in the South West, where the country, the Mexican border, and the reputation of the Apache each contributed to the delaying of pacification, was the issue long in doubt. Here, too, the problem was one arising not from comparable resources but from that of trapping mobile and elusive raiding parties.

The army had been set a thankless and disagreeable task, for which it was neither prepared nor equipped. Indian wars had always threatened to blemish, in a campaign of minor military significance, reputations won in wars of historic importance. The risk was made much greater by politicians' refusal to maintain a credible military force after the occasion of its necessity and glory had passed. Veteran Revolutionary officers commanded inexperienced men and lost prestige in futile attempts to overcome British and Indians in the Old North-West, and Civil War generals, recently accustomed to deploy divisions in the most massive campaigns of the nineteenth century, found themselves saddled with responsibility for tracking down a few hundred Indians, with a scarcely larger force at their disposal, in a vast and inhospitable region of the country.

The regular army in peacetime, as both Odie Faulk and Stephen Longstreet make clear, was neither a comfortable nor an elevating institution: life in remote Western forts and garrisons provided only hardships relieved by drunkenness and immorality. An officer committed to honest dealings with the Indians found his policy sabotaged and his career imperilled by decisions made under political pressures in Washington, failure and deception on the part of the agents of the Indian Bureau, and graft and corruption such as provided the raison d'être of the "Tucson Ring". If confidence could not maintain peace, war offered no prospect of professional glory; to defeat the Indians smacked of massacre and was at best an achievement of no apparent magnitude; to be tricked or humiliated by the enemy would destroy all chances of promotion, inevitably uncertain and slow once the opportunities of the Civil War years had evaporated. So in one trifling ambush a reputation gained on a succession of major battle-fields could be ruined.

The pursuit of marauding bands, in conditions ranging from intolerable heat to unbearable cold, through hundreds of miles of sparsely occupied territory, was not calculated to improve relations between the military and the Indians. But for the aid of Indian scouts and trackers it would have proved an impossible task, at least until improvements in communications and weapons provided the army with conclusive superiority. Railroads, telegraphs, heliographs, Gatlings and light artillery finally closed the ring around adversaries whose mobility could then be countered and whose firepower was never more than primitive and limited. Even so, the quarter of a century after the close of the Civil War saw the army almost continually engaged in a series of unrewarding and arduous operations, which could not lead to military triumph and which too often resulted only in humiliating reverses.

As the nineteenth century drew to a close it became evident that the Indian would be compelled to die in unavailing protest against the destruction of his way of life or make such terms and extract such advantages as he could from the conquerors. As early as 1877 the flight of the Nez Percés, in their attempt to take refuge in Canada, caused consternation to the first tourists in Yellowstone National Park. In 1885, less than a decade after his triumph at Little Bighorn, Sitting Bull accepted Buffalo Bill Cody's invitation to tour the United States in his Wild West Show. "The killer of Custer" sold signed photographs after performances. Geronimo, detained in Florida and Alabama after 1886, and moved to Fort Sill, Oklahoma, in 1894, was allowed on special occasions to leave his place of exile. He visited the St Louis fair in 1903, selling photographs of himself, kneeling with his rifle, face contorted with hatred, which tourists could purchase for 25 cents. A photograph of slightly later date, taken about 1906, displays another facet of his personality: he appears in shirt-sleeves and top hat at the wheel of a Pierce Arrow. Between times he had taken part together with other Indian chiefs in the inaugural parade of Theodore Roosevelt, a president well aware, by experience and personality, of the mythical potentialities of Western history. The Indian had completed the transformation from threat to emblem, from military to circus side-show.

The capitulation did not, however, solve the Indian problem, or rather the White man's problem of reconciling conscience and convenience. Clearly, in terms of numbers and of locations, the Indians, except for such an occasional unpredictable oversight as had left an Oklahoma group in possession of oil-rich land, had been relegated to the forgettable fringe of American life, a condition which the Bureau of Indian Affairs was content to accept, at least until John Collier became Commissioner during the New Deal years. Since that date there has been more interest, many proposals, and few fundamental changes, though the situation has been challenged by Indian activists such as Vine Deloria, Jr, whose *Custer Died For Your Sins* blends humour with indignation in a fashion which may appeal to those un-moved by the solemnity of other radical manifestos. But the strongest impulse behind the proliferation of works on the American Indian would appear to be the application of liberal consciences to dramatic episodes.

Stephen Longstreet's *War Cries On Horseback* and Mr Brown's *Bury My Heart At Wounded Knee* cover very similar ground and dwell on many of the same incidents: although Mr Brown offers superior documentation the major distinction between the two ac-counts seems to be that of his subtitle—"An Indian History of the American West". Whether this can be taken literally seems highly doubtful. It is rather a narrative highly sympathetic to the Indian, garnished with stylistic tricks such as indicating months by their Indian names. This avoids the basic problem of whether it is possible to write an Indian history within an American context, and permits reliance on an essentially familiar approach of relating the tale of broken treaties, harsh repression bred of total misunderstanding, self-ish acquisitory instincts, and final betrayals. The ground rules for the writing of Indian history are so firmly established that one sym-pathizes with Mr Longstreet when in a moment of irritation, he refers to its "banal quality". There was, perhaps, a banality of evil before Hannah Arendt applied the term to Eichmann's activities, and when one reads, in Mr Faulk's account, of the conditions on the train which carried eastward the captured Apaches, it is impossible to fend off a sense of premonitory apprehension. Yet what is to be made of a record of centuries of alternately incited brutality?

The Indian neither knew nor sought, except in terms so alien as to be unintelligible, justice from the White man. The clash of a sub-sistence with an exploitive society was bound to be determined in favour of the dynamic force. Numbers and strength set aside, the Indian was bound to subjugation, if only because his practice of subsistence was fatally breached by a desire to trade. The needs of the Indian were always greater than his capacity to meet the White man's requirements: a permanent balance of payments deficit could be redressed only by the surrender of land. Once begun, this process would be pursued to its logical conclusion of White satiation and Indian degradation. There is ample justification for the unease which afflicts liberal consciences.

At this late date it would seem impossible to undo the accomplished fact. One can hardly believe that, with the best law and lawyers in the world, the Iroquois will regain possession of upstate New York. If Indians exercise their right to leave the restrictions and marginal support of the reservation, assimilation would seem the likely consequence. Even if this was accepted as a desirable end to centuries of struggle for a separate existence, it would not, at a time when description as a minority has lost its pejorative sense and acquired respectability, appear appropriate as a solution to America's first racial problem. On the other hand, to advocate a return to the land would appear as inadequate a proposal as that of resolving Black grievances by encouraging Back-to-Africa enterprises. Although, in practical terms, much could be achieved by attacking the problems of inadequate aid and insensitive bureaucracy, the outcome would obscure, not eliminate, a fundamental dilemma.

The extent and forms in which Americans' perception of themselves has been affected by the Indian presence require for their description the literary audacity of a Leslie Fiedler and the historical omniscience of a Perry Miller. Yet it is clear that without the Indian the frontier concept would have lost the greater part of its impact: the conflict between civilization and barbarism could not have acquired a dramatic quality if presented simply as the conquest by man of his physical environment—this may account for the rapid decline of interest in American moon landings, which would benefit enormously as a public spectacle from the discovery of a band of Apache on a commanding height. Whatever the real or imaginary consequences of the frontier process may have been, the Indian stands in cultural and physical contrast to the expansion of American civilization, of which, however, he represents the first example. The White man must, therefore, set guilt at supersession against pride of achievement: as doubts multiply about the quality of his success, so anxiety grows to make amends for past judgments and impositions of inferiority.

If one believes that the United States has moved as far in the direction of emphasis upon material development as is compatible with the maintenance of the fabric of society, then the Indian becomes not merely a pricking of the conscience but an exemplar of the good life. Attitudes of this kind may not be borne out by statistics or acceptable to the majority, but the role of the Indian in North America has never been subject to verifiable definition; it has been the fate of the first Americans to live in a fashion which, in the eyes of their successors, has remained perpetually unreal. Whether an improved historical reputation will lead to improved material conditions remains to be seen. If it does not, the Indians will have no cause for gratitude towards their White admirers, whose support will again amount to no more than misplaced sympathy.

16

STALIN'S SPECTRE

LENIN IS ALWAYS WITH US, say the slogans in Moscow. As a proposition for everyday use, it is inescapably correct. One can't read a paper, a banner, or a poster; one can't listen to the radio or watch television without being aware that Goebbels-like assertions are being made. Lenin, packaged as an avuncular godhead, is "eternally alive". Lenin is "more living than all the living".

His Second Coming was devised during the fiftieth anniversary of the Soviet state in 1967. A huge portrait of him was suspended from a barrage balloon, hovering over his mortal remains in the mausoleum on Red Square. At night it was eerily lit by searchlights: Lenin in the sky with di-am-onds. Down below on the streets, some irreverent citizens were asking each other if they had heard the one about the old Jew who wrote to Lenin to complain about the years of delay in getting a new flat—only to be called into the local party headquarters. There he was told quite firmly that Lenin had been dead since 1924. "Dead, is he?", the Jew said. "When I want him, he's dead; when you want him, he's eternally alive."

Lenin, long dead, is safe for resurrection. Yet there is another, unofficial, canon. And in that canon, Vladimir Ilyich Ulianov takes a poor second place to the Georgian seminarist with the crippled arm, Iosif Vissarionovich Djugashvili, commonly known as Stalin. The never-to-be-formulated slogan, STALIN ALWAYS HAUNTS US, is more properly descriptive of the present Russian psyche than any forgotten-by-repetition assertion about Lenin's immortality. It was Stalin who bossed the Soviet Union for thirty of its fifty-five years of existence. It

---

ROY A. MEDVEDEV: *Let History Judge.* 566 pp. Macmillan. £5.75.

ABRAHAM ROTHBERG: *The Heirs of Stalin.* 450 pp. Cornell University Press (IBEG). £6.90.

PETER REDDAWAY (Editor and Translator): *Uncensored Russia.* 499 pp. plus 75 illustrations. Cape. £5.

NATALIA GORBANEVSKAYA: *Red Square at Noon.* Translated by Alexander Lieven. 288 pp. André Deutsch. £2.95.

Selected Poems. Edited and translated by Daniel Weissbort. 156 pp. South Hinksey, Oxford: Carcanet Press. £2 (paperback, 80p).

was Stalin who killed at least 15 million of his fellow-citizens, among them his closest military and political associates. It was Stalin who killed the peasants in the name of collectivization to achieve the Socialist Paradise.

There is hardly a family in the Soviet Union which did not suffer —in some cases masochistically—at his hand. And if you talk to a Russian family now, and it comes out in conversation that Uncle Tolya, say, died in 1938, the proper response is to raise one's eyebrows and to inquire gently, *"Tak?"*—"Was it . . . so?" *"Tak"*, they may reply, elongating the vowel sadly; or "No, no, no, it wasn't . . . so— Uncle Tolya died in his bed."

The spectre of Stalin still haunts the people. It haunts those who have set themselves up to be their leaders. Stalin is there, and many people need him. Without his memory to cling to, their lives would be nothing.

On Stalin's death in 1953 Russian schoolgirls, used to mouthing those poems thanking Stalin for living on this Earth, were ordered to let down their pigtails as a sign of mourning. At the same time, some of their mothers and fathers were crushed to death on Red Square as the body of Stalin was inserted into the Mausoleum to join that of Lenin. Stalin, after all, was the Godhead. Stalin was the Tsar. Stalin is dead; long live Stalin. What else, after all, had the Russian film industry been about for thirty years? What had *Pravda* printed except paeans of praise for the great dictator? Stalin was no mere Sun King; there was a film in which Stalin was the heart of the solar system and the sun came to Stalin. Stalin was an expert in genetics, linguistics, industrialization, collectivization, politics, art—in short, every field of human activity as understood by Soviet science. But now Stalin was dead. Not for the first time in Russian history the question was posed: What to do?

What has happened to Stalin's body since that day in Red Square in 1953 has mirrored official attitudes to his rich political legacy. Three years after Stalin's death, the "new Tsar", Khrushchev, for his own political reasons, condemned Stalin outright in a speech to the Twentieth Party Congress (a speech that remains unpublished in Russia). Two Congresses later, in 1961, Stalin's embalmed body was subjected to indignities. All primped-up in death, he was removed overnight from the Mausoleum, to the presumed posthumous pleasure of Lenin who, having found the Georgian coarse and conspiratorial in life, was now to be left in happy isolation in order to be "always with us". Stalin was planted in a patch just to the left of the Mausoleum (as you look at it from GUM), appropriately enough next to "Iron Felix" Dzerzhinski, founder of what is now the Committee of State Security (KGB).

Khrushchev, never popular with ordinary Russians because of his earthy ways (the "broad masses" can be terrible snobs), fell in 1964, thereby shuffling off Stalin's body on to the present "collective" leadership.

There is abundant evidence of a rehabilitation of Stalin from 1965 onwards, but it was only in 1970 that Stalin's patch acquired a larger-than-life bust. The bust was placed there without publicity, but the news quickly spread among ordinary Russians who drew their own conclusions at this physical manifestation of re-Stalinization. The leadership had, in any case, caused the ninetieth anniversary of Stalin's birth to be celebrated in 1969—a fact important in itself.

Today, persons unknown adorn Stalin's grave with flowers in plenty and with a regularity that ensures that they are always fresh.

Khrushchev wanted a memorial to be erected to the victims of Stalin; the present leaders erected a memorial to—Stalin. Russia is now set fair on a neo-Stalinist course for reasons which are entirely understandable, given the political upbringing of a Brezhnev. To have pursued the "harebrained" policies of Khrushchev to their logical conclusion would have meant calling into question—again—the whole continuity of Soviet history, dominated for more than half its time by Stalin. More important, it would have meant calling into question the legitimacy of the present leaders, many of whom are Stalin placemen. But, most important, to have pursued de-Staliniza-tion through to the end could have resulted in the erosion of the present leaders' power. Anyone who rules that basically anarchic country must be aware of the popular support there is for a strong leader in the centuries' old tradition of despotism and of the historical determinism that requires that he should rule absolutely or not at all. To rule absolutely, a leader like Brezhnev needs to perpetuate the Stalinist machinery of power: the all-embracing bureaucracy, within and without the party, and the all-embracing deterrent, the KGB.

All five books listed above, directly or indirectly, are concerned with the legacy of Stalin. Four of them come from Russian sources, though none has been published in the Soviet Union.

Until now there has been no concerted Soviet attempt to put Stalin and Stalinism into a balanced historical perspective. Roy Medvedev's *Let History Judge* is precisely such an attempt. Medvedev, philosopher, educationist and historian, wrote this book for a Soviet readership and, going through the proper channels, innocently presented his manuscript to Soviet publishing authorities. It was turned down. He therefore authorized its publication abroad.

In this he was following his twin brother, Zhores, a geneticist, whose books, *The Rise and Fall of T. D. Lysenko* and *The Medvedev Papers* (a masterly study of Soviet bureaucratic obstructionism in practice), have also been published in the West. Zhores also earned himself a place in a "psychiatric" hospital for a time.

Roy Medvedev's work was begun in 1962, during a Khrushchevite period that was less dark than now. It was completed in 1968, when there were already great patches of darkness across the Moscow noon. It is, by any standards, a remarkable book. It is particularly remarkable that it was written in Russia, in the most difficult of circumstances, with no official access to research facilities. Not for Medvedev, as for Marx, the rich resources of some British Museum.

Medvedev has drawn upon personal depositions, letters, never-to-be-published books, and the memory of that political long-distance runner Anastas Mikoyan in a bold and scholarly attempt to look at Stalin from the outside while he himself is still inside the system. It is an admirable feat of mental prestidigitation, for the writing is fresh and the documentation vivid and detailed. We are presented with the fullest list yet of those who perished during the purges. Moreover, there are some fascinating glimpses of that world of the 1930s: of Kaganovich's brother, for example, the Minister of Aviation, shooting himself in Mikoyan's lavatory. Medvedev, though very free with historical parallels to Stalin, is commendably reluctant to reach conclusions without a minute consideration of the evidence. He goes into the whole of the Kirov affair again and concludes that Stalin's guilt in the Kirov assassination, which triggered off the purges, "now appears plausible and, logically and politically, almost proved". He devotes equal scholarly attention to the insistent allegation that Stalin was an agent of the Tsarist secret police. After sifting all the evidence, he rejects the allegation.

Medvedev was expelled from the Party following a KGB put-up job, commonly called a "provokatsiya" in Russian, involving the publication of a manuscript by an émigré organization abroad. Nevertheless, he remains, in his own view, a true Marxist-Leninist. Therefore his book is not only an attempt to document the Stalin years; it is also one of political theory. Crudely paraphrased, the theory is that all deviations from Leninism are wrong and that Stalin was a cunning, power-hungry, but far from mad, deviant. The Dialectic-according-to-Medvedev is that Stalin was merely a fellow-traveller of the Revolution. "It was not love for suffering humanity", Medvedev writes,

that brought Stalin to the Revolution, but his thirst for power, his vanity, his desire to rise above the people and subject them to his will. For Stalin the Party was always just an instrument, a means of reaching his own goals.

After 566 pages of indictment (exposing the myth, fed by Svetlana Alleluyeva and others, that Stalin was ignorant of what was happening in his name) Medvedev reaches the following conclusion:

The Soviet Union passed through a serious disease and lost many of its finest sons. When the cult of Stalin's personality was exposed, a great step was made to recovery. But not everything connected with Stalinism is behind us, by no means everything. The process of purifying the Communist movement, of washing out all the layers of Stalinist filth, is not yet finished. It must be carried through to the end.

Medvedev has a touching faith in the underlying health of the Russian body politic. He hopes that the cancerous growth of Stalinism, fecklessly probed by the surgery of the Twentieth and Twenty-Second Party Congresses, will not prove malignant. It is an understandable hope for one who loves his country, who wishes to consider Stalin as a nightmare aberration from the true norm, and who is able to make the jump of faith back to the alleged pristinities of a blameless Lenin.

Medvedev's political theory begs many questions for those whose unenviable task it is, in studying Soviet power, to separate the actual from the desirable. First, what are the organizational faults in a self-proclaimed Marxist-Leninist state that allow a tyrant to kill millions of his fellow citizens in the name of Marx or Lenin—or in his own name, or anybody else's? Secondly, what is now to stop some as yet mute, inglorious Ivan Ivanovich Pronin from plotting and killing, as Stalin plotted and killed? Where are the checks and balances? Because of his theory, Medvedev has never to address himself to these crude but capital questions.

Above all, Medvedev ignores the question of power as exemplified throughout the whole history of the Soviet state. Lenin, who could be quite as ruthless as Stalin, understood that the Soviet Union is about power, about seizing power and then holding on to it, about using power, about abusing power. Stalin understood this. Brezhnev understands it. Medvedev will have none of this, preferring to put his faith in an as yet unpractised ideology.

The best part of Abraham Rothberg's *The Heirs of Stalin* is his final analysis of the Stalinist legacy. Here he shows a cognizance of how absolute power can corrupt absolutely not always to be found in the writings of American scholars. "What", he asks, "if the off-spring of the Revolution is truly and inevitably Stalin the cruel paranoid . . . a cancerous social and political organism gnawed by spreading malignancy?" What indeed? Especially if, like Medvedev, one would have us believe that the cancer was confined to Stalin alone.

Mr Rothberg's book is a useful summary, as its subtitle suggests, of "Dissidence and the Soviet Regime" since the death of Stalin. He sees clearly enough that de-Stalinization was never to be confused with liberalization, as it often was in the West. "People", he writes, "were not to be given enough freedom to contest seriously the decisions and purposes of the centre, only enough to fulfil the centre's purpose more effectively." In other words, there was to be a bit more carrot, and a little less stick, but the principle of centralized direction was to remain unaffected.

The title of the book, *The Heirs of Stalin*, is taken from the poem by Yevgeni Yevtushenko. Throughout the book there is a curious reverence for the obiter dicta of that talented hard-currency cultural export who is, by turns, "outspoken" and *Pravda*'s poet laureate. Equally curious is the inattention of the publishers' proof-readers— even Stalin did not slaughter the Party to the extent that only 50,000 members survived.

Mr Rothberg relies heavily on secondary sources from Moscow, including reports from Western correspondents there. There can be no substitute, however, for the real thing; particularly when, to paraphrase that *echt* dissident Andrey Amalrik, the fish have begun to speak. The *Chronicle of Current Events* is a very unofficial journal, passed from hand to hand in the Soviet Union. A recipient will read it, retype it with as many carbons as he can lay his hands on, and then distribute these copies to his friends. This process is laconically known as *samizdat* ("self-publishing", by analogy with *gosizdat* or state publishing). The *Chronicle* concerns itself with the struggle, and therefore, inevitably, with the fate, of those who want human rights in the Soviet Union. Such people are known as "dissidents" in the West.

When the *Chronicle* began publication in 1968 (long after the beginning of *samizdat* itself) its compilers, unknown now as then, could draw on a small geographical catchment area for their information. To judge from recent issues, the area is now substantially larger, comprising most of the larger "open" cities and even some that are "closed"; one must also assume that the readership is much greater. At the time of writing, twenty-three issues of the *Chronicle* have reached this country. In *Uncensored Russia*, Peter Reddaway has done an excellent job in editing the first eleven of them. He has divided the eleven issues into their subject-matter and added his own most helpful annotations. There is a section dealing with the "mainstream" of protest (Sinyavski-Daniel: Galanskov-Ginzburg), for example, and another with the protest movement in captivity. The book is illustrated with some quite remarkable and hitherto unpublished photographs of dissidents in exile and in camp conditions.

The dissidents are a heterogeneous collection of people. Some are pure Leninists of the Medvedev type, some are Christians, some are Social Democrats; others are Conservatives of a distinctly Powellite economic stamp (without ever having heard of Enoch Powell), or simply Russians despairing of that Russianness which has made Russia what it is. There is no dissident "leader" for any number of reasons: the disparity of attitudes outlined above; the tactical necessity not to provide the KGB with simply one target but to provide it with as many as possible; the fact that by being a dissident at all a man has paid a high price in courage for the freedom to think, feel, talk and write for himself as an individual. In so doing, he has opted out of the "collective", which means, through the looking-glass, that he has opted out of having any leader.

The dissidents, nevertheless, have one thing in common: courage. It is a courage unimagined and unimaginable by those who talk about the "alternative society" in the West. Many of the dissidents had fathers and mothers who perished in the purges. Many of them have a record of exile or prison themselves. In fact, having broken through a sort of sound-barrier of a courage amounting in some cases to recklessness, they have achieved that "internal freedom" of which Amalrik speaks. They have come out on the other side of some spiritual experience.

Many of the dissidents live very badly, yet they write dispassionately and with compassion. The *Chronicle of Current Events* is compiled with a factual dryness all the more remarkable for the circumstances in which it must be produced. It is difficult to be dispassionate if you are writing in one room—it may be ten feet by eight feet—in which you live with spouse and/or children. It may be one room in a communal flat, sharing a kitchen and a bathroom with, perhaps, nine other families. In such surroundings, it is difficult to achieve domestic harmony and to write dispassionately. Indeed, scenes sometimes occur which are more reminiscent of Gorki's lower depths than the brave new world presented by Soviet propaganda.

It is to this sociological soup that the KGB adds its own ingredients. Your dissident is followed everywhere by KGB agents (some of them women decked out as dowdy housewives; some of them *are* dowdy housewives). Your room is bugged by microphones, which inhibits conversation and encourages written conversation, as it were between deaf mutes. Your mail is at best opened before delivery; at worst never delivered at all. Your room is subjected to periodic searches by KGB agents who meticulously list all your books, papers and non-representational pictures and then take them away. Any Western visitors that you have may be photographed by the KGB as they leave your block, the light supplied by KGB car headlights. You run the daily risk of being arrested and put in jail for the statutory nine months' investigatory period (often exceeded). You are then brought to trial in the tiniest of courtrooms, packed from an early hour with plain-clothes KGB and a selection of rentacrowd workers deliberately misinformed about the nature of the case. The trial will be called public and your friends will not be allowed in because, true enough, the courtroom is full. Outside the court, your friends will be photographed by yet more plain-clothes KGB men and subjected to harangue and provocation by yet more rentacrowd workers, drunk from the KGB vodka provided in the courtyard round the corner. Found guilty (when was a dissident ever found not guilty?), you are sent to drag out your days in prison, in a labour camp, or in Siberian or Far Eastern exile. Possibly the worst sentence is to be sent to a psychiatric hospital (where General Grigorenko, among others, now languishes)—the most dreaded being the Serbski in Moscow. There, if you are not already mad, drugs may make you so.

It is against this background that *Uncensored Russia* chronicles with precision the fate of those men and women brave enough to say that they wish the rule of law to prevail in the Soviet Union. They rely for their wish on two documents. They are the Stalin Constitution and the Universal Declaration of Human Rights. Both of them are enforceable in Soviet law. Neither of them is enforced. The dissidents are confronted most frequently with two articles of the Russian Federation Criminal Code, articles 70 and 190-1. Both deal with "slanderous fabrications discrediting the Soviet political and social system". The maximum term under Article 70 is twelve years' "deprivation of freedom" and "exile". These two articles are enforced. *Uncensored Russia* tells us how.

The only person ever to be connected, publicly, with the compilation of the *Chronicle of Current Events* is Natalia Gorbanevskaya, born 1936, mother of two, unmarried. She was one of eight people who, on August 25, 1968, demonstrated on Red Square against the invasion of Czechoslovakia. It was one of the longest genuinely spontaneous demonstrations in recent Russian history: it lasted four to five minutes. The eight converged at the Lobnoye Mesto ("where you put your forehead to have your head cut off"), the ancient execution place just in front of St Basil's Cathedral. There they displayed their crude home-made placards—"Stop Soviet Interference in Czechoslovakia", and the like. They were immediately set on by individuals in the throng of people which is always milling about that particular place. Their placards were wrenched away and broken up. "Dirty Yids!" somebody shouted. They were physically assaulted. And as always on these occasions there was somebody, usually an old woman, but in this case a young one, who opined in the directest of terms that they should be done to death: these harridans are the direct legatees of Stalin. At this point the plain-clothes KGB operatives, who had been following the demonstrators all the way from their homes, closed in and bundled them into cars with the maximum unnecessary violence.

Five of the demonstrators (including Pavel Litvinov, grandson of the former Russian Foreign Minister, and Larissa Daniel, wife of Yuli) were eventually brought to trial and sentenced to various terms of exile. One of the demonstrators, Viktor Fainberg, lost many teeth during his arrest and in this unpresentable state was never presented for trial; instead, he was put into a psychiatric hospital, where he remains to this day.

Natalia Gorbanevskaya was not brought to trial immediately, allegedly because of her two young children, the youngest of which, not then one year old, she had with her on Red Square. Instead, she received out-patient treatment for an alleged psychiatric disorder. She used her time of freedom to compile an account of the demonstration and the subsequent trial. It is now published, in an excellent translation by Alexander Lieven, as *Red Square at Noon* (slightly abridged from the Russian original, which went by the simple title *Noon*). The book contains large parts of a transcript of the trial. Anyone who might incline to think that Soviet justice gets a bad press in the West would be well advised to read this book. If the circumstances were not tragic, it would read like some Ilf and Petrov story. Listen to that shade of Vyshinski, the Prosecutor:

The accused Litvinov and Delone were holding the banner "For Your Freedom and Ours". But what sort of freedom is intended in this case? If it is the freedom to hold such disorderly assemblies, the freedom to slander, then such a freedom does not and shall not exist. The slogan—"For A Free and Independent Czechoslovakia". Should Babitski not have known that it was just so that Czechoslovakia might be free and independent that troops of the socialist countries were sent there?

It is just worth pointing out that the Stalin Constitution enjoins, nay proclaims, freedom of assembly and freedom of conscience.

There was even a prosecution suggestion that the accused should have informed the authorities of their intention to demonstrate so that they could have had protection. One is happy to read that even in that small closed court this suggestion met with the only possible response: laughter.

Red Square at Noon is a positive hymn to the courage of men and women like Litvinov and Larissa Daniel and Gorbanevskaya herself. They came to the Execution Place knowing full well what the consequences would be. Gorbanevskaya herself was eventually brought to trial and sentenced (one uses the word advisedly) to a psychiatric hospital. Her term there ran from July 1970 until February 1972. "We commit no crimes", she writes, "that require concealment, while we are punished, as a rule, only for our convictions. And what is a conviction worth if it has to be hidden?"

Gorbanevskaya's poems, now published in a translation by Daniel Weissbort, read as tautly as may be. Gorbanevskaya has every right to be taut:

> Don't touch me! I scream at passers-by—
> they don't notice me.
> Cursing alien rooms,

I hang about alien lobbies.
But who will put a window in the wall?
Who'll stretch out a hand to me?
I am roasting over a slow fire.

The book of poems also contains, somewhat uncomfortably, a Western psychiatric judgment of whether she is mad or not (conclusion: she is not) and, more apropos, an account of her trial.

The more politically sophisticated dissidents admit that they can have little influence in changing the Russian pattern of events or even in improving the quality of Russian life. Few people, except the KGB, among the stodgy apathetic millions have heard of them, and then only through the foreign radio stations or if their trial has been pre-judged in the official press. In a word, the dissidents have no power.

Yet they go on, propelled by an inner compulsion, being picked off, one by one, at intervals of roughly six months (perhaps the KGB, too, works to a wall-chart "plan"), being sent to prison or exile for years and years and then coming back, like Amalrik and Bukovski, for more. They have got into the habit of thinking free, of thinking out of the surrounding mental drabness that contains and nourishes Stalinism. And once that habit, dearly bought, is indulged, it is difficult to shake off. Salvation has been reached.

A Western argument attaches itself to this personal salvation. The argument goes like this. The dissidents' courage rubs off on those they meet, in the camps and without. The dissidents' probity, shining through the thin paper of the *samizdat* publications, could, much more heavily concentrated, penetrate the skull even of the latter-day muzhiks. Much more thinly spread it could cover the whole of the Soviet Empire. But Russia remains Russian. Let wishful-thinking liberals ponder this cautionary tale: There are three boiling cauldrons. In each of them Soviet citizens are boiling away. A group of Western tourists is being shown the cauldrons as part of their hard-currency tour. The tourists are in the charge of a pretty young Intourist guide. "Here", she says, pointing to the first cauldron, "here are the Armenians. They are not allowed out." The Armenians boil on cue. "Coming to the second cauldron", she continues, "we have the Jews. According to the provisions of our Constitution, they are allowed out from time to time, but there is nowhere for them to go." The tourists gaze open-mouthed at the people in the third cauldron. "Who are these?", a tourist asks. The people in the third cauldron huddle wretchedly together as the water bubbles round them. "Those", the guide says, spitting, "are the Russians." "Are they allowed out?" the tourist asks. "They are allowed out at any time", the guide says. "But they rarely leave their cauldron. When they do it is only to collect more firewood. They bring the firewood back, stoke up the cauldron, and then get back in again."

17

CHOOSING A DICTIONARY

WHAT ARE today's bargains in English dictionaries? On the grounds that the latest is likely to be the most up to date, the British reader might well choose one or other of the two newest arrivals: the *Chambers Twentieth Century* or the new Hamlyn *Encyclopedic World Dictionary*. Ignoring the difference in price, his choice might be made easier by the fact that each dictionary is an extreme example of two very different types—a crammed and condensed word-book on the one hand, and an elegant, easy to use, helpfully instructive (at a some-what elementary level) "encyclopedic" work on the other.

Chambers certainly has far more words in it than *Hamlyn* or indeed any other dictionary of its size. It is true that, as befits a work published in Edinburgh, a lot of these are Scots, for it is far more generous to the speech of its own nation than any other general dictionary, the big *Merriam-Websters*, perhaps, only excepted. It is also rich in English literary archaisms, from Shakespeare, Spenser, Milton and Bunyan, more than any popular dictionary. But with all this, it contrives a noticeably larger word-list of the central stock of English common and specialized words than any of its competitors, and at the moment it is easily the most up to date of our dictionaries, with a host of recent scientific and technological words and many of the newer colloquialisms. *Anorexia nervosa, battered baby, biosphere, cold turkey* (withdrawal of drugs), *Flower People*, the new use of *hopefully*, the new adjectival use of *in, in-service, mind-blowing, pheronome, switched on, unisex*, and *velodrome* are among the items which most or all of its British rivals have yet to catch up with, and there are many others shared only by it and *Hamlyn* (together they are first with the *audiofan's tweeter, woofer* and *wow*).

Following the lexicographical revolution of the 1960s when the ancient obscenities at last made the grade of a general dictionary, *Chambers* now has them as well, albeit with some coyness of defini-tion in some cases and lack of objectivity in others (*fellatio* is judged "a sexual perversion"; *Hamlyn*, on the other hand, treats these items with the gusto and fullness they deserve).

To compress all this, plus the usual appendixes of foreign expressions, Christian names, weights and measures, and so on, within the covers of a single small, though now bloated, book of 1,649 pages, demands sacrifices elsewhere. These are in ease and clarity of layout (though the free use of bold type helps) and, often, in explicitness of definition. Everything possible is "run on", main senses are not separately numbered or otherwise marked off, and definitions are as laconic as may be, favouring, whenever possible, the "synonym" to the "analytic" type of definition, and sometimes plainly skimped or circular. Unlike its own "pocket" companion—the excellent *Chambers New Compact Dictionary*—the *Twentieth Century* has no "examples of usage" or brief "forcing" contexts to fix uses precisely.

Other British desk dictionaries, such as *Cassells*, *Collins* and the *Concise Oxford*, differ from *Chambers* in smaller or greater degree in all these respects. The *Concise Oxford Dictionary* has a smaller and at present less up-to-date word-list, but a less confusing layout for the more complex articles (which it subdivides into numbered major senses) and often more forthcoming definitions, as well as the best etymologies available in a British general dictionary.

Then there is A. S. Hornby's admirable *Advanced Learner's Dictionary of Current English*. Without exception, the *Chambers* and all other popular dictionaries assume, either tacitly or explicitly, that their users, being native speakers of English, will not need to be told that *baksheesh* does not take an article or plural, when and when not to use *the* with *church*, and that *intend*, *prefer*, *propose* (to do something, doing something) have a wider range of dependent constructions than have *hope* and *mean* on the one hand and *contemplate* and *consider* on the other. The *Advanced Learner's* is the only well-known dictionary which regularly provides information of this kind for its intended foreign learner users, in a clearly laid out dictionary of the central core of the English vocabulary, illustrated both with drawings and, liberally, with examples of usage.

At the farthest extreme from the laconic, compressed *Chambers* are the *Oxford Illustrated Dictionary*, with pictures, encyclopedic material and generous definitions, but a limited word-list, and the *Hamlyn*. The contents of the latter bear a striking resemblance to those of the big American *Random House Dictionary*, of which it is in effect a somewhat reduced and carefully anglicized version (both these dictionaries draw liberally on Random House's medium-sized and excellent *American College Dictionary*).

The "encyclopedic" element in the *Hamlyn* consists of its pictorial illustrations and the incorporation in its main word-list (it also has appendixes of the usual sorts) of, in effect, a potted world biographical dictionary, a dictionary of mythology and of literature and a gazetteer: at one opening, for example, we have *Guy Fawkes, Fata Morgana, Fatima* (the village in Portugal), *William Faulkner* and *Little Lord Fauntleroy*. Its chief innovation is the introduction to Britain of the standard American lexicographical practice of including a "Synonymy" in the main word-list; paragraphs appended to word-entries prescribing impressionistically how the members of sets like *abandon, relinquish, renounce* or *active, energetic, strenuous, vigorous* are or should be distinguished (in *Hamlyn*'s case these paragraphs mostly follow closely those of *Random House*). *Hamlyn* is a handsome book, its word-entries (following its American models) set out with great lucidity with the most common senses placed first, and its definitions clear, simple and ample. A much better dictionary for the learner than *Chambers*, but perhaps not such a bargain for the linguistically sophisticated, including the crossword-puzzlers who find *Chambers* so useful for their purposes.

The distinctive features of *Hamlyn* place it in the recent American rather than British tradition of commercial dictionary making. By comparison with most comparable British dictionaries it was generously staffed—thirteen editorial staff members and thirty-nine special consultants are listed. The major American dictionaries commonly enjoy still more imposingly large editorial staffs and draw on the advice of an impressive list of advisory editors and special consultants for numerous specialist fields of knowledge. The consequent heavy outlay naturally exacts a major (and itself costly) promotional effort to recoup this. That for the greatest modern American dictionary of English, the *Merriam-Webster's Third New International Dictionary*, when it was published in 1961 was described as "the greatest concentration of advertising ever used to promote a single book". In this case, it badly misfired.

Webster's Third was the result of more than a quarter of a century's labour by an editorial staff numbering more than 100, assisted by hundreds of expert consultants, and cost more than $3\frac{1}{2}$ million dollars to make. It runs to some 2,720 closely-packed triple-column large quarto pages in a very small but very clear type, containing some 450,000 main entries, and is doubtless the fullest inventory of contemporary English in print.

Its initial reception in the press of the United States was in general far from friendly, though British reviewers praised and welcomed it. The *Third* had broken with tradition in a number of startling ways, and these were imprudently highlighted in its publisher's own promotional literature. In order to make space for the 50,000 new words (many of them new scientific and technological terms) and a further 50,000 new applications of older words, the *Third* had jettisoned much of the encyclopedic material of its predecessor, the *Second* of 1934. It also left out many archaisms and regionalisms and ephemeral scientific terms which had appeared in the *Second*, and firmly excluded all expressions obsolete before 1755 (when Johnson's *Dictionary* was published). None of this pleased many American critics, who were (and are) accustomed to find information of most of these kinds in their dictionaries. But what caused greatest outrage was the *Third*'s abdication of what was popularly regarded as the traditional role of a Webster, that of supreme authority on correct English usage. It had opened the floodgates of permissiveness, providing a "say-as-you-go" dictionary, clearing the road to a progressive deterioration of the language of which it should have been the champion and defender.

What the *Third*'s editors had done was to abolish the register label "colloquial", replacing this by two others, "substandard" and "nonstandard", which they thought less misleading, and to adopt a policy of labelling with these terms and others such as "slang" only very cautiously and rarely. The dictionary's standard was now an informal written and spoken style, and many items were left unlabelled (as if stylistically neutral) which the dictionary's critics regarded as unsuitable for good educated use. The intensest heat was engendered by the *Third*'s tolerance of *ain't* ("though disapproved by many . . . used orally by many cultivated speakers"), *finalize* (regarded by many Americans as gobbledegook), *irregardless* and the new adverbs in *-wise*.

The traditional dictionary classification of linguistic registers into a few classes—formal, informal or colloquial, and slangy—is oversimplified. Many users of English have a command of overlapping and often intermingling registers and to assign particular items out of context to a single register may therefore be quite arbitrary. Also, in the past two generations written usage has become increasingly receptive to words formerly regarded as appropriate only to the various spoken styles, at first often for special effect but, as they become increasingly common in quite dignified settings, tending to lose their colloquial overtones and become stylistically neutralized; perhaps *hooligan, jazz, perm, snide, sideswipe,* and *gimmick* are examples. This process, which is of course not new to the history of the language (much older examples are *extra* and *mob*), seems to have proceeded most rapidly in the United States.

In these circumstances the labels "colloquial" and "slang" have become at least less certain and less easy to apply than they once were, particularly for American lexicographers, and the editors of *Webster's Third*, ignoring the fact that users of a language are always more conservative in their theory than in their own practice, courageously and honestly decided largely to dispense with them. In the event they seem to have over-reacted, and it is evident that many of the words they failed to label still retained from their history quite strong sub-literary connotations, as was demonstrated by some of the spoof passages in Webster-unlabelled jargon devised by some of their censors:

A passel of double-domes at the G. & C. Merriam joint in Springfield, Mass, have been confabbing and yakking for twenty-seven years—which is not intended to infer that they have not been doing plenty work—and now they have finalized . . . a new edition of that swell and esteemed word book.

In support of their own decisions the *Third*'s editors were in a position to point to many actual instances of the use of the offending expressions by (generally) quite reputable authors. These were drawn from their collection of 10 million quotations ($4\frac{1}{2}$ million of these culled from recent writings by the *Third*'s own staff). The 100,000 or so quotations actually included in the *Third* as illustrations of usage turn out to be predominantly near-contemporary, in a wide variety of styles, from newspapers and journals, from the speeches of politicians and from writers as varied as A. S. Eddington, Osbert Sitwell, P. G. Wodehouse and Mickey Spillane.

The discomfiture of the *Third*, especially in the matter of register labelling, had its effect on its successors and competitors in the field of "unabridged" American dictionaries. Two of these, the *Random House Dictionary* and the Houghton Mifflin *American Heritage Dictionary* are middle-to-large one-volume encyclopedic dictionaries, incorporating the usual potted literary-biographical-topographical information in their word-lists.

Without exactly naming names, the introductory matter to the

Heritage indicates that one motive for the making of this dictionary was to supply the American people with the guidance on acceptable usage which, by implication, the *Third* should have but had not given them. Certainly both these dictionaries deal expansively in "usage notes" or editorial comments on usage (another regular feature of American dictionary practice) with many of the items which had most excited the *Third*'s critics—*ain't, finalize*, and others. Both are liberal with certain register labels—"nonstandard", "informal", "slang", "vulgar". Of the two, the *Random House* is the more temperate, the crusading *Heritage* the more forthright: *Random House* accepts that *finalize* has forty years of wide currency behind it, but for the *Heritage* it is to be avoided as associated with the language of bureaucracy; *Random House* agrees that *irregardless* "does creep into the speech of good English speakers", but to the *Heritage* it is "never acceptable except when the intent is clearly humorous"; for *Webster's Third, alright* is all right though *all right* is more common, for *Random House* "it is not considered acceptable", for the *Heritage* it is "a common misspelling".

To provide its readers with the kind of guidance which its makers held "to be an essential responsibility of a good dictionary", the *Heritage* enlisted a "Usage Panel" of 105 "outstanding writers and speakers" whose opinions were canvassed on several hundred doubtful issues of usage.

The results of this were summarized and reported as percentages following the editorial usage notes which, as it turns out, sometimes overrule the panel's preferences: *simultaneous* as an adverb, 100 per cent disapproval; *ain't I* in writing, 99 per cent disapproval; *between you and I*, 99 per cent disapproval; *infer* as "imply", 92 per cent disapproval; *drunk drivers*, 83 per cent disapproval; and so on—but *drop-out* as a noun, 97 per cent approval. This particular jury was of course packed: its members were almost all elderly, very few being under fifty—they were all by definition eminent—and many were already known from their hostile reviews of *Webster's Third* to hold conservative attitudes to linguistic propriety.

Another recent major American dictionary—Clarence L. Barnhart's excellent two-volume *World Book Dictionary*—is unfortunately too little known in Britain, and is relatively expensive.

Besides dictionaries like these and the numerous smaller, more selective "Compact", "Pocket", "Little", "Junior", "Gem" dictionaries issued by the same houses, there are also numerous "School" and, in the United States, several "College" or "Collegiate" dictionaries, primarily directed at the lucrative market offered by the American educational system. All these are necessarily highly selective, for sheer reasons of space, for only very large dictionaries, like *Webster's Third*, or very compressed ones, like *Chambers*, can contain the whole range of vocabulary which a literate adult might expect to encounter—this has been estimated at 250,000 words (i.e. two-and-a-half times the size of an average book merely to list the head-words). One ground for omission of some items in several of these dictionaries has been an understandable (but perhaps scientifically questionable) desire to avoid giving offence—so not only are all obscene words rigidly excluded but so also are many of the racially offensive terms (like *guinea*, *kike*, *mick*, *spik*, *wop* and *yid*, though *nigger* and *polack* are usually retained).

In the matter of word-histories and etymologies, among the most reliable and informative of the general dictionaries is the *Concise Oxford*, with its careful etymological linking by cross-reference of the word discussed to other words or word-elements. Another general dictionary which may be specially recommended for its etymological treatment is the *American Heritage*. In this work etymologies and etymological interrelations are handled by reference to Calvert Watkins's fifty-four-page summary account of Indo-European roots and cognates, which constitutes a valuable and unique appendix. As for the two most recent of the specialist dictionaries of etymology, the *Oxford Dictionary of English Etymology* is informative on the origin and development of meanings as well as of forms, and includes from *OED* a skeleton history of each word from Old English times; and it has the most recently discovered etymologies (such as those for *boy*, *O.K.*, and *tuck*). The vocabulary of the larger and more expensive Klein's *Comprehensive Etymological Dictionary* is swelled by a large number of recondite Jewish and other Semitic terms, terms of biological science, proper names from Greek and other mythologies and English Christian names. It is also fuller and more modern in its word-list of generic words than *ODEE* is, with words like *cosmonaut* and *sputnik*, *myxomatosis* and *streptomycin*, the West Indian *zombi* and the Scottish *clachan*. It is full and apparently generally reliable on ultimate etymologies (but behind *ODEE* for *boy*, *O.K.*, and *tuck*), but largely neglects dates of introduction and lines of development. Both dictionaries have something to offer but the "standard" work on ordinary generic words must be *ODEE*, which will be still more

valuable when, with revision, its principal omissions and few lapses
have been corrected.

The nearest approach to a full historical treatment of the English
vocabulary at a popular price is the *Shorter Oxford English Dictionary*, the two-volume abridgment of *OED*, which offers a fairly
detailed account of the historical development of much of the modern
English vocabulary, substantially fuller and for many more words
than *ODEE*. But it is, after all, only the abridgment, only about one-
tenth of the size of *OED*. For a listing of the early variant spelling-
forms, for full etymologies, for the full range of dated and referenced
quotations, for a complete coverage of the ramifications of sense of
each word, for a complete account, with dates, of all derived and
compound words, for an exhaustive treatment of phrases and for-
mulas, and for innumerable scientific and technical words, obsolete
words and phrases, rare early words, cant, dialect and Scottish
words, one must turn to the magisterial work itself.

Recent researches (by H. Aarsleff) have shown that the *Oxford
English Dictionary*'s principles of the "historical dictionary" in which
"each word is made to set forth its own life-history" derive via
Liddell and Scott's Greek dictionary of 1843 from the ideas of the
German classicist and lexicographer Franz Passow, who first formulated them in 1812. Taken up by the Philological Society of London
in the 1850s, these ideas were argued into a scheme for a major new
English dictionary by Dean R. C. Trench and others in 1857 and
1858. The final realization of the dictionary itself owes most to the
Herculean labours and the example of James A. H. Murray, *OED*'s
first copy-producing editor, who personally edited almost half of its
15,487 pages. The completion of the editorial work on this tremendous dictionary by a staff of never more than twenty-odd in less than
fifty years was, it may surprise some to learn, a remarkable record
speed (other comparable foreign dictionaries have taken or are still
taking far longer).

OED's aim was to exhibit "the history and signification of the
English words now in use, or known to have been in use since the
middle of the twelfth century". By intention it excludes recent dialect
words and forms and those technical words "of which an explanation
would be unintelligible to any but the specialist"; it also, tacitly,
excludes the taboo obscene words and sexual uses of other words. It
is not perfect. In a few instances its sense analyses clearly require re-
doing. Words and senses are missing, as a glance at the *Supplement*

of 1933 will show. It is insufficiently exhaustive; its normal limitation of one or two quotations per sense per century is inadequate to account for the regional and stylistic variety of usage at any stage in the history of the language. Yet its overall reliability and fullness are astonishingly high. All subsequent general and etymological dictionaries are very heavily in its debt. The two-volume "Compact Edition" of *OED* produced last year by reduced microphotography places the dictionary within reach of those for whom the current price of £100 for the standard (and, for ease of use still preferable) edition is too much.

As a broad survey of the history of English vocabulary up to the end of the nineteenth century, it does not seem likely that *OED* will be superseded for some generations to come, if ever. But, even before *OED* was completed, it was becoming clear that even its collection of more than 5 million quotation-examples (of which 1.8 million were cited) culled from more than 15,000 volumes of text could not account for every detail in the histories of all words either in earlier periods or in all the countries and regions where the English language has been current in modern times. Partly for this reason, W. A. Craigie, who, with Murray as the other, was one of the two Scottish editors of *OED* to whom that great English dictionary owed so much, proposed in 1919 that *OED* should be followed with a series of "period dictionaries" of English on the *OED* model. Since then much of the scholarly effort on English lexicography has gone to fulfilling Craigie's plan. So far this has borne fruit in a *Middle English Dictionary*, now completed to L, *A Dictionary of the Older Scottish Tongue* (of Lowland Scots down to 1700), begun and edited by Craigie himself down to I and now completed to N, *The Scottish National Dictionary* (of Lowland Scots since 1700), now at T, *A Dictionary of American English*, also partly edited by Craigie and completed in 1944, and *A Dictionary of Americanisms* (that is, of only those words and expressions which originated in the United States), completed in 1951.

All follow *OED*'s pattern, whereby each defined sense is authenticated by a copious array of dated and referenced quotations from original sources, including, in *MED* and *DOST*, many unedited manuscripts, and, in *SND*, much evidence from oral information. All give an abundance of information on the histories of forms (for earlier periods often very complex and varied) as well as meanings. In every case they fill in the main outlines of word-histories, as presented in *OED*, with a vast amount of new detail derived from the massive reading programmes conducted separately for each dictionary. Many whole words, a huge number of specific uses of words and details of chronological, regional and stylistic distribution not noticed by *OED* are revealed by these period dictionaries, which thus abundantly testify to the soundness of Craigie's judgment. More recently two other substantial one-volume dictionaries on the same plan have been added—a *Dictionary of Jamaican English*, and a *Dictionary of Canadianisms* (including both expressions native to Canada and others judged characteristic of Canadian language or society). Among the obvious gaps in the coverage of national varieties of English, work is actively proceeding in university centres in each area towards dictionaries of Ulster English, Australian English, South African English and Caribbean English; and a Dictionary of Briticisms is also promised by an American lexicographer. Although it perhaps poses special difficulties, since only a small minority of its many users today are native speakers of English, it seems certain that a fascinating dictionary of Indian English also could be produced on similar lines to replace the 1886 *Hobson-Jobson*, which itself anticipated the modern fashion for "regional" historical dictionaries of English. (The second edition of 1903 was reprinted in 1968.)

One period for which Craigie's plan has yet to bear fruit is that of the English of England itself after 1475. In the 1920s and 1930s a large collection of quotation examples for the Early Modern English period (1475–1700) was amassed at the University of Michigan, but in 1940 work on this was suspended in favour of that University's *Middle English Dictionary*. Since 1966, however, scholars at Michigan have put the collection in order and they now plan to make selected portions of these materials generally available by publishing the quotations themselves in microfiche form. They will be beginning next year with some 20,000 quotations illustrating the uses of the modal verbs, and other subsets of the vocabulary will follow. The basis of this enterprise is a computer archive, from which microfiche, ultrafiche and other kinds of output can be generated and which can be easily corrected and supplemented by standard computer updating methods.

Another dictionary of the "period" type proposed by Craigie was a dictionary of Old English to replace the venerated but now antiquated and in some other respects unsatisfactory Anglo-Saxon dictionary of Joseph Bosworth and T. N. Toller (a supplement to this is expected shortly from the Clarendon Press). Active planning for the new dictionary only really began in 1968, but preliminary editorial work on the textual sources is now under way at the Universities of Toronto and Oxford. It is envisaged that this dictionary will be based on a computer archive of the entire corpus of Old English texts, something entirely feasible since this totals only a few million words.

Another historical dictionary which is only just emerging from the planning stage is the *Dictionary of Early Modern English Pronunciation*, being undertaken by a group of Continental anglicists, with its editorial centre at the University of Stockholm. The aim is to assemble all available statements or indications on the pronunciations of English words by early phoneticians, spelling-reformers, grammarians and lexicographers, and to set out the results as an alphabetical word-list which will show changes in fashion, as well as "regular" developments, in this aspect of word-history.

The original plans of the Clarendon Press for *OED* had always envisaged a supplement or a succession of supplements, essential to cover accessions to the language over the period in which the original dictionary was produced (1884–1928) as well as to make good any oversights that might come to light. The first result of this was the one-volume 1933 *Supplement*, a work which, though somewhat haphazardly compiled, does indeed achieve its aims. The new *Supplement*, which will bring the history of the language down to the present day, will be in three volumes of about 1,200 pages each, of which the first—covering the letters A–G—is now available.

The new *Supplement* will contain altogether some 50,000 main entries illustrated by about 360,000 quotations, incorporating all the material of the 1933 *Supplement* and so superseding it. As well as new words (such as *bimbo, endocrine*, and *gazump*) and new uses of older words (such as (top) *billing* and the modern scientific uses of *binary*), it will take in older words in current use which had not been included in *OED* and carry the history of these back to their beginnings—examples are (*a wee*) *deoch an doruis*, popularized by Harry Lauder but previously long established in Scots, and the taboo sexual words. The new *Supplement*, being edited by a staff of about twenty, is based on a carefully planned reading programme by a corps of readers energetically directed since 1957 by Dr R. W. Burchfield.

The method is essentially historical: a high proportion of the space is devoted to dated and referenced quotations covering the whole recorded history of the word or use. The *Supplement* attempts also to take in the standard vocabulary of all regions of overseas English. It remains to be seen whether, as well as labelling Americanisms, Australianisms, Scotticisms and the like, it will also overcome the insularity of most existing dictionaries, which, if they are British, label Americanisms (like *elevator*, *windshield* and the American pronunciation of *schedule*) but leave Briticisms (like *lift*, *windscreen* and the British pronunciation of *schedule*) unlabelled, and conversely. Clearly the new *Supplement* is a major event in the history of English lexicography and will be of enormous value, to the popular dictionaries among others, in establishing the vocabulary of the language as it exists today.

So far the only large-scale attempt to survey the regional, including the exclusively oral, vocabulary of the British Isles as a whole is Joseph Wright's six-volume *English Dialect Dictionary* (1898–1905), now superseded for Scots by the *Scottish National Dictionary*. As, contrary to popular belief, English dialect speech is neither dead nor static, it is arguable that a new dictionary of English dialects not only might be but should be made, on the lines of *SND* or better still the *Dictionary of American Regional English*. *DARE*, now under way at the University of Wisconsin, is based partly on excerpts from written sources—dialect literature, folklore journals, notes on regional usage published by the American Dialect Society—but also, and to a much greater extent than its nearest congener, *SND*, on fieldwork collections from oral informants by questionnaire and other fieldwork methods. It is hoped to complete this project by 1976, when the results will be presented in two forms: an alphabetical dictionary, giving forms and meanings in the usual way, with regional and currency ranges (distinguishing, for example, the age-groups preserving each usage); and a "Data Summary" of the fieldwork questionnaire providing statistics for each of several responses to a given question with the numbers and distributions—by geographical area, age-group, educational level, and occupational category—of the different responses, and in some cases a dialect map. The whole corpus on which the dictionary is based is being managed within a computer data-file, and it is intended that the data summary and the maps will be generated automatically by the computer. Thanks to a carefully limited set of directly comparable categories for the different kinds of information on each word entered into the computer system, it may even be possible to edit the dictionary itself largely within the computer system.

There are also under way two "conceptual" or "thesaurus" dictionaries (in the Roget sense), in which the synonyms will be laid out in historical (or reverse historical) order with the chronological range of currency of each one. From these it will be possible to tell the synonyms currently available at different stages in the history of English for each of a large number of "concepts", to learn for any given point in history which terms were old-fashioned and obsolescent and which the innovations, and in general to follow through the "conflicts of synonymy" in the history of English. One of these projects, by the English Language Department of Glasgow University, aims at no less than a conversion of the whole of *OED* into "historical thesaurus" form.

Among the many other decisions to be taken by a dictionary editor before he sets about his task—about the treatment of variant spellings and variant pronunciations, treatment of the etymologies, ordering of senses of multi-sense words, and others—the most central concern the selection of the word-list, the degree of refinement of meaning-analysis, and the defining style. All dictionaries of English to some greater or less degree draw on the work of their predecessors—first, generally, on earlier editions of themselves. Most of the popular British dictionaries are re-editions of works begun about the turn of the century, which in turn draw on the American *Century Dictionary*, itself based on the Scottish *Imperial*, itself based on the first *Webster*, and so on. The American dictionaries similarly exist in families, with a common word-stock and reused definitions (like the Random House-Hamlyn family).

But no self-respecting dictionary editor is content to rest solely on this ancient lexicographical tradition of plagiarism. For more recent usage and to discover neologisms, contemporary dictionaries have their own quotation-files, the largest being those of the Merriam-Webster office and the Clarendon Press. These files are the result of selective human reading and are thus costly to produce; but non-selective computerized excerpting is, with present techniques, quite inadequate to fulfil the same purposes. The quotation-files typically consist of paper-slips, each bearing a "key-word", a quotation containing the key-word, and a reference to the source from which it is drawn—a technique which, in Britain, goes back as far as Dr Johnson.

The quotation-file plays a still more central part in the historical or the period dictionary. For such works it must of necessity be very large—numbered in millions of slips—gathered by a vast reading-programme (commonly, in the English-speaking world, with the help of many volunteer readers) from a very large sample of the writings of the period covered, totalling thousands of volumes of texts. In illustrating by quotations their findings on the range and variety and the distribution in time and place and register of each sense of each word, these dictionaries inevitably also give a great deal of often otherwise inaccessible information on the thing the word denotes. Hence historical dictionaries, which also usually favour full and descriptive definitions, must also be to this extent encyclopedic. To accomplish them with their usual small staffs of five or six people demands however a long haul of sustained effort, and they frequently take generations to complete.

One useful, if obvious, principle of defining style, more regularly observed by the American dictionaries (and *Hamlyn*) than their British counterparts, is to define, whenever possible, by words more simple than the word being defined. The *Webster Third*'s new "analytical one-phrase" defining style is not wholly successful. This forbids sentence-breaks within a definition and in general any punctuation. When the notion being defined is at all complex it tends to lead to very long, breathless and involved constructions in which the reader is apt to lose his way. This example (the first part of *osmosis* sense 1) is not unfair:

the flow or diffusion that takes place through a semipermeable membrane (as of a living cell) typically separating either a solvent (as water) and a solution or a dilute solution and a concentrated solution and thus bringing about conditions for equalizing the concentrations of the components on the two sides of the membrane because of the unequal rates of passage in the two directions until equilibrium is reached.

Compare the *World Book*'s version:

the tendency of two fluids of different strengths that are separated by something porous to go through it and become mixed.

And the typically laconic (but somewhat abstruse) *Chambers*:

diffusion of liquids through a porous septum.

Gradually lexicographers of English are turning to complex modern technological devices, including computers, as ancillaries in their work and some instances of this have been noted in passing.

The new technique of publishing by microfiche or ultrafiche, whether computer-driven or not, offers a cheap method of republication of larger dictionaries which will make small demands on library shelf-space. Like the *Dictionary of Early Modern English* materials, future large historical dictionaries may cost less and take up less space, and so may be made more widely accessible, if only their editorial matter (article-headings, definitions and etymologies) and at most only a very exiguous selection of illustrative quotations is published in traditional book form, leaving to an accompanying microfiche publication the bulk of the quotations and references. At present the latter take up much of the space in such dictionaries, yet in practice they are less often read. It may be a long time before the rapid consultation and comparison of several dictionaries and their files at a computer terminal becomes a widely available resource (from the kinds of computerized library systems that computer scientists were predicting so confidently some years ago). But technologically this is of course already perfectly feasible, and lexicological studies based on the consultation by computer of two medium-sized American dictionaries have been proceeding for some years in one major American research centre.

On the other hand, it is at present impossible in practice, and it may be that it will never be possible in principle, for any machine to simulate the delicate and laborious human task of dictionary sense-analysis. This will foreseeably continue to draw on human judgment and to rest largely on the human editor's own internal system of semantics and linguistic knowledge. These he consults so as to group together what he perceives as similar examples of word-use, at present in the physical form of separate bundles of quotation-slips. Equally, the formulation of definitions to delimit and describe the senses so arrived at remains an exclusively human prerogative.

So far, despite those reviewers of *Webster's Third* who denounced it as the stalking-horse of "structural linguistics", English lexicography has not drawn heavily on the proliferating corpus of theoretic reconsideration by structural and post-structural linguists. One rather crucial difficulty is that lexicography is itself a very demanding and time-consuming task, and few practising lexicographers have found the time or energy to master as much linguistics as they no doubt should. Lexicographers would be helped by a handbook which tabulated the major and some of the minor categories into which meaning and grammar and usage can be analysed and which listed in an organized way some of the new aperçus on linguistic behaviour which lexicographers could apply in their analyses. A more visionary scheme foresees the injection of new findings by linguists into computerized dictionary files by means of rapid computer updating methods.

One kind of information which is lacking in all English dictionaries at present is the statistical. What, for example, are the relative frequencies of different competing synonyms at different stages in the history of the language? How relatively frequent, in different periods, are the different meanings or uses of a word? More crudely, how frequent is a particular word (in its several inflexional forms) relative to others within the whole word-stock over a particular period?

One dictionary now in progress which incorporates a statistical element of just these kinds is the new *Trésor de la langue française* dictionary of nineteenth and twentieth-century literary French. This refinement and others have been created out of resources beyond the wildest dreams of any British or American historical dictionary enterprise: a permanent government-supported institution devoted solely to French lexicography, a permanent staff of well over 100 people, the exclusive use of a large computer, and so on. There is no likelihood of the establishment in the English-speaking world of an institution on the lines of *TLF*, which would enable lexicographers of English to emulate and perhaps surpass its promised achievement. What is being increasingly talked about among lexicographers of English is the possibility of establishing a central bank of lexicographical data, including quotation files, available to all, and presumably in computerized form. But as yet this too remains a somewhat vague vision.

DICTIONARIES DISCUSSED IN THIS ARTICLE

Chambers Twentieth Century Dictionary (*1972*). Edited by A. M. Macdonald. xii plus 1,649 pp. Chambers. £2.50.

Encyclopedic World Dictionary (*1971*). Edited by Patrick Hanks. 1,856 pp. Hamlyn. £4.95.

The Concise Oxford Dictionary of Current English (*1964–1972*). Edited by H. W. Fowler and F. G. Fowler; revised by E. McIntosh and G. W. S. Friedrichsen. xvi plus 1,566 pp. Clarendon Press: Oxford University Press. £1.75.

The Advanced Learner's Dictionary of Current English (*1963*). Edited by A. S. Hornby, E. V. Gatenby and H. Wakefield. xxxii plus 1,200 pp. Clarendon Press: Oxford University Press. £1.60.

Oxford Illustrated Dictionary (*1962*). Edited by J. Coulson, C. T. Carr, Lucy Hutchinson, and Dorothy Eagle; illustrations edited by Helen Mary Petter. xvi plus 976 pp. Clarendon Press: Oxford University Press. £4.

The Random House Dictionary of the English Language (*1966*). Edited by Jess Stein. xxxii plus 2,059 pp. New York: Random House. Distributed by European Book Service. $30.

The American College Dictionary (*1947–1969*). Edited by Clarence L. Barnhart. xxviii plus 1,444 pp. New York: Random House. Distributed by European Book Service. $6.95.

Webster's Third New International Dictionary of the English Language (*1961*). Edited by Philip Babcock Gove. 2,720 pp. Springfield: Merriam-Webster. Distributed by Bell. £32.50.

The American Heritage Dictionary of the English Language (*1969*). Edited by William Morris. 1 plus 1,550 pp. New York: American Heritage. Distributed by Trans-Atlantic Book Service. £4.50.

The World Book Dictionary (*1963–1969*). Edited by Clarence L. Barnhart. 2 volumes: 124 plus 2,266 pp. Field Enterprises. £16.

The Oxford Dictionary of English Etymology (*1966*). Edited by C. T. Onions with G. W. S. Friedrichsen and R. W. Burchfield. xvi plus 1,025 pp. Clarendon Press: Oxford University Press. £5.

A Comprehensive Etymological Dictionary of the English Language (*1971*). Edited by Ernest Klein. xxvi plus 844 pp. Elsevier. £11.75.

The Shorter Oxford English Dictionary on Historical Principles (*1944–1959*). Edited by William Little, H. W. Fowler and J. Coulson; revised by C. T. Onions. xxii plus 2,515 pp. Clarendon Press: Oxford University Press. £8.25.

The Oxford English Dictionary (*1933*). Corrected reissue with Introduction, Supplement and Bibliography of *A New English Dictionary on Historical Principles*. Edited by J. A. H. Murray, Henry Bradley, W. A. Craigie, and C. T. Onions. 13 volumes: 16,570 pp. Clarendon Press: Oxford University Press. £100.

The Compact Edition of the Oxford English Dictionary (*1971*). Complete text reproduced micrographically. 2 volumes: xvii plus 4,116 pp. Clarendon Press: Oxford University Press. £32.

Middle English Dictionary (*1954–*) Edited by Hans Kurath and Sherman M. Kuhn. A-L2: 40 parts. Ann Arbor: University of Michigan Press. Distributed by Trans-Atlantic Book Service. £1.60 per part.

A Dictionary of the Older Scottish Tongue (*1931–*). Edited by William A. Craigie and A. J. Aitken. A–N, 26 parts: £5.20 each. A–L, 3 volumes: £16.85 each. University of Chicago Press.

The Scottish National Dictionary (*1931–*). Edited by William Grant and David D. Murison. A–T, 34 parts. Edinburgh: Scottish National Dictionary Association. Subscription £50.

A Dictionary of American English on Historical Principles (*1938–1944*). Edited by William A. Craigie and James R. Hulbert. 4 volumes: 2,600 pp. University of Chicago Press. £45 the set.

A Dictionary of Americanisms on Historical Principles (*1951*). Edited by M. M. Matthews. xvi plus 1,946 pp. University of Chicago Press. £11.25.

A Dictionary of Jamaican English (*1967*). Edited by F. G. Cassidy and R. B. Le Page. lxxi plus 489 pp. Cambridge University Press. £6.

A Dictionary of Canadianisms on Historical Principles (*1967*). Edited by Walter S. Avis. xxiii plus 927 pp. Scarborough: Gage $25.

A Supplement to the Oxford English Dictionary (*1972*). Volume 1, A–G: 1,356 pp. Clarendon Press: Oxford University Press. £15.

18

THE PORN REPORT

THE MOUNTAINS have laboured and the result is not so much *ridiculus mus* as wet blanket. Lord Longford's concern that his report should not foster a prurient interest in pornography has been so successful that he has produced 520 pages of almost stupefying dreariness. If the *Longford Report* is the bestseller it is expected to be, it will profoundly disappoint more readers than most pornographers will let down in a lifetime. It is ill-written, repetitive, diffuse and unspecific about the nature of the evils it is tackling; and its legal recommendations embody a mindless moral populism—of a conservative and middle-class kind—which is not only repulsive in itself, but inimical to just those measures of legal and penal reform which Lord Longford has spent his time promoting.

The report is not so much an analysis of our present confusion about the nature of social and individual order and disorder as an exhibition of that confusion. It consists very largely of a series of personal statements of fear and anxiety about the contemporary world, together with a few guesses about the causation of sexual and criminal deviance. The grounds for alarm are not just multifarious, but internally contradictory, as are the committee's sociological and psychological allegiances. Most of the committee, for instance, seem to want more psychological research of the kind reported on by the Presidential Commission on Obscenity and Pornography; but David Holbrook and Mary Miles dissent from this, and Mr Holbrook himself, of course, considers contemporary laboratory psychology to be the same sort of schizoid manifestation of our cultural disarray as

---

Pornography: The Longford Report. 520 pp. Coronet. Paperback, 60p.

MAURICE GIRODIAS (Editor): *The Obscenity Report.* 256 pp. Olympia Press. Paperback, 50p.

ALAN BURNS (Editor): *To Deprave and Corrupt.* Technical Reports of the United States Commission on Obscenity and Pornography. 192 pp. Davis-Poynter. £2.25 (paperback, £1.50).

JONATHAN MILLER: *Censorship and the Limits of Permission.* 24 pp. Oxford University Press for the British Academy. Paperback, 30p.

pornography is. It remains unclear throughout just what the committee is trying to prohibit with its new obscenity law; the apparent,
though probably unintentional, tactic is to swing rapidly from talking
about what one can buy in the back rooms of specialized bookshops
to talking about what one can buy on Paddington Station, as if the
fact that the former revolts Mary Stott is a good reason for depriving
commuters of the latter. And there is a great deal of loose talk about
"sexual perversion" as if homosexuality, solitary masturbation, and
the rape of juveniles were all on a par and could usefully be discussed
under the same heading; Peter Grosvenor takes a fierce line against
homosexuality, for instance, but Lord Longford makes a point of
recalling his own support for the Wolfenden Report many years ago.

Some of the writers pick usefully large and identifiable targets:
Malcolm Muggeridge, for example, picks his usual target—the
modern world. "The irresponsibility of drivers on motorways, the
bland acceptance of the facts of world poverty by the rich nations of
the West, and the threatened breakdown of our own social services"
are all symptoms of the same sickness as pornography. Any doubts
about the sociological reliability of this view are dismissed on the
strength of the statements of the apostle Paul "in circumstances very
similar to our own". Anyone still restive is informed that "in this
particular field the Christian's insights into the nature of reality are
the only valid ones". It is a pity we didn't know this before the *Oz*
trial, though there will no doubt be doctrinal conflict about just how
juries in future are to receive the Christian message—by direct
inspiration, attention to the Bible, or perhaps by adding a Bishop to
the judicial bench?

Mr Holbrook produces a secular version of the same feeling that
we are all heading down the Gadarene slope. In his case, the claim
seems to be that pornography is both cause and effect of a modern
schizophrenia, whose causes are not very clearly stated but appear to
involve childhood trauma as analysed in the theories of Melanie Klein
together with an adult adherence to the epistemology of Hobbesian
materialism. The doctrine is not very plausible as presented here,
especially when it is supported by such curious historical claims as
"the civilization of the Renaissance would not have been possible
without the Christian emphasis on marriage and the family". Yet, of
course, there is much that is perceptive and admirable in what Mr
Holbrook has recently been saying. His scepticism about the merits
of classroom-based sex education is not to be lightly dismissed; nor

is his hostility to the simple-mindedness of much that popularly passes for psychology. Yet, even here doubts creep in: he writes as if an enthusiasm for existential psychology would convert everyone to his point of view, while R. D. Laing stands as a very visible proof that this simply is not so. And there is a strange unawareness of how exposed his position is; he describes intellectuals as particularly schizoid, and attacks them for always trying to be "doing rather than being", but never stops to wonder what they will make of the fact that this year he seems to have published seven books and edited two others.

At the more mundane level of trying to ascertain what effects pornography has on its readers, the committee has some success, after a negative fashion. That is, they show up the inadequacies of some of the research from which the American commission concluded that pornography had no effect beyond temporary sexual arousal; and they are quite properly rude about the claim that sexual offences in Denmark dropped by 25 per cent as a result of the repeal of the laws against obscenity. (As almost all the world now knows, the drop is largely accounted for by the fact that some activities such as indecent exposure were taken out of the ambit of the criminal law.) But the committee's characteristic incapacity for making appropriate analytical distinctions makes even this aspect of its work less than helpful. What they failed to see is that the question of the effects of pornography falls into several components; in the first place, one wants to know whether the sexual stimulus provided by pornography is a stimulus to do those things which are pornographically depicted or simply a stimulus to obtain sexual satisfaction in ways which the viewer or reader usually employs. Obviously we would be alarmed if the customers for photographs of flagellation went out and began to flog unconsenting persons; if they made love to their wives with more enthusiasm, we might not be alarmed at all.

And at this point we need to distinguish quite carefully among the objections we may have to various kinds of sexual activity. The committee show little sign of distinguishing between the harmful, the sinful, and the filthy, nor do they seem very clever about recognizing the distinction between those activities which will harm us or cause misery irrespective of the social estimate of them and those which only make us miserable because of social disapproval. It is for this reason that the comparison between air pollution and moral pollution is not much good even as a rhetorical device. It depends not at all on social attitudes whether polluted air gives us cancer or other forms of lung disease; it seems to depend entirely on social attitudes whether we are distressed by, say, masturbation. Of course an attachment to Christianity blurs such distinctions quite effectively, since it suggests that our cultural norms embody truths about Creation. Those who think Christianity false and its morality confused are likely to want to make such distinctions rather frequently.

The vagueness of the committee's targets and the woolliness of its moral position mean inevitably that it has locked itself into just the position Lord Longford did not want to occupy. That is, the *Report* looks like an attempt simply to freeze social *mores*—the whole tissue of ideas about morality, decency, normality and deviance—exactly as they were a few years ago. Oddly, the belief on which the attempt is founded—that greater sexual freedom is the beginning of anarchy—is one the committee shares with Maurice Girodias, and as so often we seem to have reached a point where the conservatives and revolutionaries believe each other's nonsense and make life difficult for persons living in the same society with them. M Girodias's *The Obscenity Report* looks suspiciously like an opportunistic attempt to share Lord Longford's limelight, for it reprints such familiar favourites as the Danish report which led to the loosening of the law in 1967. It is, however, notable for an introduction in which M Girodias claims that the "Sexual Revolution" is "the great motor of the moral, intellectual and political movement which is fast transforming the world". And connoisseurs of the absurd will relish equally President Nixon's speech denouncing the report of his commission; more than ever, *Our Gang* looks like a case of art imitating an inimitable nature.

Lord Longford's committee, however, speak of Mr Nixon with some respect, and in the last resort their appeal is to the same "common sense" position:

The commission contends that the proliferation of filthy books and plays has no lasting effect on a man's character. If that were true, it must also be true that great books, great paintings and great plays have no ennobling effects on a man's conduct. Centuries of civilisation and 10 minutes of common sense tell us otherwise.

And the *TLS* Commentary on the series of articles about obscenity and censorship (February 25) took a fairly similar view. Now, there are at least two immediate things to be said. The first is that it is philistine to treat art as if its point were largely utilitarian; what we value in Mozart is Mozart's music, not a sort of moral tonic. The second is that anyone who does take such a utilitarian line is going to be hopelessly disappointed; George Steiner has written of his incomprehension that a man might be deeply moved by Mozart and yet run a concentration camp. But such examples multiply without number. And the converse consideration is that from men with sexually deviant tastes there has come extreme beauty; Proust watched rats being tortured in a homosexual brothel, and *A la recherche* is neither more nor less marvellous as a result.

The mistake embedded in this utilitarian view is to suppose that art literally tells us something or literally persuades us to behave in some way or other. Of course, the issue is desperately complicated, and there may be art-forms which preach a message in this direct way, and that message may alarm us enough to want at any rate to make sure the other side is heard; but ten minutes' common sense is not the only apparatus we need.

What most writers and readers will be anxious about are the committee's legal recommendations. It is at this point that Kingsley Amis and Elizabeth Jane Howard dissent on behalf of the novelist and his readers. The committee's view is that two major changes are needed in the existing law. The first is to scrap the present definition of obscenity in terms of depravity and corruption and to replace it with a definition in terms of an object's outraging "contemporary standards of decency or humanity accepted by the public at large". The second is to remove the present defence in terms of "public good". The committee seem to think that this would enable convictions to be secured without too much difficulty and without obstruction from expert witnesses, and they are probably correct. But the bland assumption that the recommendations offer no threat to freedom of speech and publication is simple-minded.

In the first place, it assumes that past gains in terms of what juries will and will not find outrageous are impossible to erode; given the committee's own ambivalence about whether the acquittal of *Lady Chatterley's Lover* was the last of the good decisions or the first of the bad, this is hard to swallow. In the second place, the temptation to employ the law for political purposes will remain as strong as ever, and the underground press can presumably be jumped on more readily if it cannot assemble liberal academic, literary and legal support. In the third place, it is dubious whether in a morally pluralist society such as ours there is the kind of consensus on what is outrageous which would make the operation of the law predictable and fair. In the fourth place, it is not much better than the prosecution of the class war by other means to make standards of what is publishable depend on the mere say-so of juries (which are largely middle-class and middle-aged) and judges (who are largely upper-class, old and isolated).

Anyone whose interest in the whole topic has not been exhausted will find Jonathan Miller's British Academy lecture a refreshing change from the silliness to left and right. He brings to the whole topic a genuine common sense and a dispassionate clarity which is long overdue. Dr Miller is quite prepared to restrain the public display of pornography in the interests of not distressing people who are upset by the sight or who fear the effect on their children. But he is sceptical about the damage pornography does, and quite sure that the damage done by a fiercer law would be worse.

The *feebleness* of pornography he analyses in terms of its obsession with "consummatory" rather than "appetitive" behaviour. The distinction is borrowed from Sir Charles Sherrington, who observed that within a species consummatory behaviour was stereotyped and mechanical, whereas appetitive behaviour varied widely. Thus "Gwendolen Harleth and Cleopatra differ from one another not by virtue of their performance in bed, but in the subtle programmes of encouragement and procrastination that lead to the final relatively monotonous conclusion".

The *fear* of pornography he analyses in terms of Mary Douglas's *Purity and Danger*. Concepts of cleanliness and pollution are, on this view, symbolic representations of our perceptions of social order; an increased concern with threats to them represents a rather confused perception that social order is in a state of flux. Since social and intellectual change occurs faster than ever, it is

small wonder that symbolic representations of order and stability, such as are represented in the various systems of etiquette and decorum, are reasserted with fresh enthusiasm, and their violation condemned with a shrillness quite out of proportion to the danger involved.

But as Professor Douglas herself has said, it is not much use tackling the question at the level of the symbol rather than that of the social order thus symbolized. Or, in Dr Miller's words: "Our current concern with obscenity and pornography merely delays constructive social action and presents . . . an image as absurd as that of someone trying to adjust their dress before jumping from a burning building."

INDEX

This index, in addition to referring to articles and reviews in the present volume, also shows other major reviews of the year which have appeared in the *T.L.S.*

Date references and page numbers in *italic* are to articles and reviews in the *T.L.S.* not reprinted in this volume. Page numbers in parentheses are given only where the reference is not immediately obvious from the article.